CROWDS AND PUBLIC ORDER POLICING

For my wife and sons, Selahaddin, Nureddin and Bedreddin

Crowds and Public Order Policing

An Analysis of Crowds and Interpretations of their Behaviour Based on Observational Studies in Turkey, England and Wales

Dr IBRAHIM CERRAH

Police Academy, Ankara, Turkey

Ashgate

DARTMOUTH

Aldershot • Brookfield USA • Singapore • Sydney

Published by
Dartmouth Publishing Company Limited
Ashgate Publishing Limited
Gower House
Croft Road
Aldershot
Hants GU11 3HR
England

Ashgate Publishing Company
Old Post Road
Brookfield
Vermont 05036
USA

British Library Cataloguing in Publication Data
Cerrah, Ibrahim
Crowds and public order policing : an analysis of crowds and interpretations of their behaviour based on observational studies in Turkey, England and Wales
1.Crowds - Turkey 2.Crowds - England 3. Crowds - Wales
4.Collective behaviour 5. Spectator control - Turkey
6.Spectator control - England 7.Spectator control - Wales
I.Title
302.3'3

Library of Congress Cataloging-in-Publication Data
Cerrah, Ibrahim.
Crowds and public order policing : an analysis of crowds and interpretation of their behaviour based on observational studies in Turkey, England and Wales / Ibrahim Cerrah.
p. cm.
Includes bibliographical references.
ISBN 1-84014-004-6 (hardbound)
1. Riot control. 2. Crowds–Cross-cultural studies. I. Title.
HV8055.C47 1997
363.3'2–dc21 97-22752
CIP

ISBN 1 84014 004 6

Printed and bound by Athenaeum Press, Ltd.,
Gateshead, Tyne & Wear.

Contents

List of Figures

Preface

This book, which aims to analyse crowds and interpret their behaviour, is mainly based on observational studies in England and Wales and Turkey.

Between February 1992 - February 1995, observations were made of 33 crowd events. These took place in Turkey, England and Wales, and all of which involved a large police deployment. In addition, informal interviews were conducted in both countries, involving key figures in areas of police public order training and practice. Further, visits were made to training sites and public order units, to familiarise the author with public order policing in both countries. Finally, the author has attended three major public order courses organised for the senior officers of British police forces.

This book analyses the underlying assumptions contained within the existing theories in the field and attempts to adjudicate on the validity of both classical and modern contributions to the understanding of the field. Two hypothesis are considered, first: *'Crowd phenomena like other social issues cannot be examined within the boundaries of a single discipline'.* This has led to development of a theory, the 'Combined Factors Approach' (CFA) which attempts to examine the behaviour of crowds using a multitude of factors.

The second hypothesis is *'In terms of exercising their function in so-called public order events, the police, far from being a neutral institution serve and protect the interest of its political masters and the ruling classes rather than serving the entire community'.* Observations of existing public order policing practices suggests the validity of a radical and Marxist argument, that the police are an apparatus of the state and therefore of the ruling classes.

The book concludes that any public order policing, regardless of the political system it serves, will tend to be relatively paramilitary and oppressive. Civilian public order policing practices need to take account of an approach which appreciates a wide combination of levels of understanding as represented by the CFA. Finally, it is argued that the more public order policing policy reflects the potential level of understanding promoted by the CFA the less emphasis on paramilitary techniques will be deployed as tactics of last resort.

Acknowledgements

No researcher is ever alone in undertaking a research project. It is with great pleasure that I begin by thanking my wife, for her enthusiastic support and unwavering encouragement over the years that I have spent writing this book, and for my sons Selahaddin, Nureddin and Bedreddin for the sacrifices they have unwittingly made.

This work is the result of six years effort, and in that period I have encountered the usual difficulties and problems associated with carrying out this type of long-term project. In addition, of course, I have had the added problems of writing in a foreign language and through an alien culture.

In the course of writing this book I have received help from a number of people to whom I now express grateful thanks without, of course, implicating them in any of its shortcomings. Although my debt to scholars in the field is evidenced in the bibliography my indebtedness goes beyond the names contained therein. Chapters of my work have been seen and commented on by a number of scholars and police practitioners in the field. I am also pleased to acknowledge the help of many people who have given me ideas and information - sometimes without knowing it - which have been used in this book.

I warmly acknowledge the invaluable comments made by Ilhan Bardakci, an eminent Turkish historian and journalist living in Bonn, Germany; Professor Salim Al-Hasani of the University of Manchester Institute of Science and Technology; and Dr John Hoffman, Department of Politics, University of Leicester, for their reading of chapters four and making valuable contributions and comments on it. Secondly, I would also like to thank Dr J. S. McClelland, Department of Politics, University of Nottingham, for his reading of chapter two, and Tony Moore, an ex-superintendent of the Metropolitan Police, for his reading of chapter seven and the conclusion. Thirdly, I would like to thank Asaf Hussain, the General Secretary of the Islamic Rights Movement, author and sociologist, and Reverend Dr Clinton Bennett of Westminster College, Oxford, for the valuable comments made on chapters four and five of the book. Finally, I cannot conclude without mentioning Jean Baxter, who proof-read the whole text several times and also made a number of invaluable comments both in terms of its English and the contents.

As the book was heavily dependent on observations, interviews and visits made at a number of public order events, training sites and schools, I would like to thank the numerous officers of the British police force in general, and New Scotland Yard and the Metropolitan Police, for the opportunities afforded to facilitate my visits and arrange my accommodation. Regarding the Turkish side of the project, I also thank those who kindly agreed to be interviewed.

I would also like to thank Superintendent Michael Lofthouse and Chief Inspector D. J. R. Pryer, of Kent County Constabulary, for the *Public Order Awareness Course*, which I attended in their force. Chief Inspector Ken Redfern and Inspector Steve Huntbach have been extremely helpful and therefore deserve warm thanks for enabling me to attend the *Major Sporting Event Command Course* and the *Bronze/Silver Commanders Course*, at the Greater Manchester Police, Sedgley Park Police School. Finally, I would also wish to personally acknowledge the kindness of Dr David Waddington, to whom I owe the permanent membership of the ESRC seminar series, which was again a source of invaluable information and inspiration.

Undertaking a Ph.D. project and writing a book obviously depends upon an accumulation of written material. Here, I would like to thank library staff at the Bramshill Staff College where I was able to have access to invaluable resources. I am particularly grateful to the librarian Sue King for arranging my visit and the hospitality she gave during my stay in the Bramshill Police Staff College.

Finally, all members of the staff of the SCSPO deserve thanks as I have received a great deal of help and co-operation from them within the research period. I particularly thank Adrian Beck and Ilyas Ülgür for their generous help and expertise in drawing the charts and figures used in the book. I would also like to thank Professor John Benyon, the Director of the SCSPO, Dr Mike King, my supervisor Nigel Brearley and Bernadette Hayes for their continuous support, encouragement and co-operation during the research period and my stay at the Centre.

List of Abbreviations

ACPO	Association of Chiefs of Police Officers
AFO	Authorised Firearms Officer
ANL	Anti Nazi League
BCP	British Communist Party
BNP	British National Party
CCTV	Closed Circuit Television
CFA	Combined Factors Approach
CID	Criminal Investigation Department
CK	Cevik Kuvvet (equivalent of PSUs in Turkey)
CPU	Central Planning Unit
CS	Corson & Stoughton (tear gas)
CSPO	Centre for the Study of Public Order
DEV-GENC	Devrimci Genclik (the Turkish Revolutionary Youth)
DEV-SOL	Devrimci Sol (the Turkish Revolutionary Left)
EGM	Emniyet Genel Mudurlugu (The General Directorate of Police)
ESRC	Economic and Social Research Council
EU	European Union
EUROPOL	European Police
GMP	Greater Manchester Police
HSE	Health and Safety Executive
ILL	Inter Library Loan
IRA	Irish Republican Army
IVP	Inter Varsity Press
MACC	Mutual Aid Coordinating Centre
MP	Metropolitan Police
NCCL	National Council for Civil Liberties
NCIS	National Crime Intelligence Service
NRC	National Reporting Centre
NF	National Front
NUS	National Unions of Students
PAS	Public Address System
PKK	Kurdistan Workers' Party
PMR	Police Mobile Reserve
PNC	Police National Computer
PSI	Police Studies Institute
PSU	Police Support Unit

SO19	Special Operations 19 (London Metropolitan Police firearms unit)
SPG	Special Patrol Group
SWP	Socialist Workers Party
TC	Turkiye Cumhuriyeti (Republic of Turkey)
TDKP-GKB	Turkiye Revolutionary Communist Party
TFU	Tactical Firearms Unit
TIKKO	Turkiye Workers' and Peasants' Freedom Army
TKP	Turkiye Communist Party
TO18	Territorial Operations (Metropolitan Police Public Order Training Centre)
TO20	Tactical Operation (London Metropolitan Police Public Order Branch)
TSG	Territorial Support Group
TUC	Trades Unions Congress
UK	United Kingdom
UNL	University College London
US	United States
YARE	Youth Against Racism in Europe

Introduction

> An examination of the nature of policing at different times and different countries will reveal a number of variations. Styles will vary according to political, economic, social and cultural conditions (Alderson, 1985, p.70).

A democratic society presupposes the right of the individual to protest peacefully on any issue. The principle underlying the law allows individual freedom to be exercised provided the law is not breached. Yet the maintenance of order during any public event such as political demonstrations, marches, protests, sporting events, pop concerts and carnivals has always been one of the most sensitive problems facing the police. The need to control what some commentators see as 'the mob' without recourse to the army was one of the strongest reasons for the creation of the police in England and Wales, in 1829 (Mark, 1977, p.86; Waddington, 1987, p.37).

For a number of reasons crowds are usually perceived as a potential law and order problem. At the simplest level there are problems of routing and maintaining traffic flow and access for emergency services. Crowds also attract petty criminals because there are situational opportunities such as anonymity for exploitation and petty crime. However, in some circumstances crowds present problems of an entirely different magnitude and type and can be perceived as posing a threat to the authority of the state. The recent crowd movements in eastern Europe and Algeria have demonstrated that crowds, as has been the case throughout history, have a potentially important role to play in the political future of nations.

The dilemma of maintaining the peace during a demonstration or any other similar public order event, without risking or undermining the right of individuals to express their grievances and opinions, has moved public order policing into the centre of political debate and controversy in Britain, a debate which also occupies the government of all democratic countries.

Contemporary issues partly stem from the influence of conventional crowd theories like those formulated by Le Bon on public order policing practices. Despite a substantial shift from a policing of crowds based on the understanding of crowds along classical lines, such as Gustave Le Bon (1841-1931), Gabriel Tarde (1843-1904) and Scipio Sighele (1868-1913) there is a danger of ignoring the socio-psychological determinants of crowd behaviour. This research, through critical attention to the underlying assumptions contained within existing theories, attempts to adjudicate on the validity of both classical and modern contributions to the understanding of the field.

This book, *Crowds and Public Order Policing,* is an analysis of crowds and interpretation of their behaviour based on observational studies in Turkey, England and Wales. The primary aim of these observations was to explore the nature and inner dynamics of crowd activities and to draw lessons for appropriate public order policing practices in both countries.

An examination of the nature of policing in different countries will reveal a number of variations. Styles will vary according to political, economic, social and cultural conditions. Even where the police system itself has one dominant or seemingly universal character, closer examination of the police in practice will reveal differences of emphasis. To be able to maintain order, in both countries, the police have different equipment and use different tactics. Turkish policing represents, to a greater extent, a paramilitary policing model, whereas the British police has until recently been regarded as one of the few examples of non-military or consensus systems of policing.

By examining two different crowd and public order policing systems which display variations at historical, socio-cultural and political levels, it is hoped that a number of common characteristics will be revealed regarding the universal characteristics of the police. I do, however, acknowledge that complete objectivity is an ideal which is desirable but difficult to attain. The author has been aware, throughout the preparation of this book, of his own subjective viewpoint, and has attempted to achieve an objective result. He has also, however, utilised this personal cultural and religious subjectivity in the formation of the central tenets of this work. This is, perhaps, obvious in his writing but it is hoped that he has brought the notion of universality rather than bias to the issues discussed here.

Broad Objectives

Both historically and today, public order policing has been a fundamental factor in police development and is crucial to an understanding of the political purposes and ideology of the police and its political masters. More importantly, in recent years, a number of issues have been raised concerning public order policing with reference to inner-city riots and picket-line violence and the methods of policing violent crowds, especially in relation to the introduction of sophisticated equipment, methods and tactics.

This research will concentrate on theory constructing rather than theory testing. However, as commonly held any research will inevitably involve some basic theories as a starting point. Even in theory-building research the importance of preceding conventional theories must be appreciated. Theory has a crucial role in any social research. It is said that 'when one does not know what one is looking for, one does not understand what one finds'. For this reason, theories help interpret the meaning of observations and highlight their significance. They help us 'understand what one finds'.

Various forms of observation and interview methods used in combination throughout this research, will serve to construct a theory. "..theory construction is a process which begins with a set of observations, (i.e. description) and moves on to develop theories of these observations. It is also called grounded theory because it is based on observations - not simply armchair speculation" (De Vaus, 1990, p.12). In other words, theory comes after observation rather than before although prior theories are taken into account.

On this point it must be made clear that making a set of observations may not always or even normally lead to development of new concepts or a new theory. Attempts to make sense of a set of observations will often use existing concepts and theories. If concepts and theories developed by others seem like reasonable summaries or accounts of what the researcher has already observed they will be used as well. There is little point in continually 'reinventing the wheel'. Where observations are new or different or are not adequately summarised by existing concepts and theories, then existing ideas may be adapted or modified. This research, like any other research, will involve a constant interplay between observation and existing theories, the collection of further facts to test the existing explanation and refinements of the existing explanation to develop new theories.

In order to achieve this end, besides carrying out extensive reading in relevant academic literature, thirty three observations have been made at various crowd events which had been deemed by police professionals to require deployment of large numbers of police officers. A number of visits were made by the researcher to various public order training centres in Turkey, England and Wales in order to familiarise with the nature of police public order training and its impact on actual events. Therefore, this research is mainly the product of the observations at crowd events, interviews with relevant people, visits to police training sites and schools.

Hypotheses

The research aims to make an analysis of crowds and the respective public order policing practices in the two countries to demonstrate the extent of the validity of the following hypotheses. These apparently different hypotheses are, in fact, interrelated and complement one another.

The literature review conducted by this research analysing the contributions of both in classical theorists such as Le Bon and his contemporaries and some modern crowd theorists and thinkers such as N. J. Smelser (1962, 1968 and 1972), J. Benyon (1986, 1987 and 1993b), S. Hall (1987), P. Scraton (1987), and D. Waddington et al. (1989) Waddington (1992) has led to the following hypothesis. The crowd phenomenon like other social issues cannot be examined within the boundaries of a single discipline.

Most crowd activities involve direct or indirect expressions of grievances and dissent, which fall within the boundaries of biology and psychology. In the Combined Factors Approach which was generated by the research these *constitutional* factors are defined as 'immediate' factors. However, these grievances and dissent are mostly directed towards the existing social and political arrangements, which constitute the *institutional*, or 'delayed' factors and fall within the boundaries of sociology.

As with individual behaviour, crowd behaviour is subject to two kinds of determinants; the 'immediate', (constitutional) and 'delayed', (institutional) factors. Policing practices which do not take into account these two factors are inadequate and are bound to be perceived as being paramilitary and oppressive.

The second hypothesis which this book attempts to validate is that in terms of exercising their functions in so-called public order events, the police, far from being a neutral institution, serve and protect the interests of its political masters and the ruling classes rather than serving the entire community.

This hypothesis derives from the Marxist writings in the field including K. Marx's own works (1975) and some of his followers such as A. Gramsci (1971) and L. Althusser (1971). This hypothesis has also been defended by a number of contemporary broadly Marxist and critical criminologists such as S. Hall (1987), P. Scraton (1987), and J. Lea and J. Young (1984).

Specific Questions

Throughout the text various aspects of crowd and collective action were analysed and this has led the researcher to address the following specific questions, which are, in addition to the main objectives of the research, a by-product of the research. Some of the questions which the research aims to address are concerned with the influence and role of crowd movements in democracies. Why, for example, is the response of democracy towards crowd movements in Algeria any different from that of the Russian experience? Does this imply that democracies are essentially hypocritical and not always tolerant to the demands of crowds and therefore elements of its public?

The last chapter, which is devoted to the implications and application of the Combined Factors Approach (CFA) to existing public order policing practices, will address issues such as the use of sophisticated riot control equipment and the deployment of public order trained units. It will also consider whether such rigorous methods and tactics are inevitable and unavoidable and, if so, how violence can be limited. The role and importance of protective police clothing and equipment on the crowd in terms of escalating violence will also be dealt with within this context. Finally, taking into account the cultural, historical and other variations between Turkey, England and Wales, this research looks at the lessons to be taken from each other's police practice in terms of public order policy.

In order to be able to address these issues and explore the nature of existing public order policing practices and training, a series of interviews were carried out in a number of public order training schools and sites and a number of key figures in police training have been informally interviewed. Regarding the nature of public order policing practices at ground level, 33 observations of crowd events have been made both in Turkey, England and Wales.

One of the aims of these observations and interviews has been to explore the impact of the existing academic wisdom in the field of public order policing practices at ground level. The research has discovered that despite a great deal of work done in the field its impact on public order policing practices has been a piecemeal and very slow moving process. Much of the police training and practices in both countries, particularly in Turkey, remain in line with classical crowd theories.

General Outline

The book consists of seven chapters, each one dealing with a particular aspect of the issues concerned and at the same time leading to a general conclusion. Each chapter constitutes the development of the theory which will formally be presented in chapter six.

The first chapter consists of two main sections and the first section of this chapter is devoted to the methods used by the researcher. The methods used by the researcher include 'literature review', 'interviews', 'courses', 'seminars' and 'observations'. As observations are the main source of information of the research a particular emphasis has been placed on the various aspects of this method. The second section of this chapter is a review of the literature which led to the development of the research strategy. The literature review is again divided into two; the first part is devoted to a comparison of *classical and modern crowd theories,* while the second part is concerned more with recent studies in the field of *crowds and public order policing.*

The research begins with chapter two, devoted to classifying existing crowds with a special emphasis on pre-event policing arrangements. Within this descriptive chapter existing pre-event arrangements will be examined, rather than ideal circumstances. Since a good description is the basis for a sound theory, it is important to begin with an objective view and unless something has been described accurately and thoroughly, attempts to explain it will be misleading. For example, as a descriptive statement it might be said that a particular crowd is violent and then policing arrangements will be made on the basis of this assumption. However, if the description is inaccurate and the crowd are not violent the response will be both inappropriate and, as it will be argued potentially precipitate violence. Therefore, this chapter will include descriptive accounts of crowds and public order policing in both countries.

One of the findings of chapter two is that crowds and public order policing cannot be explained in relation to merely physical factors. Therefore, chapter three divides the crowd into two integral parts, the 'physical' and 'non-physical' components. The first component deals with physical elements such as the participants, leaders and the police. The police are mentioned only briefly within this chapter as this element will be elaborated later (chapter seven). Non-physical components of the crowd include certain controversial concepts such as 'suggestibility', 'rationality' and 'the collective mind'.

The research has found that crowds, unlike other social institutions, have only a temporary existence. It was also found that crowds are very much influenced by the nature of existing political and social establishments and arrangements. As this study is comparative the researcher also had to compare and contrast the relationship and perceptions of crowds to certain social institutions such as 'the state', social 'classes' and 'the police'. Consequently, issues such as 'political violence', which refers to the use of violence on a wider scale, has also been examined within chapter four.

Chapter five is a further step towards the construction of the theory of the book and deals with the causes of crime in general and disorder in particular. As the perception of crime and disorder in England, Wales and Turkey have been very much influenced by the two dominant religions, Christianity and Islam, a non-secular interpretation of crime and disorder has also been included in the argument.

The observations made throughout the research period have demonstrated that the causes which lead to the gathering of large numbers at certain times and places cannot be explained by psychological determinants alone. However, to cite only the political, social, and economic factors in attempts to explain crime and disorder is also insufficient. Therefore, the argument of this book is that the causes of collective gatherings and of crowd violence can be found with an approach which combines both 'socio-economic' and 'socio-psychological' factors. Indeed, even apparently materially oriented and motivated crowd events usually, if not always, involve non-material elements which can be understood from a psychological rather than a sociological perspective. Accordingly, 'lack of political representation' and 'relative insecurity' have been identified as factors which relate to the political and socio-psychological state of individuals. These elements obviously have less material connotations and influence on the individual compared with 'poverty' and 'absolute deprivation' which affects the individual directly.

In addition to an analysis of public order policing practices this research, in chapter six, attempts to contribute to the development of a new approach, the Combined Factors Approach (CFA), which attempts to combine both the 'immediate', (constitutional-biological and psychological) and 'delayed', (institutional-environmental and social) factors in the understanding of crowd behaviour/action. As Nelken (1994, p.232) has pointed out, "The introduction of a comparative aspect can help in the reformulation of central problems in criminological theory". After explaining the *constitutional* and *institutional* factors separately a combination of these two factors in the workings of crowd behaviour/action is analysed. The resulting combined factors model is then applied to one of the observations involving the demolition of squatters' houses in Izmir (Appendix 1, observation 12). In the rest of this chapter, the implications of this model on the remaining observations have been pointed out briefly. This chapter concludes with the comparison of this model with some recent crowd theories such as Smelsers's (1962) *Value Added Theory* and Waddington et al.'s (1989) *Flashpoints* model.

The last chapter of the book is devoted to the application of the Combined Factors Approach to crowd events and its implications for public order policing practices. In line with the general theme of the book, this chapter proposes that as with other crowd phenomena the police handling of crowd events should take into consideration both *institutional* and *constitutional* factors. Accordingly, the police planning of events should be made on this basis, involving long and short term arrangements. While short term arrangements take into consideration the cultural, psychological and contextual factors of a given crowd event, long term arrangements require multi-agency efforts to tackle the structural roots of a problem which involves social, political and economic spheres. Any public order policing policy which ignores one of these mutually inclusive elements is bound to be perceived as paramilitary and coercive.

The book concludes that crowd handling by the police is very much influenced and determined by the police perception of crowd events, which is in turn influenced by the political and ideological understanding of a particular regime. In this respect, public order policing practices mirror the police force and the state which that force serves. To sum up, the nature of the relationship between the state and its subjects can be judged by the way it handles the frequent opposition which arises from various grievances. Public order policing practices are therefore a clear indication of the state and the nature of a particular regime. The research has also discovered that the direction of change of policing in general and public order policing in particular, in both countries, seem to be divergent. Finally, there is an affinity and correlation between the nature of regimes and peculiarities of each country and the *policing systems* and *policies* by which they operate.

1 Research Methods and Literature Review

Introduction

> In the practice of comparative research, the problem of incommensurability emerges already in the phase of data gathering (Sztompka, 1990, p.48).

The rationale of the traditional comparative method is to seek uniformities in the sea of differences; to show that certain regularities hold in other societies as well, or that they hold for other categories of people, or that they extend to other social characteristics.

Obviously comparing two different public order policing systems will impose great difficulties on the researcher. "In the practice of comparative research, the problem of incommensurability emerges already in the phase of data gathering. For example, it becomes manifest when questionnaires are addressed to respondents from disparate societies, for whom seemingly similar questions appear to have quite diverse connotations" (Sztompka, 1990, p.48). Sztompka has argued that the dilemmas of comparative inquiry stem both from the plurality, variety and heterogeneity of ways in which members of various societies envisage the social reality to which they belong, and from the plurality, variety and heterogeneity of ways in which *sociologists* envisage social reality from the perspective of various theoretical orientations with which they identify. It has become clear that comparative research is far more difficult and complex than it first appears and although this method seems easier in principle, unfortunately its purist aims are basically unattainable.

Despite these difficulties and complexities, any comparative study will lead to a number of useful conclusions. It is hoped that the conclusions which have arisen from this research will be of help in public order policing practices in both countries. This has been one of the primary aims in conducting this comparative research between the Turkish and British public order policing systems. In order to achieve its aims, various techniques and methods have been used during this research and it is believed that relying only on one method, particularly in social sciences, would not be adequate.

Methods of the Research

The research on which this book is based is an observational analysis of crowds and public order policing practices in Turkey, England and Wales over the period from February 1992 to January 1995. This work is the result of observations of many crowd events which took place within the research period. A number of large crowd events were observed, including the Notting Hill Carnivals of 1992 and 1993, and many events in Turkey which attracted huge crowds, such as the funeral of the late Turkish president T. Ozal.

Northern Ireland and Eastern Turkey have been excluded from the scope of the research as these areas are policed with extraordinary policing methods. In Turkey observations and interviews took place in Ankara, Istanbul and Izmir as they are the first three major cities of Turkey and therefore experience more crowd events compared with other cities.

During this period, I enjoyed the help and co-operation of many police services such as the Metropolitan Police (MP), the Greater Manchester Police (GMP), Kent County Constabulary, Avon and Somerset Constabulary and the Leicestershire Constabulary. Although my observations were not limited to London, most of my observations actually took place in London as a major centre of national cultural focus. I was given prior notification of any forthcoming events in London, via fax messages which I received regularly from TO20 (Public Order Branch at New Scotland Yard). However, I was unable to attend every event due to considerations of time, expense and distance. Therefore, I have been selective and concentrated on crowd events that were either large, posing significant safety considerations and/or predicted to be potentially contentious or violent based on appreciation by TO20 and/or media accounts. For this reason, a number of important spontaneous events which took place during the empirical period have been omitted.

In terms of privileged access, I faced no great problem from the British police in terms of the observation and recording of crowd events with my personal camcorder. For instance, I made video recordings at a relatively violent demonstration which took place in London, on 16 October 1993 (Appendix 1, observation 25). By way of contrast, a week later, during my visit to Paris Police Headquarters (Prefecture De Police), I was informed, by French police, that I needed to apply for permission if I wished to make any recording of a crowd event in Paris. I faced similar problems and treatment when I visited the German police a week later. I was searched and then allowed into the police premises which is something I only experienced once in New Scotland Yard during a period of five years in the UK.

My access to some documents and some stages of public order operations in the UK were limited, to some extent, for reasons of confidentiality and secrecy. First of all, I am a foreign researcher and secondly, some of the documents were limited to police use only. Even if I had been a home research student I would have faced the same problem. Thirdly, I did not insist upon obtaining more information than that which was volunteered to me, since I believed that the information which I obtained was sufficient. I was also sure that trying to obtain more information would harm my future relations with the police authorities and limit my access to future events. Finally, my access to crowd events in Turkey went no further than the access I have had in the UK.

I would like to emphasise at this stage that I received a very warm and co-operative approach from many British police forces, particularly the Metropolitan Police, at many events. At the Notting Hill Carnivals of 1992 and 1993, for example, I was taken to all stages of the carnival and shown the workings of police communication networks and the command structure. In addition to that, at many events which took place in Leicester (Appendix 1), I was involved at all stages of police work, beginning with briefing procedures and ending with debriefing.

Methodological Literature Review

Any research will involve the collection of data and a variety of methods and techniques may be used for data collection, but the most common and appropriate ones for this research are the literature review of existing studies, interviews (particularly unstructured interviews) and various types of observation. As usual with comparative studies, the comparison of public order policing systems in Turkey and Britain will impose particular problems and difficulties. In the following accounts the advantages and disadvantages of these methods will be discussed with reference to the research area.

The research begins with an extensive reading concerning the field of crowd events and collective violence (Bienen, 1968; Nieburg, 1968, and 1972; MacFarlane, 1974; Tutt, 1976; Frank, 1976; Harington, 1976; Rottom, 1976; Archer, 1977; Finkel, 1989; Salmi, 1993). A substantial amount of scholarly documents have been consulted and it has been found that there are a relatively large number of books, journals and articles in the field. Some of the written data has been documented in the bibliography. In addition to this, new and fresh ideas on the area have been followed by the inclusion of periodicals such as *The Police, Policing, Police Review, Social Studies Review, The Job, Ilim ve Sanat, The Light*

Trends, The Fountain and other related journals. But the difficulty which I faced was the lack of scholarly texts, either in English or in Turkish, concerning the Turkish side of the research and I was able to consult only three short official documents dealing with all aspects of Turkish public order policing (Emniyet Genel Mudurlugu, 1983a-b-c). So far I have found only a few scholarly written books and theses completed on the subject (Gundogdu, 1985; Akinci, 1990; Ece, 1991; Erkal, 1993, Ozcan and Caglar, 1994). The text books used in the Turkish National Police Academy and other police cadet schools are very similar to each other and consist of reiterating similar information which is based on the practical experience of senior officers rather than being scholarly written works (Tek, 1980; Hatipoglu, 1986; Oguz and Sisko, [undated]; Senel, [undated]; Akgun 1986, 1988; Tomruk 1989; Toker and Dilmac 1990; Gungor and Kavalali, 1990; Buyukdogerli, 1992). Therefore, as indicated in the following review of methods, this gap will be filled by the deployment of other research techniques such as observation and interview.

The bibliography includes books in three languages, English, Turkish and Arabic. Because of the lack of recent scientific investigations and data regarding the Turkish side of the research I have used very early Arabic sources some of which were written several hundred years ago (Mawsili, 1975; Farra, 1983; Ibn Khaldun, 1987; Mawardi, 1989; Tabrizi, 1991). Mawardi, for instance, lived between 975-1058 and Farra 990-1065. They made great contributions in their masterpieces, both called *Al-Ahkamu's Sultaniyya,* which can be related to political constitutions of the present time. In addition, the *Qur'an*, the holy book of Islam, and *Hadith*, (the tradition), the sayings and deeds of the prophet Muhammed have been cited because prior to the establishment of the modern Republic of Turkey (TC) Turkey was greatly influenced by these two powerful religious texts.

Regarding official documents in the UK, although I greatly enjoyed the help and co-operation of various police forces, my access to some official documents was limited to some extent. For instance, I was not able to have a copy of the Public Order Manual, prepared by ACPO, although I had access to it for reference on a few occasions (*The Times* 3.11.1992; Tan, 1992). However, the observations were backed up by official documents and operational orders which were volunteered to me (Phillips, 1986; Ankara Constabulary, 1992; Greater Manchester Police, 1980a-b; Leicestershire Constabulary, 1991, 1992a-b-c-d-e; Metropolitan Police, 1987; 1991, 1992, 1993a-b; O'Reilly 1993; NCIS, 1994). Other publications I consulted include National Council for Civil Liberties (NCCL) publications, such as (NCCL, 1968), Street (1972) Cox (1975), Grant et al. (1978) and Thornton (1985), and these have been very valuable sources of information.

I also spent a period of four days at the Bramshill Police Staff College where I had access to numerous books and official documents with few limitations. Some of the official documents in which I was interested at The Police Staff College library were marked 'Restricted for Official Use Only' or for 'The UK Police and Government Officials Only'. Therefore, the research's literature review has been to some extent restricted and does not cover some important and relevant official documents. However, I was convinced from the access I had to some of the so-called 'secret' documents that at least some of them if not all, contained no vital information which was unavailable from public sources.

In addition to using the available books and other documents at the library of the Centre for the Study of Public Order and the library of the University of Leicester, I made use of the British Library via Leicester University Library's Inter Library Loan (ILL) service.

Interview Programme

Interviewing is a vital first hand source of information about a particular area. It usually takes place between two people, sometimes three, occasionally more. It must be noted that an interview is not merely conversation and that not all the talk that goes on between people is an interview. An interview as a first hand source of scientific information should have prescribed elements and be carried out under controlled conditions. Therefore, the interview technique which will be used in this research can be defined "...as a meeting of persons face to face, especially for the purpose of formal conference on some point" (Madge, 1975, p.144). As the definition implies, interviews must involve selected people to be interviewed for selected topics. Since textual data concerning the Turkish police was limited this gap has been filled by interviews with Turkish officers (Appendix 2) some of whom were middle rank police officers who were already working in public order units in three major cities: Ankara, Istanbul and Izmir. Face to face informal interview methods were found to be more appropriate as structured and formal interviews were found to increase the level of reluctance to answer sensitive questions.

During the research period two types of interview were deployed. In the first type of informal interviews certain key figures in police forces in Turkey such as the Chief of Izmir Cevik Kuvvet (CK) 'Rapid Action Unit' and some officers who were responsible for the training of Cevik Kuvvet units in Istanbul and Izmir were interviewed (Appendix 2). Similarly, in the UK, some officers from the Metropolitan Police (MP) training centre at

Hounslow and the Greater Manchester Police (GMP) at Sedgley Park Police Training School were informally interviewed.

In addition, towards the end of the research project a formal interview programme was carried out among 20 officers of various ranks from Sergeant to Chief Superintendent. All the officers interviewed were working in Cevik Kuvvet Units of three major cities of Turkey, Ankara, Istanbul and Izmir. The officers in question were also responsible for the training of rank and file officers working in their units. The aim of these interviews was to obtain some information about the nature and problems of existing public order policing practices in Turkey. Similar information was easily available from books and official documents in relation to British pubic order policing. The findings of the interview programme are distributed throughout the text but the main discussion on this aspect of the research is contained in chapter seven.

Courses and Seminars

Three major public order courses were attended during the research period which were run by two police forces. The first course attended was a 'Public Order Command Awareness Programme', run by Kent County Constabulary (Central Planning Unit, 1992a). This was designated for senior officers to enable them to take local command during localised community disorder and riot situations (Appendix 2). All the courses were organised by the Central Planning Unit (CPU) which provides standard training programmes for most of the British forces.

The remaining two courses, the 'Bronze/Silver Commander Course' and the 'Major Sporting Events Course', (Central Planning Unit, 1992b) were run by the Greater Manchester Police (GMP). The first course is designed as a preliminary course for those officers new to command. It addressed issues connected with understanding how a riot develops and escalates, and encourages officers to resolve these problems at an early stage. The course places importance upon briefing officers attending to quell the riot, and tactics and manoeuvres appropriate to the level of disorder. Several exercises in the classroom and simulated practical scenarios are undertaken to allow officers to experience at first hand problems associated with riotous behaviour (Appendix 2).

The second course, the 'Major Sporting Events Course', was designed to improve the knowledge, skills and understanding of officers taking command of such events and focuses on the pre-match, during the match and post match dynamics of dealing with those people attending. Emphasis was placed on intelligence-gathering from all sources so that contingency plans and match orders reflect an appropriate level of police presence to ensure the smooth passage of the sporting event (Appendix 2).

Permanent membership of the Economic and Social Research Council (ESRC) seminar series has also been a source of invaluable knowledge and inspiration (Appendix 2). Throughout these seminars a number of distinguished scholars and police practitioners made presentations, discussing contemporary issues in the policing of public disorder (King and Brearley, 1993; Waters and Brown, 1994; Huntbach, 1994; Brewer, 1994; Saunders, 1994). Among the members there were D. Waddington, J. Benyon, P. A. J. Waddington, Robert Reiner, John Brewer, Michael Keith and many other prominent and influential advisers, theorists and practitioners. The list also include police practitioners from major police forces such as Chief Inspector Louisa Elliston and Inspector Keith Wood from New Scotland Yard, Superintendent Michael Lofthouse from Kent County Constabulary and Inspector Steve Huntbach from the Greater Manchester Police. All the courses and seminars have been very informative and beneficial for my understanding of the nature of police perception of crowd events and the deployment of police personnel strength and resources.

Observations

The primary method of this research has been observation. Therefore, it is worthwhile to define and examine the types of observation used in more detail (Lee, 1969; Johnson, 1975; Rose, 1982; Jupp, 1989; May, 1993). As a method, participant observation refers to the collection of findings obtained by participating in the social world of those the researcher is studying. This involves assuming a role in the social group, or on the fringes of it, and observing, reflecting upon and interpreting the actions of individuals within the group.

Participant observation has been defined as a method of gathering evidence based on complete and accurate recording of events as they occur, giving minimal interference with those events. It is also defined as a "...period of intense social interaction between researchers and subjects in the milieu of the latter, during which time data, in the form of field notes, are unobtrusively and systematically collected" (Bogden, quoted in Kidder, 1981, p.280).

It must be emphasised that although the methodology of participant observation is appropriate for studies of almost every aspect of human existence, it is especially appropriate for explanatory and descriptive studies, and studies aimed at generating theoretical interpretations.

"Through participant observation, it is possible to describe what goes on, who or what is involved, when and where things happen, how they occur, and why - at least from the standpoint of participants things happen as they do in particular situations" (Jorgenson, 1989, p.12).

Observational methods have been used in a number of studies in the field which were designed to penetrate and explore the inner workings of the British police. Some of these works are S. Holdaway's (1983) *Inside the British Police,* D. J. Smith and J. Gray's (1985) *The Police and People in London*, D. Hobbs's (1988) *Doing the Business*, and R. Chesshyre's (1990) *The Force*. Finally, P. A. J. Waddington's (1994) work, *Liberty and Order*, is of particular interest as it is based on observations and interviews and carried out almost at the same period as this research.

In the coming sub-section the pros and cons of participant observation will be examined in detail. This section will make it clear that the participant observation method is more complex than it first appears and imposes a number of problems on the researcher. For instance, most prospective participant observers encounter problems gaining access to the related field very early in their research. At one level, this has not been a particularly difficult hurdle for me in so far as I have been a police officer and presently I am a lecturer at the Police Academy in Ankara. Although I am an overseas research student, to some extent I was regarded as one of 'them' and my personal contacts with a number of senior and junior police officers in the Leicestershire Police Constabulary confirmed that this would be the case throughout my research. I was treated, on most occasions, as an overseas colleague rather than being an outsider or a hostile (!) researcher. I have not been guaranteed access to the operational culture of police work, as would perhaps have been the case for a home research student. However, I faced similar difficulties in terms of gaining access to the Turkish police, even though I am a serving police lecturer within the same organisation.

These observations become scientific when the data is gathered systematically and is related to other data also systematically gathered for the purpose of uncovering a general principle of human behaviour. As in other methods in the social science, participant observation demands rigorous training of observers, sensitive description, careful sampling, and appropriate caution in interpretation.

On this point, it must be made clear that participant observation has not been used as a single method in a particular research area. As McCall and Simmons (1969) have pointed out, "...it is probably misleading to regard participant observation as a single method" (p.1). In this research, it has been used in combination with other methods as in the case in Smith and Gray's (1985) work, *The Police and People in London*. "While observation is often important, unstructured interviews and conversations usually provide particularly valuable data" (Rose, 1982, p.112). Accordingly, I deployed other methods such as interviewing and attended three major public order courses run by two British forces where opportunities arose for unstructured interviews.

Observation encompasses a wide range of activities. "It can embrace observation which is overt or covert, highly structured or highly unstructured, and of course, there is a variety of approaches between these two extremes" (Jupp, 1989, p.56). For instance, Kidder, (1981, p.264) divides participant observations into three. They are " (1) systematic observation of natural behaviour, (2) participant observation and ecological inquiry of natural settings, and (3) archival research of natural treatments".

According to Cohen and Manion (1989, p.122) "...there are two principal types of observation - participant observation and non-participant observation. In the former, the observer engages in the very activities he sets out to observe, and often, his 'cover' is so complete that as far as the other participants are concerned, he is simply one of the group". Non-participants, however, are not actively involved in the group activities they are investigating and eschew group membership (ibid.123). Depending on the level of participant involvement, Spradley (1980) classifies participant observation into five categories. These vary between 'complete participation' and 'non participation' and among these two extremes there are 'active', 'moderate', and 'passive' participation.

The best illustration of the non-participant observer role is perhaps the case of researcher staying behind or between the police line or violent crowd, coding up every three seconds the verbal or other form of exchange between the violent crowd members and the police by means of a structured set of observational categories. Most of the observations undertaken for this book were made at various public order training sites. These were less complete compared to the observations carried out at crowd events.

It has become clear from the definitions previously discussed that unless participant observation involves some elements, it cannot be regarded as a source of scientific information. In order to observe everyday behaviour in a systematic way so that we see differences that we might otherwise miss it is vital to take into consideration the following elements. Observation thus becomes scientific when it (1) serves a formulated research purpose, (2) is planned deliberately, (3) is recorded systematically, and (4) is subjected to checks and controls on validity and reliability.

Within this limited chapter on methodology, it is obvious that all the elements of participant observation cannot be dealt with in detail.

Therefore, I have been selective and focused on the last two elements; recording and checks on validity and reliability.

One of the most important elements of participant observation is the recording of what the researcher observes. Depending on the situation, recording can be made in different ways. "The most complete records are those made on the spot. Memories are faulty and tend to be selective. When events are filtered through an observer's memory, the observer's report is bound to emphasise one person's idea of what is important and to de-emphasise everything else" (Stern, 1979, p.25). Yet, for some research projects, especially where the researcher is a covert participant, neither note-books nor tapes are practicable and notes must be made from memory as soon as possible after the event.

> Because the observer is often not able or does not wish to write full notes while at the site, the observer should be trained to make mental notes of what is observed in situ, then the notes jotted down immediately after leaving the scene, and finally full field notes, which are the conversion of the jottings and mental notes into a running log of observations. These should be written as soon as it is feasibly possible to guard against memory loss and conceptual distortion (Kidder, 1981, p.281).

In short, "...good participant observation field notes include actual quotes, clear distinctions between 'fact' and 'impression', incorporation of unusual or inexplicable events, explicit rendering and bracketing of feelings and hunches, and comments on the benefits and costs of the data gathering methods" (Kidder, 1981, p.281). In the earlier observations I was using note-taking during the event where it was convenient and appropriate. If it was not appropriate notes were made from my memory at the earliest available opportunity. In the later observations in both Turkey, England and Wales recordings were made using a personal camcorder.

The physical presence of the participant imposes some difficulties in terms of recording as well as influencing the behaviour of the observed (Waddington, 1994b, p.207-213). This negative influence is so crucial that sometimes it is impossible to use the participant observer method because rules prohibit it or because the presence of a third party or stranger would modify the behaviour under observation. More especially in situations where observers are visible, subjects tend to suppress negative behaviours, increase desired behaviour, and reduce overall activity.

The negative influence of the observer on the observed has been acknowledged by both the observer and observed in a number of previous studies. For instance, Smith and Gray (1985) who grounded their research in the direct observation of day-to-day policing in London over a two-year period, have remarked that, "...we have to assume that the presence of the researcher was something of a restraining influence; also there were indications that this was so" (Smith and Gray, 1985, p.303). In addition to that, they quote an experienced sergeant in a crime squad giving the following account of the way he would behave towards the researcher.

> You're not a fool. You know that things are not done properly in this job at times. Now I'm not going to do anything seriously wrong in front of you, but you must know that we all have in the past. I'm prepared to be as honest as I can with you. In other words, I'll give you 90 per cent of the truth (Smith and Gray, 1985, p.304).

They were also told by a Chief Inspector right at the beginning of their research that, "...if there are police officers who beat people up in the cells, they are not going to do it while you are watching" (ibid.303).

In order to eliminate or at least to minimise the negative influence of the observer's presence, McCall and Simmons (1969, p.95) suggest that, "...when the observed becomes convinced that the observer's attitude toward them is one of respect and interest in them as human beings as well as research subjects, they will feel less need for concealing, withholding, or distorting data".

This might be the case in some certain social researches done in areas of education or in similar services. But, in a controversial area such as public order policing and training, I do not believe that this will reduce the level of restraint of the observed, although Smith and Gray (1985) argue that "...the longer the observer is with them, the more the officers tend to settle back into their usual pattern of activity" (ibid.302).

Smith and Gray (1985) concluded that after a long period with a group they came to know a great deal about what went on even if they had not seen it all themselves. Once the role of observer has been established the course of events may be altered even when the observer is temporarily absent. Perhaps the only solution to this problem is to attempt to predict what would happen in an unobserved situation from what had happened in the presence of the observer, but this is unacceptable as scientific data.

It would appear that there is no way of entirely eliminating the negative influence of an observer on the observed. The mere presence of the observer means that movements are made and orientations are developed toward him which would not otherwise have occurred. Therefore, an important decision must be made in any systematic observation of natural behaviour concerning the obtrusiveness of the observer. For this very reason, investigators choose to conceal the fact that the subjects' behaviour will be influenced by their knowledge that they are being observed.

Good relationships formed between observer and observed, although desirable, can never obviate the influence of the observer's presence and it remains impossible to measure how much the observed acts have been influenced by the observer. To find out how much an observer's activities have changed events, we would have to observe the events, if possible, both overtly and covertly in order to see how much difference there is. This is, of course, impossible for practical reasons and therefore we can never be sure how much the research process has changed the people and events being studied.

Participant observation can be criticised in terms of recording and the influence of the presence of the observer. Such researches have also been criticised by many on the grounds that the accounts emerging from participant observations are subjective and biased, reflecting the belief and desired outcomes belonging to the mindset of the observer.

The reliability of participant observation sometimes is questioned. Defined conventionally, "...reliability refers to the extent to which a procedure, especially measurement, produces the same result with repeated usage" (Jorgensen, 1989, p.37). Besides this, Kidder (1981, p.266) has remarked that "...social scientific observations are reliable to the extent to which they show consistency and stability in their scoring. The most familiar meaning of reliability is the degree to which two or more observers agree on their observations".

Some critics raise questions about two types of validity in participant observation-based research. Comments about the subjective and idiosyncratic nature of participant observation studies are to do with its external validity; how do we know that the results of a particular piece of research are applicable to other situations? Fears that the observer's judgement will be affected by his close involvement in the group relate to the internal validity of the method and the results of a particular piece of research become questionable.

The problem of reliability and validity stems from the problem of subjectivity. One of the main aims of participant observation is to see social phenomena as it is in reality but researchers see social events as they are or in a way that fits their research remit. In deriving conclusions from a particular observation the researcher may subjectify the findings of this research by mixing them with his personal bias and prejudices. These are questions which are not only relevant to this particular research but to all studies with a sociological base.

Literature Review

The research begins with an extensive reading covering various aspects of crowd, crowd behaviour and collective violence. It is appropriate to divide the existing studies in the field into two broad categories. The first group deals mainly with theoretical and academic issues. Under this section, classical theories and their relevance to contemporary crowd events have been reconsidered and some eminent classical theories will be analysed and compared with modern crowd theories.

The literature review carried out for this research shows that despite the existence of numerous studies on the theoretical aspects of crowd and crowd behaviour (La Piere, 1938, 1949; Lipset and Smelser, 1961; Park, 1967; Bienen, 1968; Appelbaum, 1970; Mungham, 1977; Lindzey and Aronson, 1968a-b, 1969a-b-c, 1985; Gaskel and Benewick, 1987, Leeds, 1992; Marshal, 1992a-b), there are only limited scholarly assessments of the practical implication of these works on public order policing practices (Brown, 1982; Brewer, 1994; BSSRS, 1985; Fine and Millar, 1985; Fruin, 1993). On the other hand those works which have practical implications (Janowitz, 1968; Deane-Drumond, 1975; Sloan, 1984; Institute of Criminology, 1992) seem to be based on the experience of serving police officers and lack academic qualification. Hence, more recent works on crowds and public order policing practices will be examined with a particular emphasis on issues of crowd violence and their practical implications on police operations. Therefore, the second group of works deals with more practical issues such as the implications of theoretical works and their application to public order policing practices.

In addition to secondary data obtained from the literature review, complementary social science research techniques have been deployed and among these are interviews and observations. The researcher also attended three major public order courses designed for senior police officers in the UK. This chapter ends with an examination of the advantages and disadvantages of observational methodology, the main method employed in this research to obtain first hand data.

Existing Studies

Before occupying myself with relatively recent works in the field, some of the major crowd theories which have played a pioneering role in public order policing policies and practices up to the present time must be assessed. Existing crowd theories in this field can be grouped broadly under two categories. In the first category, there are those of G. Le Bon

(1892, 1898) and his contemporaries such as G. Tarde (1890), S. Sighele (1892a-b) and later S. Freud (1940 and 1994). Their theories are mostly based on the assumption "...that the nature of the crowd and its activities can be explained in terms of the internal dynamics of its psychological process, without reference to the social context" (Waddington, 1989, p.4). It is important to note that not all crowd theorists fall under this broad category nor do they share the same opinions to the same extent.

Throughout this research, this group of collective behaviour theories will be referred to as 'classical' crowd theories. It is of primary importance to note that although these theories are mainly based on the psychological aspects of crowd behaviour, at least some of them can be seen to implicitly acknowledge the role and influence of social factors on crowd formation and action.

In contrast to the 'classical' crowd theories the second group of theories concentrate on the social aspects of crowd behaviour. Some of the most eminent are, Smelser's 'Value Added Theory' (1962, 1968); Turner and Killian's (1962) 'Emergent Norm Theory' and Clark McPhail's 'Social Behavioural/Interactionist' theory (SBI) (McPhail 1971, Miller 1985). There are also those who regard crowd action as socially meaningful and purposeful (Bienen, 1968; Connery, 1968; Nieburg, 1968; Tilly, 1970, 1974; Young and Taylor, 1973; Parry et al. 1978; Lea and Young, 1984).

These theories attempt to introduce an alternative approach to general crowd behaviour including crowd aggression and violence. In addition, there are some eminent theories which do not aim to improve crowd theory as a whole, but which explain crowd crime and crowd violence from a particular point of view, and these are worth mentioning in this context. The theories are 'Relative Deprivation' (Gurr, 1970) and 'Subcultural Theory' (Lea and Young, 1984).

The second group includes those theories which regard crowd gatherings as more 'collective action' than 'collective behaviour'. These are classified as 'modern' crowd theories. On this point, it must again be emphasised that these theories do not completely rule out the psychological, or at least social psychological aspect of human behaviour in crowds (Reicher, 1984 and 1985), referring implicitly and indirectly to the role and importance of psychological motives of collective behaviour. The most important point rests on the question of priority and emphasis, not on complete denial. While the classical crowd theorists, for instance, give priority to psychological motives, the modern theorists give priority to material factors and focus on the social motives of human action.

Being unable to examine and assess every crowd theory, the research has concentrated on a typical example: Le Bon's 'social contagion theory' as an example of classical theories and this is compared with

Smelser's 'value added theory' representing modern theories. During this comparison and assessment, other crowd theories will be brought into the argument where appropriate.

Classical and Modern Crowd Theories

Defining collective behaviour in terms of aroused emotion is intended to set collective behaviour apart from the social action that occurs within institutionalised relationships or formal organisations. Gustave Le Bon is often identified as the founder of this trend which concentrates on the anti-social tendencies of crowd behaviour. A similar emphasis on the anti-social tendencies of crowd behaviour can be found in the writings of the late nineteenth century pioneers of crowd research, the Frenchman G. Tarde (1890) and the Italian Scipio Sighele (1892a-b). J. V. Ginneken (1992) in his book *Crowds, Psychology and Politics, 1871-1889,* points out the intriguing similarities between the works of French theorists Tarde, Fournial and Le Bon and the Italian Sighele, all of whom published significant research within a four year period. Sighele produced *La Folla Delinquente* in 1891, Tarde published two major articles in 1892-3 and Fournial's *Essai sur La Psychologie des Foules* was published in 1892. In 1895, Le Bon's most influential and widely acclaimed work, *The Crowd*, was published. Here Le Bon echoes the findings of his contemporaries that crowds are usually highly emotional and irrational, destructive rather than constructive and in need of strong leadership.

In *The Crowd* Le Bon boldly states that all crowds exert a profound and inherently negative influence on people. He describes this influence as a contagious or rapidly transmitted mental unity that emerges whenever people interact in a group. The quotation below best describes his view of the individual in the crowd:

> ...by the mere fact that he forms part of an organised crowd, a man descends several rungs in the ladder of civilisation. Isolated, he may be a cultivated individual; in a crowd, he is a barbarian - that is, a creature acting by instinct (Le Bon, 1969, p.32).

His discussion of the effects of the crowd on individuals builds to the conclusion that the crowd transforms rational, law-abiding people into violent, irrational enemies of the state. He maintains that the contagious mental unity of crowds reduces the mental capacity of enlightened and cultured people to the level of 'those inferior forms of evolution' such as women, savages, and children.

It is evident that Le Bon's emphasis on the crowd's influence on the individual was greatly affected by the crowd violence which he witnessed in his time. In his work, however, he found a number of vitally important crowd attributes which are the result of collective action and behaviour. His narrow perspective of the crowd phenomenon focused only on violent crowds and the psychological manifestation of their behaviour. Le Bon generalised his own observation to include all types of crowd, regardless of nationality, their ethics, habits or customs failing to regard the crowd phenomenon from a broad historical or cultural perspective.

His argument implies that all members of a crowd lose their individuality and act as one single body controlled by a 'collective mind'. For him, contagious mental unity overcomes the individual's rational capabilities. People in the crowd do not reflect on the outcome of their actions; perceptions are distorted and feelings of power emerge that become the basis of attack on authority. Divested of critical ability and powers of reflection, people within the crowd are incapable of respect for social standards, conventions, and institutions.

Numerous peaceful crowd events and a number of studies in the field of collective behaviour have made it clear that Le Bon was mistaken, in at least, two ways. Firstly, he was wrong to assume that all crowd movements and activities are revolutionary and against the authority of the state. Secondly, he failed to see that not all crowd members are united by one cause and motivated towards unanimously held aims and goals (Turner and Killian, 1962; McPhail and Miller, 1973). It is now evident that not all crowd actions are revolutionary with an aim of overthrowing governments or to destroy the state (La Pierre, 1938, p.540). The observations upon which this study is based have reached a similar conclusion. The empirical elements of this study have found that apart from certain crowd events which involve extreme politically motivated participants with a peculiar political context, the majority of large gatherings merely wish to air a particular grievance, or influence a particular authority in order to modify its policies to suit the needs of the protesting crowd. The bulk of crowds are relatively benign in their attitude to the state and established authority. In Western democracies this type of action is frequently tolerated and far from being regarded as a revolutionary movement, it is instead regarded as a fundamental right of the citizen, and governments can be, and are, influenced by mass protest.

Moreover, a number of recent studies on crowd participants have proved that crowd action is not as unanimous as Le Bon had imagined. Rather, the crowd acts unanimously on a particular subject for a short period of time. Turner and Killian (1962) argue that total uniformity of mood and behaviour within the crowd is seldom observed, the majority of crowd acts occurring in small sub - groups of 3-9 individuals. Within crowds various motives for participation exist, diverse feelings are in evidence and many types of behaviour can be observed. Some participants may be seeking excitement or cultural/subcultural expression. Police and protest leaders who are present are concerned with maintaining order and tranquillity. Seldom will all these people express the same feelings or act in unison. In line with this assumption, difficulties have been encountered in classifying crowds under definite and definitive groups (see chapter two).

It has become clear from my personal observation of numerous crowd events, both in Turkey and England, that some groups of demonstrators join the protests or demonstrations for the obvious cause of the demonstration in question, but in addition, they have their own peculiar reasons too. A good example of this is the presence of the members of Turkish 'Revolutionary Left' (Dev-Sol) at two recent 'Troops Out Marches' organised by the Irish Community (Observations 14 and 27). The participation of the members of Dev-Sol was very much determined by a desire to support a cause which was felt to mirror their own oppression. Besides supporting a group who are in a similar situation to their own, at the same time they were manifesting their own particular dissent towards the Turkish state (Campbell, 1994) as well as towards the British state, in an indirect way. The same participants were seen carrying their usual banners at many other demonstrations throughout the year (Observations 25 and 28).

It might be more appropriate to classify those participants who take the opportunity to express their grievances at every available and suitable opportunity as 'professional demonstrators'. These groups may be seen as regular promoters of their own concerns and what they identify as kindred or related interests. Certain groups such as gay rights activists, the Socialist Workers Party and the British Communist Party (BCP) can be considered under this category.

In abstract terms, recent studies have shown that not all crowds are revolutionary and that there is no unanimity between all crowd members as Le Bon had described. At this point, it could again be argued that Le Bon's crowd theory may explain one particular type of crowd or violent crowd, from a very limited perspective. It does not include all types of crowd nor all aspects of crowd behaviour.

Although he is more concerned with the psychology of the crowd, Le Bon does not completely ignore the social determinants of crowd action. One such attempt is apparent in a passage in which Le Bon attempts to refer to the underlying reasons and a causal explanation of crowd action:

> ...a more attentive study of these events shows that behind their apparent causes the real cause is generally seen to be a profound modification in the ideas of the people (Le Bon, 1969, p.13).

With this statement Le Bon acknowledges that individual acts are determined and influenced by certain motives which derive from long term factors; the acts of individuals forming a crowd cannot be the mere product of participation in a crowd . The crowd does not first create ideas and then act on them; rather each individual has his/her own ideas before joining a crowd. If Le Bon is arguing that the crowd may modify or exaggerate the idea, and therefore the actions of individuals, he may be right to some extent, and this has been accepted by the majority of the crowd theorists. However, the argument that the crowd completely dominates the individual mind, is now usually rejected. Although recent crowd theories disagree with Le Bon on the question of crowd influence on the individual, they implicitly accept the indirect influence of the crowd on its participants. For example, subcultural theory examines the individual's behaviour not as an isolated act committed only through individual motivation, but within the context of the individual's subculture. Lea and Young (1984) represents a revitalised form of subcultural theory, merging radical criminological concerns with earlier American subcultural theories. In fact, this is a way of indirectly accepting the influence of the group or crowd on individual behaviour. For this theory, the individual's behaviour may not make sense in isolation but it does make sense when it is examined within the context of its subculture.

Apart from the influence of the crowd on individual participants the psychological make-up of each individual may determine the type of crowd and the level of its action. There is often a variation in crowd behaviour at similar events in different countries. This can be described as a correlation between the general cultural and educational level of the crowd and the outcome of its collective action. For instance, if the individuals who constitute the crowd are violent, or personally frustrated and have low cultural and educational and intellectual levels, the outcome of such crowd activities may be more violent compared with a crowd whose members know their political rights and can calculate the consequences of their action. This suggests that it is not merely the size of the crowd or the action of joining with the crowd that makes the individual violent and aggressive, rather there may be other more remote determinants which shape and influence the outcome of crowd behaviour. It does not, however, follow that a crowd of individuals who have a high level of achievement, educationally culturally and financially, do not or will not act violently. In line with this proposition, this book will argue that crowd action, and individual action, are the product of both political, social, cultural *(Institutional)* and biological and socio-psychological *(Constitutional)* variables.

The conclusion to be drawn from classical crowd theories as represented by Le Bon is that the crowd is always intellectually inferior to that of the isolated individual and that crowd action, whether it is violent or non-violent, is less rational and meaningful when compared to individual behaviour. When subcultural theory is applied to crowd violence a similar rationality can be discerned. When a violent act committed by a mob is analysed, it may seem irrational and meaningless but when this particular act is considered in a determined context and examined from a particular subcultural point of view, this act may, to some extent, be meaningful and rational. Therefore, throughout this research it is asserted that when crowd violence is examined in isolation from its wider context, it can be perceived as rational and meaningful and as having fundamental social significance.

Crowd behaviour is perhaps one of the most meaningful of collective human activities. Throughout history crowds have gathered to accomplish things which individuals were unable to achieve. Crowd behaviour is socially and politically meaningful and, to some extent, rational. The signifier produced by crowd violence may neither be considered nor calculated and therefore cannot be deemed unjustifiable. However, this does not completely refute the rationality of crowd action. It is the task of social scientists to receive the message broadcast by crowd violence and identify its rationality. Paradoxically, the potentially conservative implications of classical theories that deny the rationality of crowds in their opposition to existing social arrangements may be seen to imply an absence of responsibility for the action of individual crowd actors. In traditional legal terms 'mens rea' is removed or compromised, removing the responsibility of the individual to the criminal law.

With regard to individual responsibility and the rationality of each act, every individual is responsible for his or her violent action during a confrontation; whatever the causes of violence, nothing can remove individual responsibility or justify violent actions. Violence in crowd action, however does not deny the overall rationality of crowd action. Since violent acts are a response to, and a reflection of, the failure of existing political and economic arrangements, the message given by violent crowds must be received and taken into consideration by responsible authorities by disregarding its apparent irrationality compared with individual action.

Crowd violence is not as irrational as Le Bon and his followers have argued, nor is it as rational as some contemporary crowd theorists have imagined. When violence is examined as isolated acts, the crimes committed by individuals and by crowds are irrational, but when examined contextually they may transmit a message and therefore be rational and meaningful.

Using this argument, this research does not deny the overall rationality of crowd violence and accepts the message which can be taken from it. However, it does not glorify or justify crowd violence on the basis of the rationality specific to its participants. The following accounts tend to place stress on the social rationality of crowd violence by glorifying it to some extent. Throughout history, crowds have mostly been the victims of violence rather than the perpetrators of it. Therefore, to glorify crowd violence and rationalise its violent activities will not change the end result of that violence.

Not all crowd movements become violent during the early stages of their formation and activities. This is the case not only for contemporary crowd events but also for historical crowds. Crowd violence has often been the result of many peaceful attempts and failures to gain some fundamental change in the existing social, political and economic structure (see 'Political Violence' in chapter four). Therefore, this is not an appropriate point to begin the examination of crowd violence in its final stage which might involve overt confrontation between the crowd and the representatives of the existing system, the police or the army. For this reason, recent crowd theorists begin their studies by exploring the roots of conflict rather than concentrating on the last stage of a long process. The theory that is developed in this book, the Combined Factors Approach, is an attempt to combine the *Constitutional* and *Institutional* factors into the causal explanations of crowd behaviour and the violence exhibited in particular.

In one of the most influential analyses of crowd behaviour, *Theory of Collective Behaviour,* N. J. Smelser (1962) defines collective behaviour as people's uninstitutionalised efforts to reconstruct the basic determinants of social behaviour. Although Smelser's theory of collective behaviour seems to be influenced by traditional classical crowd approaches, it can also be seen as an attempt to draw attention to the social meaning of crowd action. These basic determinants - the components of social action - refer to elemental forces, other than individual personalities, which order, regulate and direct behaviour within a society. The most general component of social action within a society is the set of social *values,* or shared *beliefs* identifying the goals toward which the members of the society should strive.

However, it is not always possible to identify universally held social values which every nation has in common. There are inevitably degrees of difference from one country to another. While in developed Western countries, social values such as personal achievement, activity, hard work and status have priority over non-material achievements and status, in Eastern countries and cultures this may not apply to the same extent, and emphasis may be put upon abstract values such as justice, honour, chastity and family values. Since cultural difference has a significant importance in this research, which is based on the comparison of two different cultures and police organisations, it is worth mentioning the influence of cultural determinants on crowd behaviour as well as on the police in more detail in the coming chapter.

Smelser suggests as the second component of social action *societal norms* which are explicit and implicit rules governing the pursuit of values. Much of criminal and civil law in both England and Turkey, directly or indirectly regulates the manner in which the value of personal achievement is perceived.

The third component of social action is *organisation of motivation,* which refers to the specific implicit and explicit requirements accompanying statutes, roles, groups, and organisations that constitute the social structure of a society. The final and most immediate component of social action are the *situational facilities* - tools, skills, and knowledge of the environment - that people have at their disposal.

For Smelser the components of social action, which have been briefly mentioned above, can be constructed by institutionalised means. All societies use a number of means varying from education processes, the media and the law, in order to restructure the components of social action.

Smelser also argues that the components of social action can also be restructured through uninstitutionalised means. That is, the restructuring occurs apart from and at times counter to, traditional channels of authority, decision making, communication and sources of political and economic power. Smelser terms this *collective behaviour.* The uninstitutionalised restructuring of values, norms, organisation of motivation and situational facilities occur as collective episodes.

After defining the components of social action, Smelser argues that the emergence of the crowd, in order to restructure the components of social action, is dependent upon appropriate *social conditions,* (structural conduciveness) the requisite degree of *structural strain,* specific perceptions of *such tensions* (generalised beliefs), a *precipitating incident* and, in the absence of adequate preventive control mechanism, *mobilisation by activists.*

Smelser's Value Added Theory, offers a 'several factors occurring together' explanation of collective behaviour in order to answer the question of why people depart from institutionalised means of change and take up uninstituonalised means. This method means, simply, that all five determinants must exist before a collective episode can occur. Further, the likelihood that a collective episode will occur increases as each determinant is initiated. A hostile outburst, such as an inner-city riot, can be triggered by a seemingly insignificant event that fulfils the final determinant. The Flashpoints Model which was introduced recently by Waddington et al. (1987 and 1989) and Waddington (1987 and 1992) bears a resemblance to Smelser's theory. Like Smelser, Waddington argues that the likelihood of violence increases at each stage and it might be possible to prevent the occurrence of violence at each stage by taking appropriate steps. As in Waddington et al.'s Flashpoints model, Smelser's theory indicates that before any collective behaviour can occur the following value-added determinants must exist in turn:

Structural Conduciveness This is the most general value-added determinant of collective behaviour. In the broadest sense, 'structural' refers to the basic parameters imposed on behaviour by culture. Cultural values and norms entail world views within which collective behaviour operates. For instance, in a country where there is no minority group nor any ethnic community, any race oriented riot is ruled out by structural unconduciveness. But this determinant is not permanent and unchangeable. If the same country has substantial numbers of immigrants then structural conduciveness becomes possible.

Structural Strain For Smelser, all collective behaviour results from some form of strain within the social system. Structural strain refers to inconsistencies between the values and norms of a society or to conditions of material deprivation established by the distribution of situational facilities of a society.

Generalised Belief The third value-added determinant is a generalised belief that prepares participants for action when structural conduciveness and strain are present. Generalised beliefs emerge through process of rumour, milling, suggestion and social contagion. Le Bon's social contagion theory focuses on this stage of crowd behaviour and the most significant difference between Le Bon and his followers and contemporary crowd theorists rests at this stage. Le Bon began to examine crowd behaviour from this stage, over-simplifying the former two determinants. He stretches this stage so wide that it includes all crowd types and activities. Therefore, perhaps it is more appropriate to argue that his crowd theory is incomplete rather than charging it with complete inaccuracy.

It is evident that not only Le Bon, but also some modern crowd theorists have pointed out the importance of this determinant. Blumer (1975) implies the same determinant when he argues that remarkable events create tensions which dispose people to behave like a crowd. He maintains that once underlying tensions are created people move about in an aimless and random fashion, which he calls 'milling'. Turner and Killian (1962) describe this determinant by dividing crowd behaviour into two, as 'traditional' and 'emergent'. They insist that collective behaviour is basically social behaviour, guided by both traditional and emergent norms. Even in crowded settings where excitement is high, people retain critical ability and a sense of personal motives (Reicher, 1984 and 1985). But what Turner and Killian call the 'emergent norm' is regarded as the product of the 'collective mind' by Le Bon. It implies that, regarding a norm as 'emergent' will not make it as rational as the long-established traditional norms.

In abstract terms, whatever name has been given to the outcome of collective behaviour, it will not change the level of rationality of crowd behaviour. The following quotation makes it clear that the 'emergent norm', established during the process of generalised beliefs, is not a product of well considered, reasoned and calculated decision. Right or wrong, it is a spontaneous reaction to a spontaneous action. Therefore, it is, as the name implies, less considered and has emerged as a reaction to a particular situation.

> As crowd behaviour develops, there is communication of mood, imagery, and a concept of what kind of action is appropriate. These are 'emergent', not traditional. While they are related to the past experiences and previously held norms and attitudes of participants, they constitute new products of the interaction in the particular situation (Turner and Killian, 1962, p.83).

Le Bon regards collective action as a purely irrational product of the crowd under the influence of its leaders. When it comes to making a realistic comparison and judgement between a well considered decision by an individual, or an institutionalised group of people who have expertise on a particular subject, and the decision taken by a crowd as an 'emergent norm', it is apparent that the former is relatively more rational than the latter. Not only the critics of the collective mind and behaviour but even advocates of the rationality of collective behaviour implicitly confess the inferiority of the product of the 'collective mind'. But, as it has previously been asserted, this does not lead to the conclusion that no form of collective behaviour is socially and politically rational and meaningful.

Mobilisation for Action The fourth value-added determinant is the mobilisation for action. Given conduciveness, strain, and a generalised belief, a susceptible population must be brought into action.

Action of Social Control The final value-added determinant in Smelser's model is the action of social control. Institutions and leaders confronted by imminent and ongoing collective episodes can act to (l) prevent (2) redirect, or (3) accommodate collective behaviour.

Since this determinant is very much related to the response to collective behaviour of a particular state and its controlling agencies, the police and army, this stage will be examined in more detail in a later chapter.

Smelser's theory departs radically from the social psychological tradition of the analysis of crowds and other collective behaviour - the tradition of Tarde, Le Bon, Freud and others, whose theories are based primarily on psychological variables, whether of the 'superficial' types such as imitation, sympathy, contagion, and suggestion or the 'deeper' types such as projection, regression, and transfer of libidinal ties. On the other hand, Smelser does not completely refute the involvement of psychological factors. Rather, he argues that psychological variables, "...such as suggestion, projection, displacement, and fetishism are products in part of social determinants" (Smelser, 1962, p.21). However, Smelser is accused by Currie and Skolnick (1972) of frequently relying on official riot control manuals for empirical descriptions of the 'hostile outburst', without so much as suggesting the need for exercising caution in the use of such sources. This reliance inevitably leads to an underestimation of the role of agencies of social control in the origins and the content of the collective violence itself, rather than merely affecting its outcome.

The theory emerging from this study sees the psychological metaphors as raw materials possessed by the individual to be shaped, upgraded or degraded by external factors ranging from the smallest social unit, the family, to wider ones such as the state and all its institutions, such as schools, churches and the judicial system. Moreover, the interactive aspects of social behaviour applies to psychological as well as social dimensions. It is misleading to focus on the hidden psychological motives of one set of participants in a protest situation while leaving the other factors unexamined.

All of this should not be taken to imply that this research rejects the attempt to investigate the social aspects of crowd events. Therefore, instead of focusing only on social or psychological factors of crowd events and collective behaviour, combined factors theory is an analysis of the crowd and its behaviour from an approach which combines both *institutional* and *constitutional* factors. And this research is only an attempt to draw attention to the need to combine these factors into the causal explanations. However, the theory aims to combine constitutional factors into the argument without ignoring or underestimating the significance and importance of political and social factors.

Recent Studies on Crowd and Public Order Policing

An understanding of the causation of mass disturbances is important both in terms of police response and necessary political response. Apportioning blame for the causes of disorder is, of course, important, for it influences the public and official responses to these events. But the attribution of causation to one or another aspect serves merely to blame rather than explain. Recent arguments in this field go on like a chicken and egg story; which comes first? Do police equipment and tactics provoke the crowd and escalate the riots or do the crowds themselves have an inherent tendency to riot? The existing studies which will briefly be explained, seem to be influenced by the political perspectives of their advocates.

Existing studies in this field are usefully categorised under three broad headings as the *conservative*, *liberal* and *radical* perspectives. Since the studies carried out in this field are shaped according to these three main perspectives, it is worth starting with an explanation of this broad trichotomy.

The conservative view regards collective violence as 'rare', needless, without purpose and irrational (Taylor et al. 1975, p.21-22; Benyon, 1987, p.26; Pugh, 1990). For such commentators riots are caused by 'human nature' and 'criminality'. They assume that existing social structures are adequate and desirable and there can, therefore, be no justification or necessity for violent agitation. This view is upheld mainly by Conservative politicians, police officers, some authors and certain sections of the mass media.

The liberal view sees violence as inevitable under certain conditions, such as high unemployment and widespread social disadvantage. The radical perspective, however, regards collective violence as purposeful, structured and politically meaningful. It is seen as a normal, legitimate and effective means of protest by groups who have no other opportunities and who are experiencing real deprivation and injustice (Benyon, 1987, p.26-27).

When one looks at the existing studies the influence of these perspectives can be clearly traced. For instance, P. A. J. Waddington (1985a, 1985b, 1987 and 1988) a sociologist and ex-police officer, challenges the academic wisdom that sees black rioters as 'victims' and white ones as 'hooligans'. Contradicting liberal academics such as J. Benyon and J. Solomos (1987) and others, he argues that "...because a riotous group has a plausible grievance does not establish that the grievance is the cause of the riot" (Waddington, 1988, p.36). He argues that what is smuggled into the argument at this point, under the cloak of causation, is very often a moral sympathy for the group in question.

Most academics, like many politicians, recognise that young blacks in British society are very often socially deprived and discriminated against, feel sympathy for their plight and therefore feel less inclined to condemn their riotous behaviour. Yet, this does not establish that injustice causes rioting. Waddington concluded that, "...indeed the evidence of 'white riots' points to the opposite conclusion, for they riot despite the absence of any plausible grievances (Waddington, 1988, p.36). It seems too difficult to disagree with Waddington's claim while a number of white participants were seen in inner city disturbances such as the Brixton (1981), Handsworth (1981) and many other similar inner city disturbances. Neither police brutality towards some sections of society nor deprivation and poverty theories seem to explain adequately the cause of these events. "Poverty is a necessary but not sufficient cause of riot. Neither poverty, racial difference nor police harassment are alone sufficient. Nor is the problem one of a lack of integration" (Fielding, 1991, p.77). On the contrary, while liberal and radical arguments argue that poverty, deprivation, police harassment and brutality are important causes of these disturbances, the conservatives have repeatedly argued that, those areas with the greatest deprivation and decay would be most susceptible to rioting. But Gaskell and Benewick's (1988) research shows that the situation is not nearly so simple. This study compares three areas in Northern England, all of which suffer very similar levels of deprivation such as unemployment and decay, but only one of which, Moss Side, suffered rioting. As the authors remarked, "there is obviously no simple correlation between deprivation and crowd incidents" (Gaskell and Benewick, quoted in Waddington, 1988, p.36).

However, it is still widely held by academics that despite the slight decrease in the recorded crime rate (5.5m in 1993) there is still a link between the general economic level of a nation and the crime rate (an interview with Robert Reiner, BBC 4, *Five O'clock News,* 19 April 1994). Just a few days after this interview, in another interview the Conservative Home Secretary Michael Howard denied any link between crime and unemployment (BBC 4, *Seven O'clock News*, 26 April 1994). The broadcasting media, where politicians frequently exchange views on crime and related matters, has been a rich source of information (BBC2 Public Eye, Tackling Crime, March 1992). Dramatic incidents such as the James Bulger case, a three year old boy abducted and brutally killed by two boys aged ten and eleven, or violent events involving large numbers of people such as the inner-city riots of the eighties receive heavy and widespread media coverage.

People participate in riots for various reasons and although it is always possible to find some common characteristics it is not always feasible to categorise or explain all the riots through one perspective. The reasons why people riot is still open to question and none of these three broad perspectives and individual explanations seem to be able to provide an answer. Yet, there is no reason why the answer to this question should not be investigated beyond the received ideas of these three perspectives. Therefore, this study will consider crowd action from outside these broad perspectives rather than trying to fit the facts to one of them.

In the final chapter of the book, the focus of the research will be on police equipment and tactics during crowd events and an examination of their role in the escalation or de-escalation of violence. There will be no discussion of the legitimacy or use of this equipment and tactics or the role of the police in these conflicts. However, since the way in which this equipment is deployed is seen to be very important in escalating the riots, the role of the police will be examined. It is a commonly accepted fact that the role of the police is somewhat limited and is not the only cause for riots. "The police do not create social deprivation or racial disadvantage, they are not responsible for the disadvantage of the ethnic minorities" (Scarman, quoted in Das, 1988, p.113). Hence, demonstrations, protests and even inner-city disturbances are seldom directly about policing. If the riots are the result of basic flaws in the existing system (as the liberals and radicals have argued) police can do little or nothing about it. It must be noted that "...[although] the police may have no direct influence over the cause which exercises protests but they have major influence over the course of protest, including the image disseminated in the all-important media reports" (Fielding, 1991, p.79).

Apart from those writers already mentioned, T. Jefferson, a Marxist sociologist of the police, examined the purposes and methods of the police handling of public order problems. In his book, *Paramilitary Policing* (1990), he divides public order events requiring a paramilitary response broadly into four categories; (a) preparation; (b) controlling the space; (c) controlling the crowd; (d) clearance. He made it clear that whilst this particular description fits no one such occasion, its general features embrace them all (Jefferson, 1990, p.84). With regard to protective clothing and equipment he claims that the riot control technology only serves to exacerbate the situation.

Another researcher, D. Waddington (1989) and his colleagues attempted to identify 'flashpoints' of disorder by investigating various public order events. The model "...combines reference to the antecedent conditions (the 'tinder') with a highlighting of interpersonal interaction (the 'spark'), thus involving both psychological and sociological perspectives" (Waddington et al. 1989, p.2). Their research advocates that any theory of public disorder must recognise its collective nature, group behaviour being different from individual behaviour.

The 'flashpoint' model comprises six components namely *Structural, Political/Ideological, Cultural, Contextual, Situational* and *Interactional. Structure* deals with strain theory, *Political* and *Ideological* with alienation from or lack of representation to the dominant political group. *Culture* deals with values, group identity, class values and subcultures, *Contextual* with media sensitisation, communication and previous conflict. *Situational* deals with the physical setting, the organisation of the crowd and the police and the absence or presence of any symbolic targets. Finally, *interactional* deals with the breakdown of situational norms and the rejection of arbitration. The 'flashpoints model' rejects any single theory for causes of public disorder and combines the views of the conservative, liberal and radical perspectives. Compared with Smelser's 'value added theory' Waddington et al.'s *Flashpoints* model is a further step towards a multidisciplinary approach to crowd events.

In line with the 'flashpoints model', this research has reached a conclusion that is rather subjective if not biased regarding collective behaviour, as either rational or irrational, reflecting the personal perspectives of a particular social scientist. As Waddington et al. (1989) pointed out, "...collective behaviour does not have to be either irrational or rational but may be both" (p.5). However, as collectives are made up of individuals then in any given situation different people may have different reasons for being present. Therefore, in the following chapters it will be argued that every action committed by a human being has a varying degree of rationality and is full of socially meaningful messages, but may not be justifiable.

Perhaps crowd behaviour is much more rational and socially meaningful in comparison with individual behaviour. Gatherings of large numbers or groups to demonstrate their opposition or grievances on a particular point reflects to some extent the appropriateness of their cause (Reicher, 1984). One or two individuals may be entirely irrational in their actions, but a crowd comprising tens of thousands of individuals cannot, either by chance or as a result of an irrational decision, gather, demonstrate and act in unison for a completely irrational and meaningless cause. This does not necessarily lead to the conclusion that any large crowd is always right and acts perfectly rationally. But we can receive socially meaningful messages concerning the crowd from these activities as well as messages about the general state of society, without rationalising or justifying these acts.

One of the most important findings introduced by Waddington et al. (1989, p.157) is that "...disorder is not a random occurrence in a unique set of circumstances. There is a common pattern or dynamic, underlying apparently diverse events". In an otherwise well-researched and informative contribution, they try to establish that certain arrangements or incidents were the 'flashpoints' of disorder during various demonstrations they had witnessed in Sheffield. For instance, the decision by the police to disperse a large crowd of miners following a demonstration held during the strike was, they maintain, the cause of the disorder that followed. However, from their description of events one might equally conclude that the cause of 'flashpoint' was the behaviour of the crowd in refusing to comply with the police instructions.

The attribution of causation to one or other aspect serves merely to blame rather than explain. The debate on these issues is like a pantomime where one side says 'the police caused the violence' and the other side says 'Oh no they didn't!' and the first group says 'Oh yes they did!'. No progress is made and no meaningful discussion takes place.

In the wake of the inner city riots in the 1980s, a number of studies have been carried out by academics such as Edwards (1994), Rowe (1994) Matthews (1994) and Benyon (1993, 1994a-b) as well as police practitioners such as Elliston (1991), Brightmore (1992), Morrell (1992), Francis and Matthews (1993), Hesse (1993) and Elliston (1994) at the Centre for the Study Of Public Order (CSPO), University of Leicester.

One of the reasons why police practitioners and even senior police officers have been interested in studying crowds in recent years is to enhance their capacity to respond to crowd events. They feel that any strategies and tactics used require a sound knowledge of the nature of the crowd. Whether the crowd is seen as 'client' or 'opposition', such understanding allows ground commanders to mobilise resources in advance of anticipated crowd manoeuvres and to implement tactics to prevent the crowd seizing the initiative or causing danger to its constituent members, promoting an opportunity for an early resolution to the problem.

The police admit that in the past they may have paid too little attention to an understanding of crowd psychology and therefore were unable in some instances to deploy manpower and resources in a preventive role. Rather, they have mobilised as a reaction to crowd movement with the risk of confusion and loss of the initiative which would then have to be regained (Greater Manchester Police, 1980, p.1). For the above reasons senior officers in recent years have allowed or even encouraged their officers to study public order policing and related matters, besides introducing new and sophisticated public order training methods and tactics (Weeks, 1990).

Recent studies and publications concerning the police in general, and public order related issues in particular, have been carried out by academics some of whom have had practical policing experience. These include R. Mark (1977, 1978), S. Holdaway (1979, 1983), P. Wright (1985a, 1985b), T. Moore (1986, 1988, 1990), P. A. J. Waddington (1991, 1994b). On the other hand, numerous studies concerning the field, have been carried out by many academics such as J. Benyon (1987, 1993), G. Northam (1988), D. K. Das (1988), R. Greaf (1989), Waddington et al. (1989), T. Jefferson (1990), D. Waddington (1992), L. Johnston (1992) and many others.

More recently a number of new works have appeared in the field such as E. Cashmore and E. McLaughlin (1991), M. Brake and C. Hale (1992), P. Panayi (1993), M. Keith (1993, 1994), and I. Waters and J. Brown (1994). Some of these works have added a new dimension into the field by examining the role of special constables and women officers at public order events (Heidensohn, 1992 and 1994; Leon, 1994).

Michael Keith's work (1993) titled *Race, Riots and Policing* refutes the broad generalisations in the field of riots as he believes that "Generalisations, by definition, exclude the significance of the historically and geographically specific" (Keith, 1993, p.18). However, he acknowledges the possible usefulness of typologies by saying that "It may sometimes be possible to produce useful descriptive typologies, as with the 'flashpoints model' developed in Britain in the 1980s".

Finally, P. A. J. Waddington (1994b) published *Liberty and Order*, which is based on his observations carried out almost at the same period as this research. His work has many similarities to this research; both are primarily based on personal observations of public order operations which took place in London and interviews with a number of officers of various ranks.

For those academics and authors who have policing experience such as P. A. J. Waddington and are sympathetic towards the police, the introduction of technology and sophisticated equipment into policing and particularly public order policing, is regarded as necessary and inevitable. They sometimes demand more rigorous police tactics and methods. On the other hand, the authors and researchers who fall into the second category, such as Northam (1988) and Jefferson (1990) are very critical of this drift towards technological and managerial sophistication of equipment and tactics and argue that this has moved the British police into a more militarised position and has compromised the traditional British police image.

Unfortunately, the majority of the studies in this field tend to come firmly down on either side of what has become a two-sided argument; while one side blames the police handling of public order events for escalating violence, the other side blames the crowd for being violent and not complying with police instructions. Therefore, it will be argued in this research that although the existing studies have emphasised a number of crucial points they fail to consider the problem from each other's point of view or to acknowledge that the answer is far more complex, involving an interplay of many variable factors.

In another study, G. Northam, (1988) strongly criticises police tactics and methods and the deployment of Police Support Units, (PSUs), in full riot gear at public order events. He argues that the British police have drifted into a paramilitary force and this drift has been a piecemeal response to deep-seated perceptions of increased threat among the police officers. He continues to argue that the officers who walk on streets as community bobbies today are equipped and ready to take them by force tomorrow. "The important milestones and motives of this policing revolution have been inadequately reported" (Northam, 1988, p.31). He urges that "...in a democracy which maintains the tradition of policing by public consent, the public has not been informed, much less asked, about the most far-reaching recent changes in police strategy (ibid.30).

Contrary to those arguments which strongly oppose the deployment of paramilitary equipment and tactics, one of the most eminent advocates of this paramilitary drift, P. A. J. Waddington lists a number of points which, for him, makes this drift inevitable and unavoidable. A number of articles and books have been written by him concerning the issue (e.g. Waddington, 1984; 1985a; 1985b; 1987; 1988 and 1992). He attempts to justify the process of militarisation of British policing on the basis of the argument that the acquisition of such technology need not be associated with an escalation of violence. He refers to Bayley, saying that "...the skilful manoeuvring of heavily equipped squads controls violent protest with comparatively little police violence" (Waddington, 1987, p.41). He claims that, in general, "...well-protected officers have less incentive for taking pre-emptive action from fear of injury" (ibid.41). Jefferson (1987), however, argues that there is a stronger reason for rejecting paramilitarism. Against Waddington's claims he says that a profane view of the dynamics of paramilitary policing leads to only one conclusion: such policing has an inherent capacity to exacerbate violence.

Again, the argument goes on like a 'chicken and egg' story and becomes a vicious circle. While one side insists in arguing that paramilitary equipment and tactics and deployment of public order trained police officers increases the level of violence, the other side opposes this argument by saying that, deploying untrained, ill-equipped, often unsupervised officers with neither a coherent strategy nor tactics has frequently produced both ineffectual policing and encouraged the use of excessive force (Mackenzie, 1988, p.857).

The arguments have moved towards the question of whether Britain should have a nationally based riot police, in other words, a 'third force'. While a number of authors have written for and against the establishment of a continental type 'third force', others have argued that Association of Chief Police Constables, (ACPO) co-ordinated PSUs have already created an ad hoc third force if not a *de facto* one (Cerrah, 1991).

Finally, recent studies are more concerned with understanding crowd psychology not only because of the fear of crowd violence but for the safety of the crowd members as well (Brearley, 1991 and 1992; Smith and Dickie, 1993). As crowd movements have become less violent, imposing less real threat to the existing political regimes in democratic countries, the studies have moved from *safety from the crowd* to *safety of the crowd*.

Summary

So far, some of the contrasting studies in this field have been briefly mentioned. From this account it has become clear that the arguments are surrounded by established bias and prejudice in the sphere of British policing practices. The literature review has also shown that there is insufficient information concerning social and socio-psychological aspects of crowd behaviour. This research aims to keep a balance between the above mentioned variables in its examination of crowd behaviour.

It would be more appropriate, perhaps, to re-examine the problem from a relatively objective point of view. This study, carried out by an overseas research student, may highlight various points which might have been missed by home researchers. In order to further enhance this objectivity the methods and techniques, mentioned earlier within this chapter, have been found more appropriate and convenient by the researcher.

2 Classifying Crowds

Introduction

> The fascination of crowd psychology lies in the fact that it seeks to account for behaviour that shows clear social coherence - in the sense of a large amount of people acting in the same manner despite the lack of either pre-planning or any structural direction (Reicher, 1984, p.1).

The crowd is one of the earliest institutions established by humankind. Its only significant difference from most other institutions is its temporary existence. There are crowds which gather on a regular basis for material or non material gain, such as religious ceremonies, hunting packs and armies, even commuters on the railway system. In addition, crowds gather for routine and everyday events such as funerals, weddings, feasts and festivals. Those crowds which gather to fulfil a social function or a duty, are encouraged, even praised, as performing a positive human activity. However crowds have also been regarded as somehow sinister when they gather for a political purpose.

It must also be recognised that crowd activities are subject to social evolution, just like any other human institution. Besides maintaining some of their founding components, such as material and non-material elements, namely participants, leaders and the third parties, which can be an opposing crowd, the military, the police or any other controlling and regulating body, the nature of crowd behaviour is subject to evolution. It is for this reason that the definition and classification of crowds made many years ago, may no longer be accurate and may fail to embrace all the present crowd types. We need to reconsider the contemporary phenomenon of the crowd and re-assess it and its activities in an historical context.

In line with this argument crowd theories themselves demonstrate a level of evolutionary development. For example, today's theories on crowds differ greatly from the earlier ones, such as Le Bon (1898 and 1969), Sighele (1892) in Rule, (1988) and Tarde (1890) in Rule, (1988) in their approach to crowd movements as well as collective violence. Contrary to earlier studies, which tend to see crowds and collective action as primarily psychologically motivated, irrational and politically meaningless, modern studies stress the rationality and social importance of crowd actions even when they take a violent form. For some modern theorists, all forms of collective action are meaningful, rational and politically purposeful (Tilly, 1963 and 1970, in Rule, 1988). In this sense it is believed that it is more appropriate to regard crowd movements as 'collective action' rather than as 'collective behaviour'. This implies that crowd movements are not the outcome of random psychologically determined human gatherings, but that perhaps they are more rational and politically purposeful than any individual action.

Despite this shift in the academic arena from a psychological explanation of crowd events to an acceptance of a socially meaningful interpretation, the police response to crowd events has traditionally been on classic lines, based on an understanding of classical crowd theories with an expectation of violence or similar problems when they have to deal with certain crowds. This assumption has frequently been reinforced by events which have resulted in clashes between a crowd and the police and which themselves provide the antecedent conditions for such conflict to be maintained and to spiral.

It is vitally important that the police understand the nature of a particular crowd for two reasons. First, in order to mobilise personnel strength and material resources effectively and efficiently, and secondly, in terms of preventing unnecessary risks of harm or violence by provoking an otherwise peaceful crowd. This stems from the assumption that, in an ideal politically democratic situation, in which a right to assemble is asserted, the purpose of police intervention should be to maintain peace and order, rather than merely act to disperse crowds. In recent years, many social and political movements involving crowds have become institutionalised, self-regulated and less threatening in terms of posing the potential to embark on mass violence. Therefore, studies on crowds and policing practices have moved from safety *from* the crowd to safety *of* the crowd itself (Brearley, 1991; 1992; HSE 1993; Au et al, 1993a; 1993b; Smith and Dickie, 1993).

In line with many other present studies in the area, observations of this research have revealed that it is not very helpful, or even possible, to define and classify crowds from one point of view. Brearley and King (1993) admit facing a similar problem, in their paper, *Policing Demonstrations: some indicators of change*, by saying that: "We are aware too that there is some problem with our four categories of public order policing event, especially in that they are not necessarily mutually exclusive" (Brearley and King, 1993, p.4). Crowds can be defined in many ways and classified under different categories according to different points of view, including the views of those charged with the control and/or safety of events.

The following classification, which is based on the researcher's literature review as well as his own research findings and direct participation and observation in various crowd events both in Turkey and the UK (Appendix 1), has led the researcher to classify crowds in a fluid variety of ways rather than placing them under one title or category.

Crowds and Public Order Policing

It is argued in this research that the problem of crowd behaviour must be examined from both psychological and sociological perspectives and that earlier writings are of limited relevance today, since there has been a considerable change in perspective away from the approach initiated by Gustave Le Bon and his contemporaries, who saw the crowd as irrational, degenerate and pathological. In contrast, contemporary crowd theorists such as Smelser, (1962 and 1968) and Waddington et al. (1989) concentrate on the social and political aspects of crowd behaviour by neglecting or deliberately ignoring the psychological aspects of crowd behaviour. As Waddington et al. (1989) point out, recent theories of crowd behaviour and public disorder, like the social scientific analyses of other social problems "...such as crime, the study of crowd or public disorder seems to have been bedevilled by the search for some single cause. Whether psychological sociological, or political, such causes tend to be extracted and presented in isolation from other variables" (p.3).

It is not the aim of this research to develop an entirely new crowd theory; it is, rather, to provoke future studies or apply the existing theories to a given crowd event. An awareness of the weakness of existing accounts is imperative and so this research begins by examining the reasons why crowd theorists have differed in their views of crowd behaviour and collective violence. This question can be looked at from a number of angles. First of all, the differentiation of their views may stem from the nature of social science itself; that similar, or even the same social events can easily be observed and evaluated from different points of view. Secondly, a crowd theorist may establish a theory on one observed type of crowd and formulate a theory for all collective behaviour. As McClelland (1989, p.326) has remarked, referring to the conventional crowd theorists, "...they saw different crowds, or that they saw different aspects of the same crowds". Or perhaps they saw what they wanted to see and their comments are consistent only with their own point of view. In other words, they constructed a crowd theory not on the basis of what had occurred in the crowd but on what they wanted to see and observe.

The main goal of this research is not to examine all aspects of crowd behaviour, but to concentrate instead on the social and democratic implications for effective and efficient policing of each crowd type. This research includes a broad range of crowd types, from relatively peaceful crowd events, such as carnivals, pop concerts and sporting crowds, to potentially violent crowds such as political demonstrations and rallies, spontaneous inner-city riots and some other crowd movements such as 'New Age Travellers'. Each crowd event will be examined in the context of police and crowd relations with a special emphasis on crowd control equipment, strategy and tactics.

The word 'crowd' in itself suggests a phenomenon resistant to ordinary classification. Is the crowd politically motivated, or simply an extension of ordinary criminal activity; is it purposive or rational, or pathological, was it a youth riot, a copy-cat riot, a race riot, or an anti-police riot: was it planned and organised or spontaneous? A number of writers, in the past century and in our time, have discussed and classified crowd behaviour in terms of biological categories, in terms of pathological, animal or instinctual drives opposed to rationality (Le Bon, 1969). For instance, S. Freud wrote of crowd psychology in terms of the crowd's unconscious acceptance of a leader's 'parental' authority (Freud, 1940, p.99, and 1994, p.87). Consequently, there are as many crowd classifications as there are crowd theories.

This research introduces a new classification of existing crowds referring 'organised' and 'unorganised' crowds. It has become clear that all existing crowd types could be inserted somewhere within this classification. The peculiarity of this classification is that 'being organised' is a common characteristic for all crowd types and also a very important consideration for police pre-planning of crowd events. Before introducing this classification, attention needs be drawn to other dimensions of crowd types for two reasons. The first is that crowds can be seen and classified, although not universally, from different points of view. For example, a crowd, besides being classified under a particular heading as either 'organised' or 'unorganised', at the same time can be classified as 'violent or peaceful', or 'dissenting or consenting'. Again various crowd classifications have been introduced emphasising limited psychological variables. The second reason is that inadequacies and exclusiveness of these above mentioned classifications indirectly demonstrate the universality of the classification of this research. Therefore, the above mentioned classifications are used as a yardstick or perhaps a further step towards the understanding of the classification of this research.

As indicated earlier, each crowd, in modern societies, has some implications for policing. Even the most peaceful ones have 'something' to do with policing and control to facilitate the event, and to control its impact on other aspects of the society, the physical environment, or control its participants in the interests of themselves or others. It is these 'somethings' which constitute the scope of this research.

As already outlined, the crowd phenomenon has various dimensions to study. This study will mainly concentrate on the aspects of crowd events relevant to their control rather than examining all features of crowd behaviour. It will inevitably include reference to some crowd events which may be judged by official agencies to have potential for disorder but which remain orderly for a variety of reasons.

Classifying Crowds

The argument of this book is that it is very difficult, if not impossible, to put all crowds under a particular classification. Therefore, I partly share the view with P. A. J Waddington (1994a) that, "...crowds are, by their nature, complex multi-faceted phenomenon about which we are able to learn relatively little". However, I firmly believe that classifying crowds in one way or another is generally helpful in dealing with large numbers of people, particularly for those who are responsible for the control and regulation of crowds.

From the policing point of view, it is useful to classify crowds and draw a distinction between various types of crowds, since they do not all require the active intervention of the police. It is just as important to know when not to intervene as it is to know when to exercise police authority. However, it is equally important to be able to recognise the type and nature of a crowd that may easily evolve into an uncontrollable crowd if appropriate action is not taken.

The following quotation makes it clear how important it is, for the police and for even the crowd itself, to be familiarised with the nature of a crowd:

> Saying that a crowd is a large number of persons gathered closely together is as serious mistake as saying that mushrooms are an enlarged complex aerial fleshy fruiting body of fungus. If you cannot distinguish one mushroom from another this lack of distinction may kill you when you pick and eat them randomly (Berlonghi, 1993, p.13).

The observations made throughout the research have enhanced the view that crowds cannot be grouped together under a particular classification. However, they can be classified in a number of ways depending on a particular point of view. This research classifies crowds into three groups. The first two classifications, *Violent and Peaceful Crowds* and *Dissenting and Consenting Crowds,* are used as a further step leading to a more universal and inclusive classification, rather than being a complete classification in itself. However, it must also be noted that these classifications have some utility in dealing with a particular crowd.

The final classification, which is an attempt to introduce a universal and inclusive classification of crowds uses as its criteria, the organisational structure of crowd activities and the intensity of its individual participants. This is particularly important for those who are responsible for the maintenance of peace and calm during the occurrence of crowd events. In other words, classifying and understanding crowds and crowd behaviour must not remain an academic exercise. Effective and appropriate application and implementation is important for all those concerned.

Violent and Peaceful Crowds

Crowds have been classified into various groups in accordance with particular crowd theorists' points of view. In the broadest sense, if crowds are classified with reference to the intensity of their actions, crowds can be classified as either *violent* or *peaceful*. But this is somehow a problematic classification as we often encounter difficulties in defining an individual as violent or peaceful let alone defining the large sums of individuals which make up a crowd.

It is not the number of violent participants which makes us classify a particular crowd as *violent;* rather it is the intensity of their action and its consequences which lead to this classification. For instance, if the police injure or kill, accidentally or knowingly, a participant in a crowd event, we do not expect the crowd, let alone the other agencies such as the media and political pressure groups, to tolerate this homicide. We do not put this event into a statistical context and say that one death in a ten or twenty thousand crowd is not significant. Rather, we look at this incident in terms of its frightening consequences and the symbolic or actual threat it poses to our lives. In a similar way, the police, when responding to a crowd event, regard a particular crowd as violent or peaceful not with regard to the majority of peaceful participants but to the violence and threat they face or might face from a violent minority. It is for this reason that despite an overwhelming majority of peaceful participants, some crowd events, such as the Notting Hill Carnival, are perceived as a potentially violent and certainly contentious event by the police and this shapes some of the antecedent conditions for a specific event.

Between these two broad categories various crowd classifications can be made but all definitions fall under these headings: violent and peaceful. For instance, although Le Bon, who was one of the pioneers of crowd studies, divides crowds into various categories, all his classifications fall under the heading of violent crowds, since he sees all crowds as having and sharing the same attributes. Regardless of the fact that Le Bon sees all crowd types as one category, acting irrationally, he also accepts that "...without a doubt criminal crowds exist, but virtuous and heroic crowds, and crowds of many other kinds, are also to be met with" (Le Bon, 1969, p.19). Since not all crowds have the attributes which Le Bon attaches to them perhaps it is more appropriate to assume that he documented psychological aspects of violent crowds, rather than examining the general attributes of all crowds, embracing all types. This is a product of Le Bon's own particular historical perspective and concerns, writing at a time when, within living memory and experience, the crowd posed a threat to social stability (Ginneken, 1992).

Dissenting and Consenting Crowds

If crowds are considered from the motivational point of view, they can be grouped into two broad categories. *Dissenting* and *Consenting* crowds. Dissenting crowds are characterised by being *demonstrations*, (commonly political or industrial) *marginal group* movements, or so called *spontaneous riots* . These types of crowd have violent connotations, or at least a potential for violence, but this does not necessarily mean that all members of such groups are violent and likely to embark on violent or criminal activity.

Dissenting crowd activities, which carry a potential for violent confrontation, can threaten or question the existing political arrangements, especially when they are carried out as an integral part of some alternative political movements. Otherwise, it does not matter how violent the crowd event is, it will not threaten the existing political structure. The activities of such crowds do not go beyond influencing the settings of political agendas. Crowd movements in so-called liberal democratic regimes such as western Europe and the USA, even if they involve some degree of violence, can be viewed from this perspective. These crowds might be violent but are not revolutionary. As Gurr (1989) puts it "...most demonstrators and rioters in the United States were protesting rather than rebelling or engaging in organised violence" (p.335). These crowd activities can be seen as expressively critical as opposed to purposefully revolutionary. On the other hand, where a crowd represents and acts on behalf of a wider political challenge, such as the Russian and Algerian crowd movements in the early 1990s, it can be both violent and politically threatening to the existing regimes. These crowds are both violent and 'revolutionary'. To put it differently, most revolutionary crowds are violent, or can be violent, but not all violent crowds are revolutionary. Most crowds that remain as non-revolutionary crowds, because the bulk of their participants lack this essential element i.e. being a part of an alternative political movement; that is, a crowd movement has crucial historical and political importance when it takes place within a wider political context and a significant portion of the participants adhere to a genuinely alternative, reasonably coherent programme of change.

Crowd movements and violence in relatively democratic and liberal countries, such as western Europe and the United States, might be damaging and costly, but they are not as politically threatening as they are in rigid and totalitarian or less democratic countries where there are fewer or no legitimate forms of grievance expression. Flexible regimes accommodate the crowd movements in two ways. Firstly, by allowing crowds to gather and air their grievances within the established channels, i.e., rallying, protest marching and so on. Sometimes other crowd events can indirectly serve the same purpose, such as football crowds, festivals and carnivals such as the Notting Hill Carnival. Secondly, flexible regimes do not 'fall apart' or resort to spectacularly repressive control techniques when they face a violent crowd confrontation such as the inner city riots of the 1980s in the UK and the Los Angeles riots in the United States. As the flexible regimes are not maintained by overt coercion, they can, to some extent, absorb and accommodate certain levels of crowd violence.

Conversely, crowd movements in rigid, less democratic regimes are more threatening and have a fundamentally different nature. For instance, the 'New Ruz' (Kurdish New Year) celebrations in eastern Turkey, which is akin to the Notting Hill Carnival, is revolutionary and politically threatening. While the crowd at Notting Hill serves a unifying role despite some exhibition of a spirit of struggle, crowds at the *New Ruz* celebration tend to factionalise two communities which have been living in peace and harmony for hundreds of years. It may also be argued that sectarian celebrations in Northern Ireland may be similarly regarded.

The danger for relatively democratic regimes is that despite their benign name, when the system moves towards paramilitarism and becomes increasingly totalitarian, the same problems might be experienced. In other words, it is not the name of a regime which legitimises a system; rather it is the inner workings of this system and its nature, which matters. The danger for democratic regimes is not the crowd movements, however violent they may be, but the gradual shift from real democracy which may take place without radical changes in government.

To sum up, it is not the violent participants or their violent activities which makes a crowd movement revolutionary and a threat to existing arrangements, it is the wider context of this movement which counts. It is for this reason that crowd movements, even in the form of violent confrontation serves the establishment opposition as a safety valve, defusing tension within certain groups. It is for this reason that most democracies are, to a degree, tolerant to this kind of crowd movement. In fact democracies, even those formed by an overwhelming majority, "...were found to have experienced more extensive "civil conflict" (a broad category that includes non-violent protest and demonstrations) than authoritarian regimes" (Gurr, 1989, p.335).

On the other side, are the *Consenting* crowds, or it may be more appropriate to refer to them as non-dissenting crowds. Crowds do not usually gather and demonstrate in support of policies of a particular government. Accordingly, the name does not necessarily imply that these crowds are purely consenting and do not have any grievances against the existing political and social arrangements. Rather, it emphasises the primary motive which mobilises the crowd mass. In fact, many of the so-called consenting crowds might have a grievance or concern over a particular point, besides their apparent and dominant motive. The crowd at the funeral of the late Turkish president Turgut Ozal, (Appendix 1, observations 17 and 18) was a good example of this. Despite its apparent aim and the nature of the crowd, which was well above one million according to conservative estimates, it had many political objectives concerning the selection of the next president. The banners and placards held by the crowd reflected the demands of the crowd besides its primary purpose in mourning the passing of a widely respected leader.

The following are the most popular banners carried by the crowds during the funeral services, which were held first in the capital city Ankara and then in Istanbul, the biggest city of Turkey, where president Ozal wished to be buried:

SIVIL CUMHURBASKANI - Civilian President
DINDAR CUMHURBASKANI - Religious President
DEMOKRAT CUMHURBASKANI - Democratic President

The crowd which had primarily gathered to mourn was promoting the political idea of a 'civilian', 'religious' and 'democratic' president.

The crowd at the Notting Hill Carnival (1993) is another good example of this contradiction. The Carnival is not a perfectly peaceful event despite its positive connotation, but neither is it a violent or revolutionary event, but something between the two. Despite its apparent meaning that might stem from the word 'carnival', it might be more appropriate to describe the event with two contradicting phrases; a 'peaceful event' by a crowd containing 'hostile elements'. Today many white people join the carnival and enjoy themselves perhaps much more than some black participants (Gutzmore, 1982). Contrary to popular belief, the West Indian and Black community is only represented by a minority at the event, although it is this particular community that organises it. "Two-thirds of those who attend are white, the remainder are mainly Afro-Caribbean. 60% of those who attend are from London, 20% from other parts of the UK and 20% are foreign visitors" (Metropolitan Police, 1993b). Despite the diversity of the crowd participants, the event still symbolises for many the struggle for preserving black identity and culture in a white land, rather than being a carnival for both black and white.

The quotations below, taken from *The Notting Hill Carnival Guide '93,* demonstrate the feelings of struggle and fight mixed with the carnival atmosphere.

> We are West Indians in somebody else's place, ...Carnival was simply what they had and they [the black Community] had to fight to preserve it, ...Carnival cannot and must not be separated from its genesis; if the knowledge of the struggle dies then Carnival as it was conceived is also in danger of dying (Howe, 1993, p.8-9).

On the one hand, the significant portion of the Black community perceived the Carnival as a way of struggle against a dominant and sometimes hostile culture. They felt that their culture and identity were under threat by the white community.

> Whites were encouraged to invite West Indians to tea, they called it tea and sympathy; the idea was to cultivate in you a certain social and cultural finesse and if you did that properly, there would be no racism. They were trained to mould and shape you. This created a tension which people found necessary to break through, to transcend, to be themselves. Carnival was born out of that experience (Howe, 1993, p.9).

On the other hand, they believed that, "...the carnival was under regular threat from the authorities who perceived it as a law and order issue rather than an expression of our culture" (Howe, 1993, p.9).

Although in recent years both sides have spent a great deal of effort in giving a benign carnival atmosphere to the event, the hostility, which has, perhaps, been reinforced by some violent events in the past, still can be felt throughout the carnival. Dancing, singing and the costumes which participants wear are the manifestation of a symbolic resistance to a dominant culture (Gutzmore, 1982; Edgar, 1988). In fact, events such as carnivals have often been a relatively benign way of venting grievances. Perhaps the carnival was the most peaceful way of resistance, if not a fight, against unwanted, sectarian cultivation.

> Carnival is a cultural institution which regularises and ritualises the permanent social conflict. It is a ...form of class struggle. It enables the unprivileged class to make revolution without really performing it, and to improve its social position again and again for a short period of time without even touching the society's existing power structure (Gutzmore, 1982, p.29).

These two crowd examples, one taken from Turkish and the other from the UK experience, have shown that crowds might sometimes have an additional meaning arising from an undeclared motive dominating the behaviour of the crowd. The second and undeclared motive and spirit might determine the outcome of the crowd action. From this point of view, the crowd who attended the funeral of the Turkish President T. Ozal was a political crowd besides its primary and apparent purpose. Again, crowds at the Notting Hill Carnivals have mostly, if not always, been politically expressive and dissenting crowds rather than a non-dissenting crowd. With regard to the participants, as was the case with the dissenting crowds, they might be made up of violent and non-violent participants but the overall expectation of a carnival crowd is of a peaceful and happy gathering.

A similar approach was introduced by a paper delivered at the Institute of Criminology (1992) University of Cape Town, on *Crowd Management* which deals with two types of gatherings in which the police intervene: "...first, crowds which gather to express shared grievances, and secondly, crowds involving opposing groups which gather to conflict". My observations have reinforced the notion that the crowd events which involve two opposing sides are more likely to be violent than those opposed by the police.

An example of such an oppositional event is the 'Bloody Sunday March', which is held anually to commemorate the death of 13 people killed as a result of the army use of firearms against Irish demonstrators in 1972 (Waddington, 1994b). This particular event although it is small in size involves two opposing crowds; the marchers and extreme right wing counter demonstrators (observation 14). During one of the 'Bloody

Sunday' marches which was one of the smallest events in the research period, police carried out the biggest mass arrest in London in recent years (BBC Radio Four news at 12 pm 30 January, 1993). Despite its small volume, approximately 1000-1500 participants, fights broke out when a group of extreme right wing demonstrators tried to disrupt the march, which marked the 21st anniversary of Bloody Sunday. It was reported on Radio Four that nearly four hundred people had been detained, and all those detained had been released later without charge. Conversely, at a more recent event, an anti BNP march, which took place in London on 16 October 1993, involving over 50, 000 participants, the number of those arrested was less than one hundred (*The Independent on Sunday* 17 October, 1993; *The Mail on Sunday* 17 October, 1993; *The Sunday Times* 17 October, 1993).

The Monsters of Rock concert in 1992 (observation 5), which took place in Castle Donington, is another good example which shows that it is not the size of a crowd but its nature and mobilising causes which should be the focus of attention for explaining the behaviours exhibited within it. There was no opposing group or crowd and the police kept a low profile during the concert. There was no police deployment inside the concert site and police work was mainly concentrated on monitoring the crowd using a CCTV system and maintaining the traffic flow before and after the event. During the concert, which was attended by over 65, 000 participants inside the site and almost 10, 000 people waiting outside, there were only 25 arrests resulted from fights which were mainly caused by excessive alcohol consumption. The reason for the crowd gathering in the concert was only for entertainment and no political or any other motives were apparent.

It is interesting to compare the Notting Hill Carnival with the Bridgwater Guy Fawkes Carnival which dates back to the 1605 Catholic plot to terminate a Protestant parliament (Evans, 1988:3; Comer, 1994). Despite its historically contentious nature the Bridgwater event has gradually become de-politicised and is now simply the largest illuminated carnival procession in the world (Evans, 1988:2; Bridgwater Guy Fawkes Carnival Souvenir Programme, 1994; Comer, 1994). The carnival which attracts over 120,000 people is policed by only 150 police officers including 50 special constables (Avon and Somerset Constabulary force operational order No: 119/94). The Notting Hill Carnivals of 1992 and 1993 however, were policed by over five thousand police officers (Waddington, 1994b, p.20). This comparison highlights widely differing police perceptions of large crowd events.

Organised and Unorganised Crowds

One of the end products of this research, derived from observations, is the initial classification of crowds by the police based on the experiences of past events, a classification which largely determines police pre-planning of events. It is vital for the police to know beforehand whether a particular crowd is 'organised' or 'unorganised'. It is, however, important to bear in mind that a particular crowd classified as an organised crowd, such as a football crowd, theatre audiences, or even a casual street crowd may easily change from organised passive crowd into unorganised active crowd. Consequently, depending on the occurrence of an unexpected event the nature of a crowd can very easily change, transforming itself from one category to another.

This classification particularly focuses on the initial image the police has acquired about a particular crowd even based on past experiences and this in turn influences the police pre-planning of events. For the police a particular crowd, before the assembling completed and the crowd began to act, can be seen as one of the following classifications. However, this classification does not argue that once a crowd is classified as organised or unorganised it will remain so forever.

If we look at each crowd from an organisational point of view each crowd is either 'organised' or 'unorganised'. An organised crowd does not necessarily require that all of its members act collectively with the same motivation. Moreover, organised crowds can be *active* or *passive*. For instance, a large group of people attending a political rally could be classified as an organised-active crowd. On the other hand, a group of students of the same size may well be organised but passive. The term 'organised' is a relative concept and it does not always imply concerted action by all members of the group. Although the second example group, the students, are not completely passive, when compared with the rallying crowd they can be said to be relatively passive.

In addition, when one looks at the organised-active group, it can easily be observed that not all of its members are active to the same extent. While a small proportion of the group is active and behaves violently, the majority of the crowd may still remain relatively quiet and passive. Therefore, it is a misrepresentation to argue that violence is an inevitable consequence of crowd gatherings and that those who constitute the crowd act violently and irrationally. As will be made clear on the following pages, even during the most violent crowd events, not all members of the crowd engage in violent activities. This refutes the idea suggested by Le Bon that people who as individuals were neither irrational nor stupid, could become part of a group whose unconscious collective mind obeyed his law of the mental unity of crowds.

A number of relatively recent studies on crowd participants (Allport, cited in La Pierre, 1938, p.4; McPhail, 1971; Miller, 1985, p.46) have proved that Le Bon was wrong in his assumption that being a part of the crowd makes an individual act in complete unanimity. Rather, in the most intense and concerted crowds clear differences in behaviour can be observed within the apparent unity. For instance, Mannheim (1965b) groups the crowd participants according to their level of involvement in crowd activities as; (a) the active minority, of which the most important elements are (b) the leaders. At the other extreme there are (c) the passive majority, the followers (p.648).

When we examine the second type, the unorganised crowd, it can be divided into two; the 'unorganised passive crowd' and the 'unorganised active crowd'. All crowds, in the ordinary sense, are unorganised and passive. Although they may impose a danger to themselves, as well as to other people, they have little to do with the police or other control agencies apart from routine arrangements.

The main concern here is the *unorganised-active crowds,* such as so-called spontaneous violent outbreaks of the eighties in the inner cities of the UK. It is those type of crowds which the police find very difficult to deal with and a substantial amount of police time and money is invested for the training of Police Support Units (PSUs). Dealing with these crowds occupies most of the public order training programmes. The decision to deploy PSUs and determining the number of police officers to be deployed is very much influenced by the nature of a crowd as well as by crowd numbers. The absence of an appointed leader or leadership during a spontaneous and unorganised crowd event particularly makes the police task more difficult. This is so because the lack of a leader/leadership makes it impossible to negotiate with the crowd.

A final point in this classification is the intensity of the activities of each individual member of a crowd during an event. Since not all members of the crowd are active and violent to the same extent and level, each crowd can, finally, be divided into two parts; 'active members' and 'passive members' and examined separately. This study as well as many other studies in the field of violence participation have revealed that not all members of violent crowds act in the same way. Even the most violent crowds involve relatively passive members, whose acts cannot be classified as violent.

In the final category, the crowd has been classified according to the degree of organisation and the level of activity of its participants. Since the organisation of crowds is related to the socio - psychological make-up of its participants, the involvement of individuals as active and passive has been incorporated into this classification. Crowd action is therefore determined by both the collective consciousness and the individual mind.

The classification, which has been developed in this chapter, seems to be applicable more universally. All existing crowd classifications might have a place somewhere within this classification. Not only the crowds but those control agencies such as army and the police public order units, who themselves are responsible for controlling or regulating crowd activities are also included within this classification. What is more, as a group of people the police and army units are a kind of crowd and are subject to the same psychological influences as any other crowd and there is no reason why they should be regarded as immune from the same psychological considerations.

Crowds and their Psychology

One of the important aspects of crowds, with respect to public order policing, is the psychological state of participants and its overall state. Hence, not only Le Bon and other conventional crowd theorists, but also a number of contemporary and modern studies have been concerned with the psychological state of crowds. There is a reciprocal relationship between the crowd organisation and the psychological make-up of its individuals. While the psychological make up of the participants determines the nature of crowd organisation and action, the individuals, in turn, are influenced by the organised crowd action.

A substantial amount of work has been done concerning crowd psychology, (Tarde, 1890; Sighele, 1892a-b; Le Bon, 1898; Berkowitz, 1962 and 1968; Ginsberg, 1964; Levy, 1972; Evans, 1975) and its implications for regulating and controlling crowds. Some of these works are purely devoted to crowd psychology while others partly focus on certain aspects of the area concerned (Folger, 1984; Reicher, 1984 and 1985; Sime, 1993; Berlonghi, 1993). However, there is no space in this chapter for a systematic review of the all major sociological writings on crowd psychology and consequently the discussion which follows will be brief and limited primarily to crowd behaviour which falls within the scope of this particular research.

Before moving on to the existing psychological crowd classification it must be noted that classifying crowds according to psychological variables has usually been perceived with suspicion by modern crowd theorists. This is partly so because most psychologically based classifications follow the line drawn by Le Bon (1898) and his contemporaries, G. Tarde (1890) and S. Sighele (1892a-b). Indeed the earliest works on the crowd were written by criminologists discussing the basis upon which to punish crowd participants - should all be considered guilty or just a criminal core of ringleaders who incited the others? (Ginneken, 1992). However, some modern crowd theorists have turned their attention to the psychological aspect of crowd participants and have formulated an entirely different perspective. It is argued that some crowd behaviour, if not all, shows clear social form and cannot be explained in terms of the individualistic theories that dominate crowd psychology. As the quotation from Reicher (1984, p.1) makes clear, "The fascination of crowd psychology lies in the fact that it seeks to account for behaviour that shows clear social coherence -in the sense of a large amount of people acting in the same manner-despite the lack of either pre-planning or any structural direction".

In order to fully explore the nature of crowd behaviour and to improve appropriate responses to the problems raised by a crowd event, it is important to analyse the crowd from the psychological point of view. The following is an attempt to do this by Varwell (1978, p.82) who defines four main crowd types as follows;

> *1- Aggressive:* 'Aggressive' clearly describes the sort of situation where a crowd is intent upon destruction of some sort or another.
> *2- Escapist:* A crowd may be intent upon escape. These circumstances may arise when a serious fire or explosion occurs in a dance-hall or in a busy hotel, when what was originally a passive crowd becomes frightened.
> *3- Acquisitive:* A crowd may become acquisitive and begin looting for various reasons.
> *4- Expressive:* The purpose of the crowd may be expressive - it may be primarily concerned with the expression of feelings or emotions.

In an earlier classification by Raymond M. Momboisse (1964) a similar line is followed. Again this classification roughly divides the crowds which the police might have to deal with into four main categories: 'Conventional Crowds', 'Expressive Crowds', 'Sightseer Crowds' and 'Hostile or Aggressive crowds'.

In a recent work Berlonghi (1993, p.15-17) classifies crowds under eleven broad categories, some of which are involved with psychological implications such as 'aggressive or hostile crowd', 'expressive or revelling crowd', and 'violent crowd' (Berlonghi, 1993, p.16-17). Almost all psychological classifications refer to 'expressive' and 'aggressive' states of crowds and their participants.

It is important to note that the distinction between the types of crowd is not always clear cut. It is, however, important to bear in mind that one crowd may have all four of the above mentioned elements simultaneously, or that the nature of a crowd can very easily change, transforming itself from one of these categories into another (Moore, 1988 and 1990; Appendix 1, observations 17 and 18).

It is also possible for a crowd to be classified as belonging to more than one category. For instance the mourning crowd at the late Turkish president's funeral (Appendix 1, observations 17 and 18) could be considered as a political crowd besides being a mourning crowd. Although there was no opposing crowd present, and the dominant motive was mourning the loss of the president, the presence of politically oriented banners turned the nature of the crowd into a political demonstration. The banners included slogans such as 'Civilian President' and 'Religious President' implying that some of the reasons for his popularity was his being a civilian and to some extent a religious person. It also implied the wish of the crowd that they wanted the future president to bear similar attributes.

In a similar way, a particular crowd may begin to gather as an expressive crowd, primarily concerned with the expression of discontent towards a particular group, such as the police or any other group, and the same crowd can change into an acquisitive crowd, at the same time maintaining and keeping its expressive nature. In other words, a particular crowd may express its feelings of discontent by looting or committing arson. Such a group is then also described as aggressive. Again, when a particular crowd has a violent confrontation with the police, some crowd members, if not all, become escapist, and try to leave the area.

Although the above classifications of crowds in terms of psychological behaviour may give a general idea about the crowd types, it is far from being complete or sufficient. Categorisation of a crowd using one of these four types is not always possible, as all of these attributes may be exhibited simultaneously. Crowd behaviour is also subjective. For instance, while a relatively violent crowd will be described as aggressive by some, even their most violent activities may be seen and described as expressive by others. Recent analyses of the violent acts of some groups, such as football crowds, or even the violent crowds in inner-city riots, define these acts as expressive rather than aggressive. The underlying idea is that those who have no way of airing their grievances and discontent through legitimate channels tend to use violent activities. For this group, the violent acts and looting are symbolic and reflect the discontent of the crowd rather than stemming from the criminality or aggressiveness of human nature (Taylor, 1971 and 1989; Marsh, 1978).

A similar classification was introduced by Blumer (1975, p.29), dividing the crowd into four types. He defines the first as the *casual crowd,* as in the instance of a street crowd watching a performer in a store window. The casual crowd usually has a momentary existence; more importantly, it has a very loose organisation and exhibits scarcely any unity. A second type may be designated as the *conventionalised crowd,* such as the spectators at a programmed football game. Their behaviour is essentially like that of casual crowds, except that it is expressed in established and regularised ways. The third type of crowd is the acting, *aggressive crowd,* best represented by a revolutionary crowd or a lynching mob. The outstanding mark of this type of crowd is the presence of an aim or objective towards which the activity of the crowd is directed. The remaining type is the *expressive crowd,* such as one sees in the case of carnivals, festivals and similar events (Blumer, 1975, p.29). In fact this classification was first put forward by Tarde (Ginneken, 1992, p.220 and 229) as being the four 'forms of existence' of crowds and public. Although Blumer did not cite Tarde in his work, Ginneken argues that Blumer's crowd theory and crowd classification contained elements remarkably similar to Tarde's.

Despite the similarities of Varwell's and Blumer's crowd classifications, it is clear that the crowd can be defined according to many variables leading to distinct conclusions. The main factor behind this differentiation is that it is not only the crowd's nature but the personal perception of particular crowd theorists which determines the crowd classification. Crowd theorists such as Tarde and Le Bon define the crowd on the basis of the premise that the nature of the crowd and its activities can be explained in terms of the internal dynamics of its psychological process, without reference to the social context. Even some contemporary crowd theorists, such as Canetti (1962) describe the crowd using a similar approach. His work includes a number of crowd types ranging from hunting packs and religious crowds to armies. He explains crowd violence in general as a collective desire to grow rapidly, suggesting that during this rapid growth, the crowd sees every single object which does not join in this growth as its enemy; houses, locked doors and windows are all 'enemies' to its collective will to demonstrate its social/political perspective.

Canetti implicitly, if not explicitly, justifies or even glorifies crowd violence which, for him, stems from this desire for growth. He believes that the crowd which sees those who oppose it, or do not join it, as its enemy and offers equality to all its members. For him, "...a crowd does not become a crowd until its members lose their 'burdens of distance' differences of rank, status and property" (Canetti, 1962, p.16). Canetti may be correct in his description of crowds and the justification for crowd violence but his crowd is again, like Le Bon, simply a violent crowd. His work has violent connotations and uncertainties about crowd behaviour, and his explanations differ dramatically from the rest of contemporary crowd theorists. His personal perception of the crowd can be easily seen in his classification of crowds. He broadly classifies the crowd into two types; *open* and *closed,* in terms of its desire and capability for growth. For him, the natural crowd is the open crowd; there are no limits whatever to its growth, it does not recognise houses, doors or locks, and those who shut themselves in are suspected of dissent from its objectives. He maintains that: 'open' is to be understood here in the fullest sense of the word; it means open everywhere and in any spatial, intellectual and temporal direction. "The open crowd exists so long as it grows; it disintegrates as soon as it stops growing" (Canetti, 1962, p.16).

McClelland (1989) who considers Canetti's work, *The Crowd and Power* (1962), as the masterpiece of crowd theories, accuses Le Bon of writing his book in order to frighten his readers. Yet Canetti's crowd description, explanation and even celebration of crowd violence appears to be more frightening than Le Bon's work. If the crowd is violent or can become violent for whatever reason, it does not matter very much whether this violence stems from the desire for growth or irrational crowd psychology; it is frightening all the same in that it potentially poses physical harm to all who are not actively committed to it, hence its apparent totalitarianism as a perspective. Canetti concludes his broad crowd classification by suggesting that: "...in contrast to the open crowd which can grow indefinitely and which is of universal interest because it may spring up anywhere there is the closed crowd. The closed crowd renounces growth and puts the stress on permanence. The first thing to be noticed about it is that it has a boundary" (Canetti, 1962, p.17).

Canetti's crowd definition and classification implies that all crowd types are inherently and inevitably violent. What he defines as the crowd is defined as the *mob* by McClelland. McClelland (1989) in his book, *The Crowd and the Mob* (1989) as the title suggests, clearly distinguishes the ordinary crowd from the violent mob, referring to the nature of crowd activities. In other words, the crowd is essentially peaceful and if a gathering of human beings is violent it is to be called a mob rather than a violent crowd. As indicated by Varwell (op. cit.), any type of crowd may transform from one type to another. This is true for the crowd and mob as well. McClelland has remarked that:

> The crowd could become a mob if the circumstances were right: loss of nerve by the local authority; the failure to arrest demagogues; high bread prices, perhaps, or unemployment; then the dormant passions of the crowd would turn into the active barbarism of the mob whose nature could be

> understood in a way that had not really changed since the trial of Socrates (McClelland, 1989, p.6).

From this quotation it is understood that, although McClelland's crowd is, essentially, a peaceful one, when it becomes violent it is not to be classified as a crowd any more; it is a mob.

There seems to be as many crowd classifications and interpretations of crowd violence as there are scholarly and applied professions interested in the phenomenon. In fact, most crowd theories are based on, or lead to, a particular crowd classification. Some of the formerly eminent classifications have been mentioned earlier in this chapter. On the other hand, it is clear that, it is not always possible to integrate the existing theories and classifications under definite and definitive groups. For instance, the existing crowd theories and classifications can be grouped under two main categories as classical and modern crowd theories. Recently, our attention has been drawn to the advantages of multidisciplinary social scientific approaches, taking into account political, sociological and psychological factors, effecting crowd behaviour rather than examining it within the boundaries of a single discipline (Waddington et al. 1989). For instance, Waddington et al. (1989) in their work, 'Flashpoints', based their model on 'issue-oriented' riots, after adopting Marx's (1972) and Smith's (1983, p.159) classification of crowd events as 'issue-oriented' and 'issue-less' crowd events. Marx (1972) suggests that crowd activities can be classified on the basis of two criteria: first, whether or not there is a 'generalised belief' present among crowd participants, (very often based on grievances); and, secondly, whether or not the crowd activity is intended to be 'collectively instrumental' in achieving some desired end. In short, crowd activities which are not instrumental, and where a collective belief is absent, are described as 'issue-less'.

The 'Flashpoints' model, after adopting this classification, focuses on the so-called 'issue-oriented' crowd events. However, this classification does not entirely refute the social potential of the existence of so called 'issue-less' crowd events. "By contrast issue-less riots are a reaction to social conditions, but the form of the riot behaviour and its targets do not reveal what is being protested against" (Waddington et al. 1989, p.16). Classifying crowds according to their underlying motives, is however, is not something new. In fact most crowd classifications are based either on the psychological state of crowd participants or its underlying causes and mobilising motives. For example, in a rather value laden classification, C. Tilly (1970) sees crowds as 'primitive', 'reactionary', or 'modern' (Tilly, 1970 and 1974; Field, 1983; Rule, 1988). He is one of the few who regards the acts of crowds as 'collective action' rather than as 'collective behaviour'. He also sees collective violence as purposeful and rational, that is, oriented to achieving authentic and enduring ends of those involved (Tilly, cited in Rule, 1988, p.170). However, his rather value laden classification fails to embrace all crowds.

Summary

This chapter has two primary aims. The first is to re-classify existing crowd types and the second is to draw some lessons from these classifications, in relation to the police response to crowd events. While introducing a new crowd classification, the chapter also concludes that there might be many ways of classifying crowds. Regarding the police pre-planning of crowd events the chapter demonstrates that the perceived nature of a particular crowd and the make-up of its participants is very much related to the police plan to deploy to these events.

Observations of the research (Appendix 1) in line with many other studies in the field, have shown that the police response to crowd events is shaped by experience of past crowd events, and their general perception and expectation of crowds (Brearley and King, 1993, p.10). These perceptions and expectations, in turn, reinforce and determine the deployment of police personnel power and resources for future events. For instance, the police do not see the Notting Hill Carnival as an isolated crowd event from its past; rather all preparations are made on the basis of an accumulation of experience from previous years. For the police, the Carnival still has negative connotations, despite the potentially celebratory connotations of its name and there is an expectation that it will impose public order problems.

The classical police perception of crowds was based on the assumption that *the mob has many heads but no brain.* Perhaps today's police perception of crowds has moved away from this assumption to the idea that *the mob has many heads and many brains*, and this causes the problem. It is for this reason that recent police responses to crowd events have moved from containment and control to the organisation and regulation of the crowd for their own safety and that of others who may be present. As P. A. J. Waddington (1993) demonstrated in his paper, 'Dying in a Ditch', and his recent book (1994 passim), *Liberty and Order,* the police undertook the role of helping and even organising the crowd in some recent demonstrations in London. But these changes included arrangements for safety from the crowds in an indirect and passive way (Waddington, 1993). As he concluded in his paper in question, the police involvement in crowd events has become 'a compromise' rather than 'containment' or 'confrontation'.

In addition to above mentioned general conclusions which are relevant to crowd classifications, this chapter has also highlighted to two important points. The first point is that the classification of crowds, in terms of the level of activities of would be participants, seems to be a more universal and beneficial approach for police deployment at crowd events. For the police, one of the most important points is to know what kind of action the crowd will take in certain circumstances. The second point is that the crowd phenomenon has many different aspects to examine. One of the common points, which crowds and public order policing have in common is that their beings consist of two integral parts; 'physical' and 'non-physical' components. The first component, the physical one, consists of three main elements; the crowd, its leader/leadership and control agencies; i.e. the police and the army. The second component, the non-physical elements of crowds consists of various psychological methaphors and has been the centre of much controversy since Le Bon's time. Therefore, the next chapter will be devoted to the examination of these two components.

3 The Crowd and its Integral Parts

Introduction

> ...we have a very imperfect knowledge of the human heart if we do not also examine it in crowds (Rousseau, cited in McClelland, 1989).

In the previous chapter, attempts have been made to classify existing crowds, and to re-classify crowd participants as being *organised-unorganised* and *active-passive*. This classification partly reflects the existing police perception of crowds based on past experiences and in this respect this classification is perhaps a new attempt to define the existing public order policing practices based on past experiences. It has been apparent throughout the observations carried out for this book that despite any theoretical classification made by the police, most police practices are very much in line with this classification. Demonstrations of similar sizes were policed by substantially different amounts of police officers and this has led to the conclusion that the planning of events is very much determined by the expectation of violence. This expectation is in turn very much influenced by the perception of the potential crowd using the terms organised-unorganised and active-passive.

Although the previous chapter made an attempt to classify crowds in respect of police pre-planning of crowd events, it was also asserted that crowds cannot be classified in a definitive and definite way. Despite this inability to classify crowd, the research has discovered certain components which every crowd has in common. These components, which are the subject of this chapter, are again divided into two main parts; the 'physical components of the crowd', that is participants, leaders/leadership and the control agencies of the police; the 'non-physical components' concern the crowd as well as the police and cover various invisible aspects of crowd behaviour. These include certain psychological metaphors such as 'suggestibility', the 'collective mind' and the 'rationality' of crowd behaviour.

The Crowd and Its Integral Parts

The crowd is an entity which resembles the human body, consisting of two basic parts; the body and the spirit. The mere existence of any human gathering represents the crowd's body while the motives and ideas which lead to the formation of a particular crowd is its spirit. These shared motives or ideas, which make up the spirit of crowd action and lead to the gathering of large numbers at certain places, have a crucial role in determining the kind of action the crowd will take, and consequently the deployment of police in controlling or suppressing the crowd.

As with individual behaviour, crowd behaviour is a product of many diverse physical and non-physical elements. The classification introduced within this chapter is far from being complete in its coverage of all relevant elements. However, as the main concern of this chapter is more to do with crowds and public order policing, this book's approach will be dealing with those components which have a direct influence on crowd behaviour.

This classification, while placing a special emphasis on the immediate components of public order policing, does not underplay the importance of many other variables such as the influence of the climate, the physical lay-out of the streets and the venue where the crowd gathers. Numerous studies done in the field discovered that there is a link between the season of the year and even the time of day and crowd disorder. However, although these factors might have an influence on crowd behaviour, to a limited degree, they are not and cannot be its primary determinants.

There may be various underlying factors which cause an individual to take part in the crowd. Crowds are not large numbers of people gathered randomly at certain venues and times. There is usually a cause leading to this gathering and unless policing practices take into account the underlying causes, the response to crowd events will be inadequate. The underlying causes can be accompanied by the presence of a visible target upon which the crowd can focus. In the absence of such a visible target, particularly with politically motivated crowd events, the police are usually perceived as targets. This is partly because the police are often the only available visible target and are perceived by the crowds as representatives of a state authority which is, in turn, perceived as the source of their discontent.

Crowds are not something odd, they are a part of society. They are a temporary institution existing in and created by the function and operation of society. The signifier 'crowd', has positive connotations, particularly in comparison with signifiers such as 'mob' or 'rabble'. Crowds have a temporary existence and are less durable compared with other social units but remain as a product of society. In the same way, the police are a product of society but are more organised and permanent. The existence of crowds is as socially meaningful as the existence of the police; the police represent and act on behalf of established political and social arrangements whereas the crowd may express discontent and dissatisfaction towards this establishment.

This book suggests that not every agglomeration of considerable numbers of individuals constitutes a crowd; there must, in addition, be an environmental and mental 'something' which transforms the purely factual agglomeration into a crowd in the psychological sense. Hence, the second stage refers to some of the psychological determinants which this book proposes to be the result of participation in a crowd. However, the three factors of *suggestibility*, the state of *rationality/irrationality* and the *collective mind*, mentioned in this chapter, are not, of course, the only factors which might exist in a crowd.

This book deals with two discrete crowds, the crowds which the police are supposed to be policing, and the police themselves as a crowd. As society creates conditions either directly or indirectly for the creation of crowds, at the same time it also prepares its own counter crowds, the police, to control the former. However, the nature of this encounter is very much determined by the leader or leadership of those two types of crowds. The presence or the lack of leaders and leadership, therefore, is one of the most important components of public order policing.

However, the determination of leadership fails to explain collective behaviour. The presence of a crowd, leaders and the police to control them are insufficient to explain the inner dynamics of crowd behaviour. There are often factors which influence both crowd action and the police and its practices. These are the non-physical components of crowds. These determinants are more relevant to the socio-psychological and biological aspects of human behaviour rather than remote factors such as political, economic and social arrangements.

Physical Components of the Crowd

Having indicated in a general way the principal common characteristics of the police and crowds, it remains to study these components with particular emphasis on their relevance to classical and modern crowd theories. As this research is more concerned with the relationship between the crowd, particularly the violent crowd, and the police, the research's model of examining physical and mental components of crowd behaviour will focus on certain aspects of the phenomenon. This selectivity will inevitably exclude some less dominant physical and mental components.

The components which determine crowd and police relations are of two kinds: *remote* and *immediate*. This research will focus on the immediate components of police-crowd interaction rather than examining the role and influence of remote components. But since the remote and immediate components are, to some extent, two integral parts of a whole process, the effect of remote components on immediate components will also be considered.

When a crowd-police interaction is analysed it is seen to have the following major physical components: the *participants*, *leaders,* and the *police*. These three major elements are identified as the 'physical components of public order policing'. From this starting point, the research moves on to the 'immediate mental components' of public order policing. This includes some of the most common psychological attributes of the crowd and the police. In abstract terms, this chapter is devoted to the examination of the immediate physical and mental components of public order policing. Since the police as a well organised group of people are subject to similar psychological and mental processes as the crowd, they will be examined in the same context. As mentioned earlier, remote factors such as religion, family and education, and cultural specificities have a critical influence on the manifestation of immediate components, and these will be discussed in the following chapter.

Participants

Crowd participants are not merely a collection of human beings. The crowd can be examined in terms of 'composition', which refers to the make-up of its participants, and 'motivation' and 'emotions', which refers to the behaviour of the participants and crowd as a whole under the influence of psychological metaphors. The crucial point of emphasis is the question of the power of the crowd and its unified activities. In the following account crowd participants will be analysed from these viewpoints.

Violent crowd events can be studied and analysed in terms of individual activity as well as organisational, community and societal responses. At the individual level of analysis, many questions revolve around the issue of riot participation. In this research, 'the participants', have been seen as the first visible component of the crowd and have been given priority over other components. At first glance, the participants and the leaders seem to constitute two integral parts of a whole and come into existence simultaneously, but a close examination will show that it is not the leader who instigates the crowd but rather the reverse is true. A leader may have an importance and play his role after the crowd comes into existence. Without a leader a crowd can still survive and it may have the attributes of a crowd for a certain period of time, but without a crowd, leadership becomes an abstract personal quality, rather than a reality.

As the name implies, participants are those who happen to be participating and the leaders are those who are being followed by participants. The opposition could be a rival group or the representatives of the state, the police. To understand the nature and the outcome of a crowd event it is important to establish a sense of the nature of crowd. This can be achieved by a close examination of the participants and their relationships to the leader. Hence, one of the first tasks in studying crowd events and riots in particular is to determine who is and who is not a riot participant. A number of riot participant studies have revealed that classifying people as participants and non-participants in a riot situation is not as simple as classifying people as male/female or young/old. On a superficial level crowd participants are constituted by two types of people; the first kind are natural participants while the second are dedicated and determined participants.

Throughout these observations two main types of participants were encountered. The first group of participants were those who had first hand involvement with the cause of the event. Those kind of participants were either the victims of a particular group of people or of a policy. Participants at crowd events such as the 'Bloody Sunday' demonstrations, for example, who belonged to the Irish Community and who felt themselves to be the direct victims of a particular policy fall into this first category. In industrial demonstrations such as the 'Women Against Pit Closures' march, for instance, women whose husbands or relatives were mineworkers or were directly influenced by the closures can be categorised in the same way.

The second group can be specified as 'professional demonstrators' who have no direct involvement with the cause behind the crowd movement but feel sympathy towards it. They are not the direct victims of a particular policy or a group. The presence of members of the host community in anti-Nazi demonstrations are an example of this category. These participants get involved in such demonstrations not because they are involved in the first degree, but support a cause with which they have sympathy. Their main aim is, in addition to the apparent cause, to manifest their dissatisfaction with the existing regime, or the status quo.

Both groups of participants can be seen as a 'dissenting minority' as opposed to a 'silent majority'. Whether or not they belong, politically or ethnically, to a marginalised group they represent only a small proportion of the dissident community. However, crowd movements which attract the silent majority among its ranks are much more powerful and influential than those involving dedicated members of a dissenting minority.

The variations in the motivation and the composition of crowds inevitably affects the behaviour and expectations at a particular crowd event. Even in the presence of a common target which serves, to certain degree, as a unifying influence, the minds and actions of crowd participants show distinct variations in individual goals and aims. This was the case at one observation when some members of the crowd did not want to resist the police while others urged the crowd to break the police line (observation 25).

Regarding the individual acts of crowd participants during a crowd event, the composition of the crowd must be examined closely. It often appears that everyone in a crowd is staring in rapt attention at a speaker or leader. But "...a systematic analysis of photographs or film records of such events reveal that 'crowds' are seldom completely focused on a single object, and when near unanimous focus occurs it is of a short duration. The most common form of focused or convergent behaviour within gatherings occurs among small clusters of two to five people within gatherings" (Miller, 1985, p.46). This view of behaviour within gatherings contrasts with the 'unanimity of behaviour' characterisation offered by the social contagion theory; it also contrasts with the assumption that crowds are composed of people who have the same motivation and desires.

Crowd participants do not share exactly the same common interests and motivations and they rarely act unanimously (Grimshaw, 1968 and 1972). In 1971 McPhail reviewed the volumes of riot participation studies conducted between 1965 and 1970. He found at least 215 separate individual tendency variables which had been examined in an effort to account for individuals' participation in riots (McPhail, 1971; Miller, 1985, p.26). The conclusion to be drawn from McPhail's study is that it does not only refute the conventional crowd theorists, who argue that the crowd acts irrationally in total unanimity, but it also raises doubts about the rationality and social import of crowd behaviour, a view which is held by modern crowd theorists. The question of how a violent crowd event, where the participants display many individual tendencies and motivations (Grimshaw, 1968; Quarantelli and Dynes, 1968), can be socially meaningful, is crucial. The messages to be drawn from these competing and contrasting motives are complex and inconclusive.

The complexity of the situation suggests that instead of denying the rationality of crowd action completely or giving a perfect and total rationality to crowd violence, a compromise must be found. It is feasible to argue that crowd action may not be as rational as individual action, but it may not be completely irrelevant and irrational either. The message given by crowd violence cannot be underestimated, however violent and indiscriminate it might be. In order to receive the message given by the crowd, it is important to examine its composition. Can all participants be from the criminal elements of society, as some official bodies, the police and even the media have declared, or are they generally ordinary members of society? Numerous studies on the participants at violent crowd events have revealed that the overwhelming majority of violent crowd participants were ordinary citizens and not criminals (Tilly, 1963, 1970 and 1974; Cooper, 1985; Waddington, 1989).

Information obtained from Cooper's study (1985) appears to refute police comments and press reportage, which suggest that those mainly responsible for the disturbances were either criminals or young adolescents. The same study revealed that, "...half of those arrested in Toxteth had never before appeared in criminal courts, and nearly half of these were over 21" (Cooper, 1985, p.65). Empirical researches carried out both in the UK and the USA consistently support this assertion. Ghetto rebellions in the USA and the inner-city riots in the UK in the 1980s, are characterised by the participation of a far broader spectrum of people then the media and the official picture suggest (Currie and Skolnick, 1972, p.67; Smelser, 1972).

Waddington et al. (1989, p.11) also points out that, "...disorders often involve ordinary members of the public who do not otherwise commit criminal acts". While this explanation refutes the police and the media reports, it does not explain why ordinary members of the public who do not otherwise commit crime become part of a crowd and commit violent acts during a crowd event. On this point we are forced to accept the arguments of classical crowd theories which insist upon the influence of the crowd on its participants. Unless we offer a logical explanation for those crimes committed by ordinary people we have to accept, to some extent, the conventional explanations. Their summarised argument is that ordinary members of the public can commit criminal acts when they become part of crowd. The individual leaves his/her personal responsibilities and becomes part of a unanimous activity.

While modern crowd theories have insisted upon the essential innocence of crowd members and denied the criminality of their past, they have also implied that these innocent and peaceful participants become violent when they join in a crowd. The grievances which form the foundation of the protest and of the subsequent violence become subsidiary to the acts of violence themselves. In addition, analyses of motivations and grievances must consider carefully the term 'innocence' when examining the causes of violence.

The point which this research tries to make is that while trying to rationalise crowd events, even very violent crowd confrontations, the criminal motivation of the participants must not be oversimplified. As with the classification of crowd events, crowd participants can be grouped according to their motives in various types. Turner and Killian (1962) attempted to classify crowd participants by using individual motives as the basis of five categories. Their classification categories reflect a decreasing level of personal identification with the events and issues that are part of any specific episode of collective behaviour. Unlike classical crowd theorists, Turner and Killian conclude that people retain a clear sense of personal motivation when participating in collective behaviour (Miller, 1985, p.26).

Miller (1985) in his book, *Introduction to Collective Behaviour*, provides the following quotation from Turner and Killian, which classifies crowd participants under five categories in terms of individual motives.

> 1 A person who feels a strong personal commitment, or ego involvement, with the situation at hand.
> 2 Motivation by a feeling of generalised concern. The concerned participant is unlikely to take the initiative but very likely to follow the lead of others and comply with emerging norms.
> 3 The insecure participant. People may participate in collective action because doing so offers a sense of direction and identity.
> 4 The curious participant joins in order to find out what is going on or to experience being part of a crowd.
> 5 The final category of motivation is ego detachment, often characterised by an exploitative attitude. Those who loot at disaster scenes do so because they can emotionally divorce themselves from the plight of others.

It is obvious that Turner and Killian's classification is far from being complete and in reducing motivation to five categories, they have oversimplified a very wide and complex area. As McPhail (1971) found in his study, there may be dozens of different individual motives and they can be manifested in various forms, in different cultures. The acceptance of individual motivation does not suggest that the acts of individually motivated participants are carried out without the influence of the crowd. In other words, individually motivated acts may be modified or exaggerated by the crowd. Le Bon may not be completely right when he remarked that, "...he [the individual] will be less disposed to check himself from the consideration that a crowd being anonymous, and in consequence irresponsible, the sentiment of responsibility which always controls individuals disappears entirely" (Le Bon 1969, p.30). However, he cannot be entirely wrong in his argument that the individual forming part of a crowd differs from an isolated individual. Several psychological experiments have demonstrated that groups can arouse people and diffuse responsibility. When high levels of arousal are combined with diffused responsibility, normal inhibitions may be diminished (Berlonghi, 1993, p.18). This tendency of participants to abandon their normal restraints and to lose their sense of individuality is labelled 'de individuation' (Festinger, et al. 1952).

Modern collective behaviour theories are far from offering a clear explanation of the violent acts of the crowd. Neither is it still not clear whether they regard collective action or even crowd violence as socially meaningful or who should bear the responsibility of the acts of violence committed by a crowd. If these acts are committed by individuals who otherwise do not commit crimes, why are we still denying the influence of the crowd on the participants? Le Bon has suggested that the crowd acts like a tempest, which picks up individuals, whirling and scattering them before allowing them to fall. However, each individual has responsibility for the acts they commit, although their decision may have been slightly modified by the crowd itself. It is very important to remember that each person is responsible for their own actions rather than blaming the phenomenon of de individuation for violent behaviour and crime during a crowded setting.

A participant's behaviour in a crowd situation might be influenced and accordingly modified in two opposing ways. In the first instance, a participant's act of violence can be controlled or reduced by the presence of large numbers. A participant, who can see that what he is doing or intends to do will be widely observed may refrain from committing his violent act or carries it out within the limitations of the consent of the other participants. This does not imply that violent acts committed in crowds are not really violent, but it shows that they are not as violent as most individually committed violent acts. We all know that the most appalling acts of violence are committed by criminals in the absence of other people. This leads us to the conclusion that sometimes crowds exert a positive effect on their participants when they want to commit violent acts. We see policemen, soldiers and even unarmed civilians badly injured or even killed by crowds, but we do not often witness the type of planned and deliberate murder or mutilation which so often occurs in solitary acts.

Being a part of a crowd may also influence a participant's behaviour negatively. For instance, some people do not interfere in a fight which they believe is unjust when they are an isolated individual. One of the reasons for this may be that they are fearful or do not have the power to prevent it from happening. Individuals feel themselves to be powerless and fail to interfere in an obvious injustice. The same individual becomes a hero in a similar situation when they are part of a crowd or in the presence of large numbers of observers. However, there might be some individuals, dedicated supporters of a cause or an ideal, who act with the same degree of determination as isolated individuals as well as when they are part of a crowd. However, it is commonly observed that individuals becomes more assertive and even courageous when they resist an injustice in the presence of large numbers. This fact directs our attention to the possible influence of the crowd on the individual participant.

There may be a number of reasons for this. First, participants may hope that they will receive support when they cannot overcome the problem alone. Secondly, the presence of others and their approval might intensify his/her determination. Having the approval of many people or being part of a crowd that has the same or similar feelings for a cause, will inevitably effect the participant's degree of action. Belief in the righteousness of a cause and the knowledge that there are others who feel the same may give an individual a sense that their actions will be supported, be they violent actions or positive, peaceful actions.

Since crowd violence will be analysed in a separate section, in more detail, let us move on to the second visible component of public order policing; the leaders.

Leaders

The second visible component of public order policing, the leader or the leadership, takes various shapes and forms in contemporary crowd events. This type of leadership is more complex when compared with leadership in conventional crowd events which do not involve issues of public order. Leadership can be overt or covert and moves from individualised to institutionalised leadership.

As already suggested, for most of the duration of a crowd's existence, there is a leader or leaders who exert some control over events. However, this does not suggest that leaders impose their wills on the crowds they lead. Despite the fact that the leader is identifiable compared to the complex nature of the crowd, the structure and shape of leadership may have various forms. One of the mistakes made by both classical and modern crowd theorists is that they have overestimated the role and influence of the leader on the crowd in committing criminal acts. Perhaps the crowd was influenced by its leader not only because the leader had tried to influence them, but also because the crowd was ready to be influenced. Although the existence of the crowd is largely dependent upon the existence of its leaders, acts of violence cannot be attributed only to the influence of the leader. No leader can make a crowd commit criminal acts unless participants within the crowd choose to do so. If one tries to put the crowd and the leader in causal order, perhaps it is more appropriate to assume that the leader comes after the crowd. It is not the leader who influences the crowd and determines the outcome of crowd action, rather it is the crowd who chooses the leader and puts him into the position of leadership. This does not have to be done in a formal way by democratically selecting a leader; rather it may be an informal or even a primitive electoral procedure.

The leadership in contemporary crowd events lasts as long as the leader continues to behave in a way acceptable to the crowd. This kind of leadership cannot create any fundamental change in the mind of the crowd. Leadership becomes a role of crowd representation rather than being a leader with any stable power. This sort of leadership can be called *symbolic* and temporary. When the cause which led to the creation of the crowd disappears, its leaders also disappear. Both conventional and contemporary collective behaviour theories speak of this type of leadership. As Le Bon (1969, p.118) has remarked "...these leaders are more frequently men [sic] of action than thinkers. They are not gifted with keen foresight, nor could they be, as this quality is generally more conducive to doubt and inactivity". Le Bon maintains that the intensity of their faith gives great power of suggestion to their words.

On this point it must be noted that since this research is particularly concerned with the 'symbolic leadership' of violent crowds, rather than charismatic leadership, the latter will not be dealt with in this discussion. In order to recognise the difference between symbolic and charismatic leadership it is worth looking at the main characteristics of charismatic leadership. Charismatic leaders are those who lead the crowds which they have themselves caused or formed. These crowds cannot be thought of without also thinking of their leader and the leader is a necessary precursor to the crowd. The most important point here is that the crowd does not necessarily cease to exist when the leader dies or disappears. Even after the disappearance of the leader, he/she still exerts an identifiable influence on crowds. It is these leaders and crowds which have played important roles in the destiny of nations. Religious leaders such as the prophet Muhammed and Jesus are examples of charismatic leaders who have caused fundamental changes in their followers way of life without much resistance or objection. Charismatic leaders often have a coherent and radical philosophy behind the action of their followers. These leaders are involved in action and the philosophical urge behind their cause.

After giving a brief account of the main differences between real and symbolic leaders, it is worth concentrating on symbolic leadership and to consider the role and influence of this kind of leader on the crowd during a violent confrontation. Contrary, perhaps, to general opinion, rebellious behaviour is not caused by leadership *per se*. Even when the leadership of a rebellious situation actually serves to direct the energies and activities of a violent crowd, the leader does not, by his or her own initiative and activities, cause the rebellious behaviour which they direct. The leadership role in crowd violence is important but limited; a leader cannot make a participant commit a criminal act because the participant's desire, and decision to commit a particular crime originates from the motives held by the individual. This is not to oversimplify or underestimate the role of the leader, but their role can go no further than provocation and incitement.

The leaders are not usually, as some people might imagine, extraordinary persons who influence and direct the crowd to a particular target. "Ample evidence has been gathered showing that crowds far from being hypnotised by charismatic leaders are often incited by unremarkable characters" (Gaskel and Benewick, 1987, p.3). Leadership may simply consist of a role model - the person who strikes the first blow, throws the first rock or fires the first shot or one who deliberately urges others to hostile action. In this sense, perhaps it is more appropriate to classify most of the so-called leaders as 'provocateurs' rather than full leaders. Particularly in violent public order events the leaders and targets are symbolic and there is no real leader or followers to obey them. There are provocateurs and provocation but not leaders or leadership and followers.

In confrontations, violence may occur in the absence of conscious decisions by the leadership of either side and it may actually occur in spite of a leadership decision against violence (Grimshaw, 1972, p.44). While this research aims to show that the leader's influence on the crowd is very limited, this does not deny the influence of the leaders entirely, rather it should be stressed that it is the participants who are primarily responsible for their action. Mannheim has pointed out that:

> ...it is going too far when some writers regard the leader as nothing but the personification of the emotional drives of the crowd, entirely dependent upon its whims and, without any will of his own, merely giving expression to its fleeting impulses. It is only consequent that according to this view the leader of a criminal crowd is neither legally nor morally responsible for its action (Mannheim, 1965b, p.649).

This seems an undue generalisation of a highly complex phenomenon. Perhaps it is more appropriate to accept the existence of a mutual relationship between the crowd and its leader, each one influencing the other and being influenced by it. The explanation given by Mannheim

(1965a-b) may only be relevant to the symbolic leadership with which this study is concerned and the interaction between leader and followers in charismatic leadership may not be two-sided to the same extent. But, in contemporary crowd events, as has already been mentioned, the leader is not immune to the atmosphere and the stimulus emanating from his/her followers; but is susceptible to their presence and their action.

Almost all crowd theorists have been interested in leaders and each new generation of crowd theorists has claimed that its predecessor has failed to understand the mechanism of leadership. Besides categorising the leaders as charismatic and symbolic, there are various forms and degrees of leadership, ranging from political leadership to trades union leadership and so on. Although some crowd theories give the impression that the violence of the crowd is increased by its leaders, in fact both the police and the crowd have always benefited from having a leader. Therefore, even the worst leadership is preferable to a leaderless crowd. As will be shown in the following account, this opposes the common view which suggests that the existence of a leader in a crowd event makes the situation worse for the police. However, the evidence suggests that the reverse is the case. Recent crowd events, particularly the inner-city riots in the USA and the UK, have demonstrated that violent crowds without any hierarchy and leadership are far more dangerous and difficult to deal with. For instance, the Los Angeles riots would not have claimed about 60 lives and caused many billions of dollars worth of damage to property if the crowd had been acting under a clear and overt leadership. Therefore, the established power:

> ...[the police] looks for the crowd's leaders, and sighs with relief when the crowd has specific demands; established power waits for the crowd to go away and hopes to negotiate with its leaders, thereby turning the crowd into a constituency and socialising its leader into the established power game whose rules are already fixed and in which established leaders are already adepts (McClelland, 1989, p.332).

Today not only violent crowds but also some other relatively peaceful crowds such as the New Age Travellers in Britain and criminal gangs in the USA pretend not to have a leader for various reasons. The media coverage of such groups throughout the period of observations has revealed that a number of crowd types deny the existence of any sort of leader or leadership. On the other hand, it was evident from their conduct that they had a form of leadership and hierarchy amongst themselves (Marsh and Campbell, 1978a-b; Erlen, 1992; Mouland, 1992).

Before moving on to the topic of some crowd attributes, two final points remain to be made. First, it is important to stress that not all crowd leaders are of the same type. To paraphrase Shakespeare, some are born leaders, some achieve leadership and some have leadership thrust upon them. Some crowd leaders are leaders for a moment, or for a limited period of time. Some leaders come to their crowds from the outside and then lead the crowd in its cause, but no matter where the leader comes from, or what form the leadership takes, the leader is the symbol and the cause of the unity of the crowd. In this sense, it can be seen that the leader's influence on the crowd is very limited. The leader cannot direct them to an unknown target and make them commit criminal acts and cause damage to property, unless participants wish to do so. When the leader wants to direct the crowd to a target a target will be chosen which the crowd will not object to. In other words, the violent outcome of collective behaviour cannot only be derived from the crowd's suggestibility to its leaders. It is an oversimplification to explain this complex phenomenon by suggesting that individuals who act under orders are capable of doing anything suggested to them.

As indicated earlier, there are many factors which influence a crowd event. Individuals in the crowd are bound by ties to the leader and by ties to each other, but these ties are typically seen as being cumulative because they are thought of as being basically of the same type. McClelland (1989) has pointed out that explanations of crowd behaviour which relied on suggestion and imitation have never been able to make any clear distinction between the two; leaders suggested behaviour to the crowd, some members responded, and they in turn suggested the same behaviour to the less responsive members of the crowd. The same interaction process can be in question between the leaders and the crowd; the crowd influences the leader and the leader in turn influences the crowd and so on.

The second point is that not all crowd members have exactly the same individual motives and may not respond to the leader in the same way and to the same degree. This refutes the idea suggested by conventional crowd theorists who argue that crowd members are suggestible and imitate the leaders to such an extent that they commit acts of violence under the influence of their leaders.

The conclusion which can be drawn from this is that the interaction between the crowd, its leaders and the target is too complex and mutable to admit conventional crowd theory. Acts of violence may not be committed by the influence of the leaders, they may be committed by individuals who have reason and a sense of judgement. However, it cannot be denied that the influence of the leader, during a crowd event, may modify or exaggerate the degree of criminal acts the followers commit.

The Police

So far, two of the physical components of public order policing, participants and leaders, have been analysed with a special emphasis on collective behaviour and violence. The last and perhaps the most important component, the police, will be the subject of the final chapter and this chapter will also contain the implications of the model of this research on public order policing practices.

As a type of crowd, the police are subject to almost the same considerations in terms of the interactional relationships between leaders and the behaviour of their followers. It is both historically and currently the case that the police or other officials may initiate violence, carry out destructive behaviour and may be responsible for the escalation of the merely disorderly into the tragic (Skolnick, 1969; Currie and Skolnick, 1972; McEvoy and Gamson, 1972; Levy, 1968). The role of police commanders is a paradigm of the role of crowd leader; the same dynamics which rule leader/crowd relationships can be seen to operate in the police hierarchy, although to a different extent. The variation in degree but not in nature stems from the fact that the police, as a relatively well-organised and trained crowd, is more controlled. It is again a more permanent social institution compared to an ordinary crowd and this clearly puts limitations on the degree of crowd action and the role of it leaders.

At this point, it is appropriate to analyse some crowd attributes which can be considered as non-physical components of public order policing in more detail such as 'emotionality', 'irrationality' and 'destructiveness'.

The Non-Physical Components of the Crowd

The activities of crowds are reminiscent of the human organism and its behaviour. It consists of a body, that is the participants, and the leaders who resemble its head. Crowd behaviour is guided, to some extent, by an alleged mind which for some is the source of irrational activities, and for others perfectly rational and meaningful behaviour. Whether crowd behaviour is caused by the collective mind or not, there is an undeniable relationship between crowd action and the mood which is the product of crowd presence. At every single demonstration observed for this book the presence and workings of collectively held values and norms which affected crowd action were apparent. This sharing of values and norms can be termed the collective mind.

One of the important points to explore here is whether the crowd or individuals within a crowd are as emotionally and psychologically motivated as Le Bon and other classical crowd theorists have argued. While some modern crowd theorists regard crowd behaviour as rational, thus refuting the irrationality of crowd violence, they agree that crowd behaviour usually occurs within a context of strong emotion. For instance, Couch (1975, p.76) does not distinguish crowd behaviour from many other instances of human behaviour and maintains that a sequence of interactions between a husband and wife or employer and employee can also be highly charged with emotion. What classical crowd theorists failed to see, is that emotionality is not peculiar to the crowd, rather the majority of human interactions are highly emotional. Therefore, it is a misrepresentation to see the emotionally oriented concepts such as suggestibility or irritability as purely an outcome of crowd existence. It is not the individual who constitutes the crowd, but any individual can be influenced by the suggestions he receives from outside. The person who makes suggestions to other individuals does not have to be a charismatic leader and the individual does not have to be a part of the crowd.

Emotionality, suggestibility and so on, are usually the integral parts of the human mechanism. It is not the product of a collectivity, rather the emotionality of the crowd which is the agglomeration of individual emotionality. This explanation seems at first glance, to prove the classical approach to crowd behaviour. One of the significant differences between the explanation of this book and classical approaches is that they argue that a perfectly sane and rational person in possession of reason may become irrational when part of a crowd. On the contrary, this research argues that if a person acts irrationally under suggestion, it is not because the crowd makes this particular person irrational, rather it is because this person is open to suggestion and will act less rationally and more emotionally under certain circumstances. For classical theorists the individual is apt to lose his sense of responsibility both because responsibility is divided and because his behaviour is masked by anonymity. This might be the case to some extent but the roots of emotionality and other similar feelings exist in each individual rather than being the mere product of the existence of the crowd. This argument does not suggest that the crowd and the leader have no influence on the participants, rather that they shape and direct these previously acquired feelings.

Today, "...all crowd theorists seem to agree that the 'heightening of affect' (emotional intensity) and the 'lowering of intelligence' are the 'fundamental facts of group psychology' " (McClelland, 1989, p.247). The most striking point conventional theorists argue is that the crowd makes a perfectly innocent individual commit criminal acts. It can be asserted that crowds may provide an opportunity to commit a criminal act to an individual who already has an intention and the ability to do so. The crowd cannot change an innocent individual into a criminal, but provides an opportunity to those who already have the tendencies or inclinations towards committing certain acts.

This approach takes the individual as the essence of crowd action. It sees the crowd as an agglomeration of individuals, rather than seeing it as a single body acting with a collective mind. This implies that if individuals have the intention of committing crimes, the crowd may provide the opportunity for them, but since it does not make the individual a criminal or force them into criminal activity, the crime committed by individuals in the crowd remains the product of individual decision and responsibility.

With regard to the concept of destructiveness, crowds may sometimes be destructive, but destruction is not the inevitable consequence of crowd existence. Contrary to the common view which perceives the crowd as destructive, most crowd types remain relatively peaceful. Throughout the research period, which involved over thirty observations at various events, violence was observed at only three events (Appendix 1, observations 14, 25 and 27). These were the 'Bloody Sunday Marches' of 1993 and 1994 and the 'Close Down the BNP' (British National Party) march organised by the anti-Nazi League and other left wing groups. Moreover, destructiveness is not uniquely possessed by the crowd. In the majority of cases of crowds attempting to challenge the authorities and to establish a less authoritarian political system, the number of people killed or maimed by the crowd is smaller than by those suppressing the crowd. In general, in the history of mankind, the authorities controlling the crowd have been responsible for more deaths than the crowd itself. It is a misconception to believe that all crowds are destructive and act irrationally without any restraint.

Classical crowd theories have drawn most of their conclusions from observations of violent and frightening crowd events, rather than from the far more numerous peaceful crowd protests and gatherings. Classical theorists appear to be selecting the most extreme examples of crowd action in order to support their theory. Modern crowd theorists such as Canetti and Smelser see the destructive nature of the crowd from a different angle. For Canetti, the destructiveness of the crowd is not a fundamental crowd characteristic;

> ...it is a derivative of the crowd's desire for growth and for equality; it is not the fragility of the objects which attracts crowd violence, but rather the noise of broken glass, which represents 'fresh life'; windows and doors are broken by the crowd as 'boundaries', obstacles to growth; houses are

> destroyed because the crowd fears it will be shut up again; the crowd in its nakedness everything seems a Bastille (Canetti, 1962, McClelland, 1989).

In this sense Canetti sees the crowd as a single object acting unanimously. He makes no mention of the acts of the individual in the crowd, rather referring to the crowd as a single object acting in total unity. As will become apparent from the following quotation, his explanation of crowd violence is not clear. His account seems descriptive rather than explanatory:

> The crowd particularly likes destroying houses and objects; breakable objects like window panes, mirrors, pictures and crockery; and people tend to think that it is the fragility of these objects which stimulates the destructiveness of the crowd (Canetti, 1962, p.19).

From this respect Canetti's crowd is not any less frightening than Le Bon's. For Canetti, the crowd's destructiveness and violence stems from its desire to grow and he glorifies crowd violence and destructiveness as an acceptable excuse for this desire. He maintains that, "...the destructiveness of representational images is the destruction of a hierarchy which is no longer recognised [by the crowd]" (Canetti, 1962, p.19).

Whether one agrees or disagrees with the psychological aspects of crowd behaviour there is an undeniable link between crowd existence and the acts of crowd participants during a crowd event. This inevitably leads to an examination of certain psychological metaphors which are considered as constituting the non-material aspects of crowd behaviour.

Suggestibility

Anyone who observes participants in groups or crowds, and then considers the same participants individually is forced to conclude that they often behave differently in these two general situations. In a crowd, participants will frequently do things which they would not allow themselves to do under other circumstances.

It is generally accepted that in a highly organised formal crowd, the members are bound by a double emotional tie, to leaders and also to other members of the group. This explains the 'alteration and limitation' of the individuals personality which crowd theorists have always remarked upon. Since the emotional level of each individual is not and cannot be the same, each individual response to a leader's suggestions will inevitably vary in degree. While some will obey the leader's command without reasoning and questioning, and commit violent and destructive acts, others may not listen to the leaders at all. This is related to the degree of suggestibility possessed by each individual. In abstract terms, the main source of suggestibility is the individual and their readiness to obey the leader's directions. An individual is suggestible not because of the leader's suggestions, but because the individual is open to the suggestions of others.

Classical crowd theories suggest that all members of a given race will take part in a crowd event. This approach fails before Milgram and Toch's (1969) basic criteria which asks why riot police fail to be drawn in by the rhetoric of a crowd demagogue. As Couch (1975) has argued, if crowds are as suggestible as claimed by classical crowd theorists, authorities could control riots simply by suggesting that rioters disperse and go for a cold swim. On the other hand, the individualistic approach predicts that participants will be tied to personality type. However, despite attempts to do so, no common trait has ever been found to distinguish membership versus non-membership of a crowd (McPhail, 1970).

The influence of crowd leaders and of the crowd itself on individual participants cannot be completely ignored. The crowd or the individual within the crowd does not invariably accept the suggestions of the leader because they do not always have the opportunity to apply reasoning to what they receive. This implies that in some crowd situations, the crowd may have to accept orders given by its leaders without reasoning because it has no other alternative. Lack of effective communication between crowd members and the leaders or organisers contributes to this problem. In some cases, participants cannot respond to the organiser or the leader or cannot fully understand what they are required to be doing. Therefore, suggestibility does not always occur in the full sense for practical reasons.

Suggestibility does not occur only between the leader and the follower, even individuals within the crowd may influence each other in different ways. Blumer (1975) introduces a model of 'circular reaction' in order to demonstrate how this works.

> [It] refers to a type of inter stimulation wherein the response of one individual reproduces the stimulation that has come from another individual and in being reflected back to this individual reinforces the stimulation. Thus inter stimulation assumes a circular form in which individuals reflect one another's states of feeling and in doing so intensify this feeling (cited in Evans, 1975, p.22).

A similar kind of 'circular reaction' can occur within small, highly organised and institutionalised crowds. The result of this kind of circular reaction can be entirely different from the circular reaction in a relatively large crowd. One of the reasons for this is that it is very difficult, if not impossible to achieve a two way interchange of view. As Ginsberg (1964) has remarked:

> Collective deliberation can only yield good results when there is a genuine interchange of views and when each member is able to throw some light on the problem under discussion based on his own observation. This leads to genuine, integrative and co-operative thinking which can produce results superior to anything any individual could have produced by himself (Ginsberg, 1964, p.113).

Emotions such as suggestibility and emotionality are reduced to the minimum level within small and organised crowds, but these crowds give, to some extent, an opportunity for a reciprocal exchange of views between the leader and the crowd. Compared with large crowds where communication works only unilaterally, from the leader to the crowd, the decisions taken by these groups may be relatively more rational and well considered. In fact, nothing can reduce the suggestibility and emotionality of human actions to the perfect minimum level and all human acts are influenced by a number of determinants. In this sense even a decision taken by an individual after a long period of consideration is not immune from emotionality and suggestibility. An exchange of views, however, reduces the level of irrationality and improves the quality or the level of the decision taken by the individuals. As Ginsberg (1964) has stated "...in unorganised crowds such free interchange is impossible. The majority are bound to be passive listeners and consequently the influence of the few who generally know something of mass psychology is predominant" (p.114).

In conclusion, individuals within a crowd may be more suggestible and act less rationally, but this is not only because they are part of a crowd, but also partly because they are influenced by the crowd's atmosphere and these conditions make them unable to reason or to judge actions properly. This applies equally to the physical senses; for instance, an individual cannot hear what is said or cannot see what is occurring in the crowd. The researcher has personally experienced a similar situation at a national demonstration in London, when at one point a substantial number of the crowd left the main rally and took another route (observation 1). As a member of the crowd he had difficulty in understanding what was going on, and in deciding which group to follow. Although the researcher followed the main rally, his decision was fortuitous and not based on information.

'Rationality' in the Context of Crowd Behaviour

Throughout this chapter it has been maintained that each crowd event has at least three dominant visible components. Classical crowd theories would argue that when these components exist violence is imminent and that the crowd will act irrationally and become destructive. This conventional approach to collective behaviour may be traced in Le Bon's distaste for the mystical loss of individuality and civilised behaviour in the crowd, an approach which has been reaffirmed in modern 'riot control' manuals, as well as in most contemporary social-scientific approaches. In line with this emphasis on individuality, collective behaviour has usually been seen as destructive and, in most treatments, inappropriate, distasteful and irrational.

In this sub-section, it will be shown that this approach is erroneous. Studies of riot participation argue for more structured crowd behaviour than classical collective behaviour theories would suggest and far more attuned to the redress of specific grievances and the selection of limited and understandable targets (Quarantelli and Dynes, 1968; Currie and Skolnick, 1972). Violence is not the inevitable consequence of crowd existence. In addition, if violence does occur it may not be as rational as some modern crowd theorists have argued, but it may not be completely irrational either. Since the act of violence may be motivated by various factors it is not feasible to rationalise crowd violence as a whole. But, as indicated in the previous account, there may be lessons and messages which can be derived from crowd violence (Nieburg, 1968; Levy, 1968). When we look at crowd violence incidents individually every act of violence is more or less rational. Whatever the condition of the crowd and suggestions of the leader, each individual is responsible for their actions. Within this context when the word 'rational' is used, it does not imply the 'justification' of violent acts. Rather, it refers to the assumption that each act of violence is committed by its perpetrator's reasoned and considered decision.

There are numerous crowd events which show that not all crowds are disorderly and violent and therefore violence is not an inevitable consequence of crowd existence. Not only supposedly peaceful events such as carnivals, festivals and pop concerts, but even the majority of potentially violent crowd events such as political demonstrations and rallies pass without any serious violence. An overwhelming majority of the demonstrations which took place within the research period have enhanced the view that expectations of violence at crowd events have been dramatically reduced.

Of course, any crowd may impose some problems in general to the police, but serious violent confrontation does not always pose a danger to the authorities. It is important to distinguish why two different crowds of about the same size, may yield different public order problems in terms of levels of disruption and violence. Is it the sheer size of the crowd which creates public order problems or are there considerations other than the physical presence of a crowd? For instance, the police did not expect violence and anticipated only routine levels of control at Wembley Stadium during a visit by the Pope in 1982. As Benewick and Holton (1987) have pointed out, the peacefulness of a crowd numbering 100, 000 reflects the view that crowd discipline may arise from intrinsic not extrinsic sources. A similar sized crowd but constituted by different participants may impose problems of public order and violence to the police at the same venue at the following week's football match. It is not terraces or fences inside the ground, nor the sheer size of the crowd which creates violence; rather there is something inherent within the individuals involved which dictates the collective action of the crowd.

Not only supposedly peaceful crowd events but even potentially violent crowd events have proved that not all contemporary crowd behaviours are destructive and revolutionary. "Following the work of Emile Durkheim, there is the strong possibility that peaceful crowds mobilised for some mass public ritual may function to express and strengthen processes of social solidarity and social cohesion" (Benewick and Holton, 1987, p.201).

The second question concerns the underlying causes of crowd violence. Is it the crowd which makes its individuals violent and irrational, and therefore leads to collective violence or are the police, the front line representatives of the state, the provocateurs of violent acts? Substantial numbers of studies show that the situation goes beyond this dichotomy; neither of these factors can be the sole cause of crowd violence. Therefore, recent studies have focused on the social aspect of crowd violence in order to examine the remote and underlying causes of crowd violence. A number of recent crowd studies which included football crowds, which are supposed to be a happy event, focused on the social aspect of crowd violence in and around football grounds (Marsh, 1978; Dunning et al. 1986 and 1990; Taylor, 1971; Popplewell, 1986; Taylor, 1989; Sir Norman Chester Centre for Football Research, 1989; Dunning, 1990). They discovered that the roots of football hooliganism or violence do not start or end in the terraces but go back to the environment where the so-called hooligans came from.

The social causes, which make the supposedly peaceful spectators aggressive and violent are insufficient to explain visible manifestation of the social disruption of crowd events. The psychological make-up of each individual, the traditional terrace culture, and the crowd's influence on the individuals, increases the possibility of violent conflict between rival fans or the police. The incident of pitch invasions, (Pirie, 1992; Gibson and O'Neill, 1993; Lacey, 1993; Ross, 1993) following the removal of so-called provocative physical measures such as crash barriers between the crowd and the pitches and reducing the number of police officers inside the stadium, fails to eradicate the roots of football violence (Leicestershire Police Constabulary Operational Order, 1992c).

Rationale of Crowd Violence

There seem to be as many explanations and interpretations of crowd violence as there are scholarly and applied professions interested in the phenomena. Some social scientists tend to see crowd violence, like all violence, as a form of interaction. It indicates that all other forms of communication have been tried and failed and that nothing is left but for the strong to conquer the weak. On the basis of this argument, it is believed that any form of violence is a rational, socially and politically meaningful action directed toward the change of existing values, norms, or system. This explanation, however, is too wide to include all forms of violence. First of all, it cannot be said that all crowd violence is directed towards an intentional and calculated goal. For instance, it is very difficult, if not impossible, to see football violence in this context. Even the inner-city disturbances in Britain and the USA were not deliberately planned and directed towards the creation of fundamental changes in the existing system. It is unscientific to rationalise spontaneous riots because this type of unplanned action does not seem to be a rational way of changing the existing inequalities in society. Riots may reflect the state of society and give some messages about society, but they cannot be as rational as some have argued.

Moreover, numerous violent crowd events of the 1960s in the USA and 1980s in Britain have shown that crowd violence does not change the circumstances which brought them into such action. La Piere (1938, p.523) argues that, "...quite often rebellious action only aggravates the conditions which have brought it about and detracts from constructive efforts to improve those conditions". Whether crowd violence changes the situation towards the good or not, at least the crowd participants see their action as an expression of their grievances (Ball-Rokeach, 1972; Grimshaw, 1968; Lanf and Lang, 1968; McCord, 1968; Ransford, 1968, p.591; Waddington, 1992, p.63). Miller (1975, p.252) says: "The majority of a national sample of blacks saw the riots as a way to call attention to their problems, express their discontent to whites, improve their conditions, and end discrimination". To some extent this might be the case, but when it comes to tackling the problem, the expected change does not take place. With regard to calling attention to a particular problem, not only ethnic groups but also members of marginalised groups and communities may be provided with the motivation and the opportunity to assert their right to equal concern and respect by means of violence.

One of the reasons why collective violence does not always yield the desired and expected result is that, it is not directed towards the real underlying causes. For instance, if members of the unemployed black and white communities attacked the police in Brixton in 1981 and 1985 and a number of different inner city areas, this does not mean that the police were responsible for the prevailing economic and social conditions. As has been repeatedly indicated by Lord Scarman (1982) and many others, the police are not responsible for the deteriorating social and economic conditions which underlie the apparent causes of the disorders. He remarked that the police do not create social deprivation or racial disadvantage and they are not responsible for the disadvantages of the ethnic minorities. Yet all incidents started with an apparently insignificant incident involving a police officer and a member of the deprived community. Since the police were perceived as the visible representatives of the existing system the hatred of the crowd was directed towards them. Therefore, whether it is related to the causes of violence or not, the object of rebellious action is always concrete and tangible. It is obviously impossible to attack such abstractions as capitalism, the ruling class, a corrupt system etc. Violent attack is, therefore, directed toward some concrete targets, a class of persons or the police for example, who are considered to be responsible for the occurrence and maintenance of all such incidents.

Crowd action and crowd violence does not always solve a particular problem. It may attract attention to particular problems, but it does not necessarily yield a positive expected result. Smelser, who sees collective behaviour as socially meaningful and problem solving, is not clear on the issue of crowd violence and he fails to explain how crowd violence solves problems. His model may be useful in explaining how a crowd movement improves, escalates and explains the underlying causes behind these events, but he does not give a satisfactory explanation of how a riot situation can solve problems. He takes the position that collective behaviour is purposeful or implicitly problem-solving behaviour. This is based on the assumption that people will not attempt to 'reconstitute their social environment' without first recognising that their social and economic environment is problematic. This approach can easily be applied to anti-democratic and authoritarian states where one class is openly suppressed by another. In those countries the violence, individually or collectively, can be seen to be directed purposefully towards the oppressive regime. Their decision in using violence may be seen as the final and therefore legitimate solution to voice their grievances, and their actions may be directed toward the reconstitution of their social environment.

In conclusion, collective violence, whether it is the outcome of a collective mind or individual mind cannot be regarded as rational as some contemporary crowd theorists have argued. On the other hand, it must be agreed that collective violence transmits a message about the general situation or particular problems which are experienced by certain groups (Berk, 1972a-b; Berk and Rossi, 1972; Campbell, 1972; Short, 1972). The messages taken from collective violence, about the inequalities and injustices of the existing system, are insufficient to justify indiscriminate crowd violence and crowd violence should not be regarded as rational on the basis of this assumption. In fact the problem arises from the differentiation between the concepts of rationality and meaningfulness. There seems to be no universally accepted form of rationality and it is a rather relative concept. Even the most irrational acts may be quite rational for others. It is not the absolute rationality of a particular act, which is significant, rather it is the perception of individuals who see particular acts from different points of view. In Western ideology the concept of rationality varies in accordance with various political and sociological views. In traditional Turkish-Islamic thought, however, the rationality of an act cannot be decided objectively. Even the most apparently irrational acts may be regarded as rational on the basis of traditional values and beliefs. Perhaps, this was also the case in the West at one time when human affairs were conducted more by religious influence than rational considerations. However, a gradual erosion of religious ideas and sentiments and the secularisation of social affairs has transformed the Western society into a more materially oriented rationality.

The Collective Mind

A crowd is not only numbers of people participating in a demonstration or a particular activity. To use a psychological metaphor one tends to think of a crowd as having one personality and mind. Those theorists who saw crowd violence as socially and politically meaningful and rational tend to regard collective violence as the outcome of an imaginary 'collective mind'. The concept of the collective mind, which has its origins in the works of J.

J. Rousseau (1952 and 1968), has been used as the basis for the justification of collective violence. It was suggested that since collective violence was the outcome of this collective mind or consciousness, it must be regarded as rational and meaningful. In order to make judgements about the rationality or irrationality of crowd violence, the collective mind from which crowd violence derives must be examined.

The collective mind is nothing but the personification of patterns of collective behaviour. It is nicely calculated to provide a philosophical justification for any kind of collective behaviour. Both classical and modern crowd theorists have regarded collective violence as the outcome of a collective mind. The only difference is that unlike contemporary crowd theorists who see crowd violence as rational and meaningful, classical theorists, such as Le Bon, see the outcome of the collective mind as inferior to that of the individual mind. In other words, both groups of theories accept the existence of the collective mind, but one group, the modern crowd theorists, justify and tolerate crowd violence by referring to the collective mind. The second group, the conventional crowd theorists, criticise the collective mind on the basis of its inferiority, compared to the individual mind. Le Bon maintains that "In the collective mind the intellectual aptitudes of the individuals, and in consequence their individuality, are weakened. The heterogeneous is swamped by the homogeneous, and the unconscious qualities obtain the upper hand" (Evans, 1975, p.13).

This account asserts that from the interaction of people in social groups or crowds there arises a collective ethos, variously termed the 'collective mind', 'collective conscience', 'collective spirit' and so on. This mind is supposed to be the directing force of collective activities and when collective interaction takes place, individuals are thought to lose identity and to merge into a whole. The spirit of force then determines the behaviour of the individual member.

Recently a new explanation has been introduced as an alternative to the problematic notion of the collective mind. It is argued that as a consequence of de-individuation participants tend to abandon their normal restraints. This causes a loss of self-awareness and evaluation apprehension in crowded settings that foster anonymity. Berlonghi (1993) maintains that, "...when self-awareness is reduced an individual will act impulsively, not be able to monitor or regulate his own behaviour, be less concerned with the evaluation of others, and will lose his ability to act rationally. When self-awareness is reduced the person is controlled more by the situation than self" (p.18). Although psychological metaphors such as reasoning, suggestibility, rationality or irrationality and so on, have their roots in the inner make-up of individuals, how a person feels in a situation is also dependent upon the emotions he perceives in others in the same situation. This means that a person may be influenced by other participants as well as the leaders suggestions.

Contrary to this argument, during the early history of social psychology, Floyd Allport (1924) attempted to construct a social psychology based strictly on the principles of behaviourism and avoiding completely the 'collective mind' fallacy. He applied these principles to collective behaviour, denying that any new forms of behaviour emerge in the collectivity. He concludes that, "...crowd behaviour is merely the sum of individual reactions" (cited in La Pierre, 1938, p.4). Allport summed up his theory of collective behaviour in the declaration, "...the individual in the crowd behaves just as he would behave alone, only more so" (op.cit.p.4).

Allport's assertion is problematic for two reasons. First of all, crowds are made up of individuals and these individuals choose to participate in a particular crowd event on the basis of their individual decision. Crowds do not come into existence randomly, but because their participants share the same or at least similar grievances on a particular topic. "The people are brought together by a common interest preparing them for a certain type of action" (Allport, 1924, p.292). This emphasis on individual predisposition has been retained, though modified during the occurrence of crowd event. While acknowledging that 'personal characteristics act as a selective factor in the recruiting of individuals to a crowd', Turner and Killian (1972, p.21) argue that "...the hundreds or thousands of individuals who converge on the scene are heterogeneous in motivation despite the similarity of their behaviour" (Turner and Killian, 1972, p.27, cited in McPhail and Miller, 1973, p.722). This implies that the seeds of collective action go back to the individual rather than being a mere product of crowd participation. Participants may be influenced by many factors before becoming a part of a particular crowd and these may have a determining influence on the participant, but their action is rarely determined by a supposedly collective mind.

Secondly, it is difficult, if not impossible, to constitute a collective mind in a crowded situation, and direct the crowd by this mind. The observations and interviews of this research (Appendix 1 and 2) have revealed that, despite all the sophisticated communication networks available to the police, it is very difficult for them, let alone the crowd, to communicate and deploy manpower effectively in crowd events involving large numbers. During pre-organised events police communication networks frequently fail and this leads to chaos. For these reasons, it is very difficult for the leaders or the organisers to change their followers minds dramatically. Individual behaviour may be influenced, but it cannot be completely directed by a so-called collective mind. From this respect, radical approaches to the rationality of crowd action, which sees collective violence as collective action, seems more feasible than the ones which propose that crowd violence is the result of collective behaviour.

This radical approach, with which the researcher partly agrees, explains collective action by refusing the concept of the collective mind. But it fails to explain why some people commit acts which they would not otherwise commit. If we are determined to give a meaning to collective behaviour which has a collective connotations, we may regard the outcome of collective behaviour as a 'collective message' derived from various motives and reasons rather than from a collective mind. This 'collective message' does not have to be the end-product of an allegedly collective mind. This approach refutes the existence of the collective mind as argued by classical crowd theories. It also acknowledges, in an indirect way, the modern crowd theories which regard collective behaviour as socially meaningful.

It may be possible to answer this question of the participation of individuals who have no previous criminal record, without denying the existence of a collective mind or blaming the collective mind for the violent acts they commit. Namely, acts of violence committed by individuals may not be merely the outcome of a collective mind, but the result of an individual having the opportunity to commit an act, by being a part of the crowd. In other words, the collective mind rarely dominates the individual mind, it only provides opportunities and acts as a facilitator. It seems that this is the reason why some innocent and peaceful people commit criminal and violent acts when they become a part of crowd.

Summary

This chapter has led to the conclusion that the crowd and police are products of society, the former having a less permanent existence and being less organised than the latter. Both crowds and the police can be seen as a social institution, while the former is created because of the inconsistencies of society in meeting the demands of its people, and the latter exist to control these dissenting individuals who want to achieve something by forming large groups. The relationship of these two crowds is very much influenced by the nature of the leadership which determines the kind of action one crowd will take when encountering the other.

The second finding of this chapter is that public order policing consists of two integral parts 'the physical' and 'non-physical components'. The first component of public order policing, the physical component, falls within the scope of sociology and includes elements such as the participants, leaders and the police. The second component is concerned with metaphors such as suggestibility, rationality and destructivness and falls within the scope of psychology.

In the following chapter the research will concentrate on the role of external factors on crowd gatherings and its mode of behaviour. These external factors range from the state and its institutions and in particular, the control agencies represented by the police and army. These institutions play a substantial role in the social, political and economic spheres of human life.

4 Crowds Against the Establishment

Introduction

> The objective aspects, territorial boundaries, the letter of the law, the monopoly of legality and police power, in themselves do not make a nation, in fact they may generate more violence than collaboration, unless a nation is built in the minds and hearts of the people (H. L. Nieburg, 1968, p.19).

In the previous chapter the general constituent components of crowd behaviour were examined and it was concluded that crowd behaviour and public order policing consists of two integral parts. The first part is the physical component of public order policing which is made up of three physical elements: the crowd, its leaders or leadership and the police. The second part is mainly concerned with the mental constitution of crowd which refers to certain attributes mainly put forward by classical crowd theorists such as Le Bon and Tarde. These attributes include concepts such as 'irrationality', 'suggestibility', 'crowd mind' or 'collective mind' and 'collective violence'. Crowd behaviour was examined from the perspective of two combined elements, constitutional (biological/psychological) and institutional (social/environmental) factors.

The observations carried out for this research and other studies in the field have led to the conclusion that any study which involves crowds and public order policing in different countries needs to deal with the inner dynamics of crowd behaviour and the social and political arrangements which shape them. The perception that the police and the public have of each other varies from one country to another and displays differences which are influenced by many cultural factors. In view of these differences this study will initially deal with related cultural concepts in England, Wales and Turkey. These include perceptions of 'crime and collective violence', 'political violence' and arguments concerning 'human nature' and its specific application to crowd behaviour in different social environments.

With regard to Turkey, it must be noted that neither sociological explanations nor political perspectives were established, or have been adopted, in the same way as in the West. The political and ideological perceptions related to crime and collective violence have usually been considered within the framework of a broadly Islamic perspective as competing school of thoughts (Safak, 1977), rather than with reference to 'outside' alternatives. Despite apparent similarities in name, Eastern (Turkish) and Western (English) conservatism greatly differs on the issue of crime and relevant concepts. Liberal and radical ideologies, however, although they were represented prior to the secularisation of Turkey within Islamic ideology as competing school of thoughts (Safak, 1977), have formally been developed mostly since the secularisation of Turkey in the 1920s and have broadly followed a similar line as their Western counterparts (Kongar, 1979; Toprak, 1993; Turan, 1993; Karaosmanoglu, 1993; Heper, 1993; Heper et al, 1993).

Collective behaviour, throughout history, has always involved conflict with the state (Spencer, 1982; Miliband, 1984; Yack, 1992; Hoffman, 1992) and has been associated with class divisions in society. Most popular crowd movements are, in fact, the ones which are politically motivated and which involve opposition to particular political systems or issues related to social interests and the distribution of social and political power. Explanations of crowd behaviour, as a method of political struggle, have also recently received more sympathy even though it involved acts of 'political violence'. While conventional crowd theories mainly see collective violence as a manifestation of contentious aspects of human nature on a large scale, many modern liberal and radical theories regard collective violence as a legitimate aspect of political struggle and as a rationally chosen means of bringing excluded or marginalised interests on to the political agenda. Therefore this book, which is based on the comparative study of crowds in two distinct nations and cultures, has led the researcher to a preliminary study of the concepts such as 'the state', 'crime', 'class' and 'the police'.

Finally, although this chapter has made use of many explanatory concepts which are mainly used by conservative thinkers such as 'human nature' and 'non-material' (spiritual) factors generally emphasising irrationality or innate 'wickedness', the argument of this book falls somewhere between liberal and radical approaches which assume varying degrees of rationality in the activities of crowds. On the other hand, it must also be noted that this argument is not merely a collection of ideas from pre-existing approaches, rather, it is a synthesis of already existing theories giving rise to a new approach, which shall be termed the Combined Factors Approach (CFA).

Comparisons between Turkey, England and Wales

This comparative study of Turkish and the British crowds and public order policing practices will not only be limited by the comparison of the two police organisations but will also involve the cultural differences and similarities of these two distinct nations. The differences, in terms of this study, manifest themselves at two levels. The first is that the police and public expectations and perceptions of concepts such as the state and the police, are very different. Secondly, different general perceptions of the causes of crime may have an important effect on the police response to crime in general, and public order events in particular. For this reason, before moving on to the issue of policing practices, it is appropriate to begin by exploring the state, class (Hobbes, 1962; Quinney, 1980; Spencer, 1982; Gamso et al. 1982; Miliband, 1984; Giddens and Held, 1988; Hoffman, 1992; Johnson, 1993), political violence and human nature which all pertain to how illegal actions, including collective violence and crime, are perceived in these widely differing jurisdictions.

In Western ideology, political considerations of crime and crowd violence have been categorised under three broad perspectives. These are, the Conservative, Liberal and Radical (Benyon, 1987 and 1993). Within these three broad perspectives and within each individual perspective there are, again, various explanations for crime and crowd violence (Tame, 1991). For instance, left realism and left idealism, which approach the problem of crime and violence quite differently, are still categorised as 'radical perspectives' (Lea and Young, 1984), due to their criticism of existing social and political arrangements which are held to make crowd and collective violence a rational choice of action for many who participate. On the other hand, even within conservative approaches there are various explanations of crime and violence (Tame, 1991). The most important point which all these perspectives have in common is that each of these categories tries to explain crime and violence by concentrating on one factor and ignoring other aspects which may influence the definition of crime. These three broad categories are greatly influenced by and shaped according to sociological explanations of crime and crowd violence. For instance, while conservative approaches reflect Le Bon's view of crowd violence, radical perceptions have been shaped and influenced by a materialistic, generally Marxist ideology. In other words, sociological explanations have shaped political perspectives and they, in turn, have influenced the overall policy of the police concerning crime and collective violence.

One of the problems faced, in terms of terminology, has been to find a means of defining existing Turkish political perceptions which can be understood relative to Western social scientific traditions. The dilemma is that despite existing secular political ideologies, the public perception of the state and the police in Turkey still very much reflects historical and traditional perceptions which are considerably influenced by Islam (Bellah, 1958 and 1961; Atar, 1983; Kazici, 1987; Mortimer, 1991). For this reason, to define the present public perception of police and state as purely Turkish would be wrong and misleading. Despite the official denial of any link with Islam, the present, avowedly secular, Turkish state still enjoys a deference which is mainly derived from Islamic perceptions of the distribution of power in a socially just society. On the other hand, it would also be misleading to define those influences which shape the perceptions of people and the police as the product of a purely Islamic ideology. Present policies have been based on the adoption of Western ideologies at the cost of forsaking Islamic ideology and there is a large degree of official rebuttal of Islamic influence (Armstrong, 1937; Turner, 1978; *The Light*, 1980 and 1981; Mortimer, 1991; Mather, 1994; Bright, 1994; Khilafah, 1994, p.10).

Throughout the text, specific references will focus on the Turkish experience, but since Turkish ideology is very much influenced and shaped by Islamic thought, the term 'Turkish thought/ideology' will refer to the Turkish-Islamic perceptions toward the research topic. Despite the gradual development of radical and liberal thought in Turkish political discourse the social circumstances prevailing have given rise to what might broadly be termed 'Turkish ideology'. This is a pervasive ideology which is broadly conservative in nature. Therefore, the concept of 'Turkish ideology' throughout the text will refer to traditional Turkish conservative ideology rooted in pre-Ataturk Islam. The term will be used in contrast to ideas emanating from Western ideology which broadly embrace the commonly stereotyped three perspectives, in England and Wales as well as other Western countries.

Turkish ideology has been greatly influenced by and shaped according to the Islamic sacred law and tradition (Bellah, 1958 and 1961; Lewis, 1961; Lord Kinross, 1965) and also reflects the cultural and historical specificities of the East. It might, therefore, be misleading to assume that Turkish ideology is based only on Islam. Besides this influence, existing cultural and traditional values and norms which do not contradict Islamic thought have been accepted into Turkish ideology. Today, even in Turkey, which is, to a certain extent, a democratic and publicly secular country, the influence of Islamic observations on crime and related matters can be clearly seen. In some cases, therefore, our explanation of crime and collective violence will have to go further than simply examining existing secular ideological arrangements, which have been in force for seventy years.

It may be appropriate to consider Turkish political history in two major stages, one having direct and declared relations with Islam up to 1923 when the modern Turkish Republic (T. C.) was established. The second stage starts with the establishment of the modern Turkish state by Kemal Ataturk, which openly rejected previously held values and norms in favour of adopting Westernised ideologies (Armstrong, 1937; Robinson, 1965; Turner, 1978, p.162-170; Sloan, 1995, p.8). This research, which is mainly concerned with contemporary crowd theories, will mainly focus on contemporary crowd events, but it must be noted that deeply rooted Turkish-Islamic perceptions still have a profound effect on the relationship between the modern Turkish state and its public. For this reason this research deals with aspects of Islamic ideology prevalent prior to 1923 which, despite efforts to reduce their practical impact in subsequent regimes and administrations, still has a substantial influence on Turkish perceptions of the relationship between the citizen and the state (Turner, 1978).

The State, Class and Crime

The observations on which this research is based have revealed that contemporary crowds, like crowds in history, neither gather nor act randomly. Nor are they, as conventional methodologically individualistic crowd theories suggest, a mere collection of psychologically motivated participants. Rather, crowd movements usually, if not always, involve expression of grievances. These grievances, dependent upon the circumstances, may be purely material, or associated with non material abstract values and norms. They may stem from absolute material deprivation as well as relative material and political marginalisation. In other words, crowds usually have something to say or are in opposition against power-holding elites and they are mostly derived from the frustrated material or social ambitions of marginalised groups, most notably among the 'lower classes'. In a broad sense, the power holding elites whom crowds oppose are the state and its control agencies; the police and army.

The observations on which this study is based, have led the researcher to study the state and its controlling agency the police and examine their implications for public order policing practices in both countries. The research has also found that besides some shared and universal points, such as the state and the police being the apparatus of the ruling classes, the public perception of the state and its agencies differs historically in the two countries. Furthermore, the research has also revealed that there is a correlation between the nature of a state and the nature of its police. Accordingly, authoritarian states tend to have authoritarian and paramilitary police forces, while less authoritarian states have less authoritarian police services.

Authoritarian State versus Just State

The Concept of 'the State' (Dawlah) has a rather different meaning in Turkish thought which stems greatly from Islam. Contrary to Western semantics, the State, in Turkish thought, has positive connotations (Murad, 1992, p.2; Bardackci, 1995). The word 'state' has many literal meanings such as, 'luck', (talih) 'welfare' (refah), 'wealth' (zenginlik, varlik) and 'happiness' (mutluluk) (Devellioglu, 1984; Dogan, 1986). The Islamic state is ideally supposed to be primarily 'the just state', rather than being only a law and order state (Ozdenoren, quoted in Gocer, 1993, p.20). The most peculiar characteristic of the Islamic state is its being 'the just state' (Taymiya, 1992; Karaman, 1993; Huseyin, 1993a and 1993b; Hatemi, 1993; Unal, 1993). In Turkish, the word 'justice' implies notions of equality rather than punishment. It implies the distribution of justice in many areas of social life before it implies the punishment of would be criminals. An Islamic State, therefore, is one which focuses on the establishment of a 'just order', rather than being a law and order state (Taymiya, 1987, p.125 ; Ahmad, 1991, p.15; Unal, 1993, p.75). The law and order state, in Western thought, gives priority to criminal justice and the punishment of criminals rather than the creation of social, political and economic justice.

The Islamic state gives priority to justice rather than law and order (Taymiya, 1992, p.125-133). It attempts to deliver justice in many areas such as social justice, political justice and economic justice (Ahmed, 1991, p.15-23). The application of penal law ideally comes after the state has fulfilled its role in delivering justice in other areas. The state has to tolerate certain crimes if it has failed to provide justice in other areas. In its ideal form, if the state has failed to provide social and economic justice for its citizens, it has no right to punish the 'criminal' for such crimes. For this reason, during the reign of the second Caliph of Islam, Omer (591-644), who is famous for his strict and uncompromising application of Islamic law, certain property crimes committed during a severe famine were pardoned or tolerated (Cawziyye, 1969, p.13-14; Zeydan, 1985, p.194-195; Udeh, 1990). As the 'spirit of justice' faded away, the state gradually began losing the consensus of the people. The state's attempts to maintain its established authority, which was established on the principle of this form of ideal Islamic justice, transformed the state from a *just* state to a *totalitarian*, despotic, oppressive and anti democratic state. Therefore, the states which are ruling the Muslim nations today are much more totalitarian than the Western 'law and order' states.

In Turkey today, the influence of religion on people can be observed in various forms, ranging from public perceptions of the state and its front line representatives, the police and the army, to the general approach to crime and violence. Despite its strict secular structure and practices the Turkish state currently enjoys the deference of the vast bulk of its citizens (Inan, 1993, p.132). This is referred to in the *Qur'an*, one of its verses stating that, "O ye who believe obey Allah, and obey the messenger, and those charged with authority among you" (*Qur'an* 4:59). Accordingly, the state and its agents, the government and police, enjoy an inherited obedience which is based on an historical perception which stems from a religious legitimacy. In fact, the state is legitimate so long as it fulfils a number of conditions which are set up by 'the Sovereign', the God. The term 'Sovereign', in Islamic usage, is one of the names of God which implies His ultimate authority and power over all creations including the affairs of man.

In Islamic thought absolute sovereignty belongs to Allah (Unal, 1993, p.83; Rahman, 1994, p.47). The rulers and other institutions are employees of the Sovereign, acting on his behalf. Indeed, the head of an Islamic community is supposed to be the servant of his people rather than being their master. This ideal was realised to a greater extent in the early days of Islam, particularly during the reign of the first four Caliphs. This notion originates from the sayings of the prophet Muhammed which state that "Lord of the nation is he who serves them" (Tabrizi, 1991, p.340; Unal, 1993, p.135). The head of a society or a state is supposed to be the servant of his subjects and the consent of those ruled is an indicator of his legitimacy. Sunni Islam assumes equality - authority ultimately invested in the community. Christianity, traditionally, has assumed a hierarchy of bishop and prince with 'subjects'. Rights and privileges accompany 'status' but also responsibilities (Bennett, 1992, p.104-105 and 1994).

Under the principle of Islamic monotheism, in which all sovereignty belongs to God, (Rahman, 1994) individuals who occupy high positions are only the employees of the Ultimate Sovereign. There is no obligation upon the subjects to follow the dictates of the state if the commands of its agents implies disobedience to the Ultimate Sovereign. This principle is related to the early Islamic tradition concerning the obedience of the ruled to the rulers which states "La ta'ate li mahlukin fi ma'siyeti'l-Halik", which means "There is no obedience to the created [rulers] in disobedience to the Creator" (Tabrizi, 1991, p.321; Turner, 1978, p.118; Unal, 1993, p.84). For this reason, the state requires obedience from its citizens on the basis of it being perceived as partly holy by the majority of the people. The legitimacy of a particular system and state is, therefore, dependent upon its obedience to the Sovereign. Furthermore, political opposition against an unjust authority is a *duty* or obligation (Mawdudi 1993: 28) rather than a right or freedom solely. It is the duty of each single person or group to warn the authorities when they see any abuse of power and authority (Taymiya, 1992, p.125-133; Mawdudi, 1993, p.28; Hamidullah 1993, p.11; Unal, 1993, p.86). This is mostly justified by referring to one of the sayings of the prophet Muhammed which states that "The most excellent Jihad is when one speaks a true word in the presence of a tyrannical ruler" (Tirmizi, 1981, Section 20, Hadith No. 4011; Tabrizi, 1991:Vol. I p.786).

While Islam requires the obedience of citizens to the authority, by the command of Allah which states "O ye who believe! Obey Allah and obey the messenger, and those charged with authority among you" (*Qur'an* 4:59) it also requires citizens to warn the authority, by any available means, whenever they see them as unjust and engaged in wrongdoings. This seems to be a contradiction, but an attentive analysis demonstrates that it is perfectly possible to reconcile this apparent dichotomy. The requirement of obedience to the authorities implies the consensus of the general public. As long as this general consensus exists, the state and its agents have the right to ask for the obedience of the public. If either the state or citizens step outside this boundary legitimacy is lost and the other side has a right and a duty to oppose it individually as well as collectively. But these rights and duties must be undertaken within the conditions which will be quoted later from Udeh (1990) and carried out within the Islamic framework (Mawardi, 1976; Farra, 1983; Mustafa, 1985; Mawerdi, 1989; Berki, 1982). The conduct of the state towards its citizens, in normal situations as well as during violent political opposition, is regulated. In the same way a number of rules are specified to guide the citizens on how to perform their opposition against an unjust authority. Collective behaviour is expected and tolerated and regarded as socially meaningful if it is carried out peacefully and within the main framework of Islamic law and tradition.

As the political systems in the West were being developed and refined to ensure the peaceful transfer or distribution of power, with a large emphasis on the democratic process, this vital field has remained largely ignored in Turkish in particular and Islamic world in general. It may be that if the Turkish state had continued in its natural development and progression without obstructions it would have developed a political system more akin to present day representative democratic systems available in the West. Presently, most Muslim states, if not all, are ruled by regimes which neither resemble their Western counterparts nor are they the natural result of the development of their own previous systems. As Huseyin (1993a and 1993b) has made it clear in his classification of the nature of Islamic sates, Muslim states which currently rule over Muslim populations fall in the category of 'munafiq' (the hypocrite) states. Huseyin claims that such states enjoy a holy obedience by the people which is not reciprocated.

Hence, the development of hegemonic control is based on the distorted interpretation of sacred writings. Marx talks of religion as 'the opium of the people' (Marx, 1970, p.131) by which he regards religious practices as a comforting illusion (Dahhak, 1993, p.32) for the lower classes imposed by the ruling classes as a means of control. Any society which depends upon an authorised religion for its laws and social mores can be seen to be exercising very tight hegemonic control. However, according to N. Kemal, an opponent of the political arrangements in later period of the Ottoman State, and many modern Muslim scholars, the despotism and tyranny was not due to an inherent savagery in Islamic law, but rather the tyranny resulting from the failure to observe Islamic law, and from the concentration of judicial, legislative and executive power in one source (Kassam, 1993b, p.15).

It is not only the religious factor which determines the perceptions of people about obeying the state without question. Turkish culture itself is full of examples which display a cultural tendency towards obedience of authority (Bardakci, 1995). A similar theme is also implied in a proverbial term 'the state father' which implies, in Turkish culture, that the state is supposed to treat its citizens as equal, just as a father would, ideally, treat his children. Not only legitimate punishment but even some abuses of power have been tolerated by the people according to this opinion. These acts are seen in the context of a Turkish proverb, often used without irony, saying that "The finger cut by the state does not hurt". This implies that citizens should tolerate any punishment meted out by the state, no matter how severe it may be. Although the immediate meaning is indicative of punishment given out by courts, in practice the term has broadened to include police and army punishments and even the abuse of physical force.

As a result the Turkish people tend to tolerate the excessive use of force by the police in individual cases as well as in public order events. Since the people are discouraged from rising against the state and its representatives by this perception, it is not very common in Turkish history to see the masses rise up against the state to react against incidents where an individual has been beaten up or accidentally killed by the police. The reason for this is that neither Turkish culture nor Islam justifies uprising against authority in these cases. Rather, the religion establishes a number of legitimate channels to express grievances and to demand justice (Mawardi, 1976; Kutub, 1981 and 1982; Farra, 1983; Mustafa, 1985; Mawardi, 1989; Udeh, 1990). Perceptions of the state, in the West in general and in England and Wales in particular, generally have more negative connotations. Any use of force by its agencies i.e. the police and the army have been publicly questioned. Perhaps the suspicion about the police practices is based on experiences rather than negativism, or perhaps a bit of both. This argument has been proved by the occurrence of inner city riots of the 1980s most of which were sparked off following apparently minor incidents involving the abuse of power by the police, but with a perceived heritage of such incidents.

Two great Muslim political philosophers were Farra (990-1065), who lived around Baghdad, and Mawardi (975-1058), who lived around Basra and Baghdad, (Kavakci, 1975, p.xi). They explained in detail the ways in which an individual or a group of people who have a grievance should seek their rights against the state and its officials including the Sultan himself (Farra, 1983, p.189; Mustafa, 1985; Mawardi, 1989, p.315-339). In fact, if the whole history of Islam has taught only one lesson, it must be the necessity of creating and enforcing the laws which restrict the powers given to a Muslim ruler and which make it mandatory for the whole society to monitor the ruler's actions and to correct or remove him if necessary.

Farra (1983) in his book, *Al-Ahkamu's-Sultaniyye,* introduces a set of rules on how to express political or any other grievances against state officials, including 'the sultan'. He maintains that the citizens have both a right and a duty to caution the rulers in peaceful and legitimate ways. He explicitly rules out violence against the state and its agents for any purpose, and concludes that government or governors must be overthrown by legitimate political means. They must be overthrown using the procedures by which they had come to power. His contemporary, Mawardi (1989) explains in more detail in his book, *Al-Ahkamu's-Sultaniyye ve'l-Velayati'd-Diniyye,* the ways and procedures of appointments and dismissals of senior state officials, ranging from religious leaders to army officers and political leaders. Refusal of any kind of violence is based on an assumption of government by the consent of the general public. In addition to that, as briefly mentioned above, a number of legitimate channels have been established should officials abuse their power and neglect their duties.

Perhaps the refusal of political violence by the above mentioned authors was justifiable and sufficient in a time when the people were ruled with their consent by just rulers. However, a more tolerant approach was necessary as the consent of the general public was eroded for various reasons including the corruption of the rulers and the system. Therefore, towards the end of the Ottoman State, a code of practice, called *Mecelle*, was prepared by a law commission. *Mecelle* was prepared according to Islamic sacred law and each of the first one hundred articles were derived from the *hadith* -sayings and deeds of the prophet Muhammed, (Berki, 1982). Each article was a commentary of either a hadith or a verse in the *Holy Qur'an*. The articles from 25-32 are related to the general use of force. The *Mecelle* does not refer directly to the use of violence against the state, but simply sets some general rules regulating the use of violence and it justifies or tolerates the use of violence in certain circumstances. This directly and indirectly justifies the use of violence against the state when it was believed that more violence would be prevented by this limited violence.

Ruler and ruled are subject to the same law and there can be no discrimination on the basis of position, power or privilege. Islam, ideally, stands for equality and scrupulously adheres to this principle in social, economic, politic and judiciary realms alike (Mawdudi, 1993, p.13). Mawdudi (1993, p.32) states that "Islam insists and demands that all officials of an Islamic State, from most senior to most junior, are equal in the eyes of the law. None of them can claim immunity from it. The most humble citizen has the right to file a legal complaint against the highest executive in the land". Looking at the workings of present Muslim regimes one can easily see how far the present rulers are from representing the ideal Islamic state. This applies not only to secularised countries such as Turkey but also countries ruled by so-called Islamic rule such as Iran and Saudi Arabia.

There are numerous examples which show that not only the rights of Muslim citizens, but all citizens including non-Turks, were protected by legitimate channels (Kettani, 1979; Esposito, 1992; Dahhak, 1993, p.154 and p.233; Mawdudi, 1993; Akgunduz, 1993a-b; Kassam, 1993a-b; Bardakci, 1995). In one instance, for example, it is related that the conqueror of Istanbul, Fatih Sultan Mehmet, was taken to court for punishing a non Muslim citizen without an appropriate formal trial (Tutuncu, 1971; Sonmez, 1989). Since the legitimate channels for the expression of grievances had been established, any act of violence directed towards individuals or institutions were ruled out. Violence is not permitted nor tolerated unless it is absolutely necessary. It is permitted as a last resort, when it is believed that more violence will be prevented by using violence (Berki, 1982, p.24-25). Violence, in this context, is to be understood in a direct physical sense rather than being indirect hardship due to political mismanagement or partiality.

When it is believed that unlawful state violence will be prevented by a limited and controlled violence this limited violence is then permitted. The deployment of violence by citizens against state violence must be carefully considered and decisions must be based on an analysis of costs and benefits (Farra, 1983; Mawerdi, 1989; Udeh, 1990; Berki, 1982; Tash, 1995). This approach fails to justify spontaneous riots which cause serious injuries and damage to property.

However, it would be misleading to assume that Turkish history has always been peaceful (Bardakci, 1995). Rather, the point which is raised is that the use of individual and collective violence is regulated by certain rules, pertaining to the people and to the state. The conditions which legitimate the use of violence by the state, can also legitimate the use of violence by the people when it is absolutely necessary and more violence can be prevented. Therefore, in Turkish history a number of collective violent events have occurred but these differ from those of the West, both in terms of motivation and legitimacy. Moreover, after the establishment of The Turkish Republic the imposition of Western ideology has led to Western types of crowd events such as industrial and political demonstrations, student protests, political rallies and the like. Today, despite the cultural and religious differences between Turkey and the Western world, the nature of crowd events and the police response to them has been moving towards the Western style, but in proportion to the general level of democracy.

The second concept related to collective behaviour and violence is the 'class' factor. There has been a marked difference between Western thought in general and England in particular, and Turkish thought in terms of understanding materially based differences in society. The deep marks of mediaeval feudal class divisions in the West are still apparent in contemporary thinking. For instance, as a reaction to this deep division, some Western radicals perceive crime and collective violence as a means of struggle to deploy against the ruling classes.

When existing radical approaches are analysed closely it can be seen that apart from a few differences they are all based on the concept of class conflict. Instead of finding a way of reconciliation they prefer to defend the working-classes and unemployed peoples' interests against the ruling classes and their representatives in the state. The impression given is that there is an on-going war and conflict between the classes. Crime is only one of the means which the working classes have to deploy in this war. This is justified, to some extent, since other perspectives particularly that of conservatives overtly defend the interest of the ruling class.

In this study two main points have arisen regarding class and crime. The first point is that although Turkish society includes many materially oriented classes, there are common characteristics relating to non-material standards and values, such as the religion, which act to unify the whole of society. The second point is that class divisions in Turkish society have not been as clearly drawn as in Western Europe (Bardakci, 1995). Furthermore, state intervention in social life, at least in theory, aims to reduce or modify class distinctions rather than favouring one class against another.

With regard to England and the rest of Europe, class divisions have been highly articulated and most crowd movements have involved grievances relating to these divisions. In recent history most crowd movements, which shook the stability of regimes in Europe, were class oriented activities such as the French Revolution (Rude, 1964 and 1981) and the food riots of England. Therefore, Marxism as an alternative to Western capitalism, has focused on the divisive nature of the class system.

The writings of Karl Marx are essentially based on the division of people into conflicting classes. He divides the people into two classes under the capitalist mode of production, the working class or 'proletariat', and the ruling class or 'bourgeoisie' (Marx and Engels, 1884, p.49; Marx 1957, 1970, 1975 and 1988; Lenin, 1969). However, an attentive study of his works reveals that between these two main classes he mentions a number of other classes which do not fit easily into either category (Ollman, 1968). The discontent against capitalism has been fuelled by revolutionary Marxist ideology and contemporary crowd movements have an inherited violent character stemming from Marxist ideology (Hoffman, 1991, p.6). Marx sees violence as the only way of achieving working goals, "...we ought also to recognise that, in most of the countries on the continent, it is force that must be the lever of our revolutions; it is to force that it will be necessary to appeal for a time in order to establish the reign of labour" (Marx, 1988, p.595).

The proletariat are in a constant struggle with the bourgeoisie and in this war they are seen to legitimately deploy all available violent means, "...they destroy imported wares that compete with their labour, they smash to pieces machinery, they set factories ablaze, they seek to restore by force the vanished status of the workman of the Middle Ages" (Marx and Engels, 1848, p.63). Marx and Engels openly declare, in the *Manifesto of the Communist Party,* (1848, p.114) that the goals of the proletariat can be attained only by the forcible overthrow of all existing social conditions. Marx argues that, "...every class struggle is a political struggle" (1848, p.65) and legitimises violence in the struggle between two rival classes. However, it is argued that "Marx did regard peaceful change as possible and desirable under some circumstances, usually where liberal institutions were firmly entrenched...This would however be exceptional" (Hoffman 1995, p.2).

In this century an overwhelming majority of crowd movements and in particular industrial disputes have gained momentum from Marxist ideology. For example, the 1960s and early 1970s were the years when most European countries, including Turkey, were shaken by student movements which had gained momentum from Marxist ideology. After state communism in Eastern Europe faded away in the late 1980s and early 1990s (Gellner, 1991; Hoffman, 1991 and 1992), at least in the practical arena, the crowd movements which once posed a real danger to the stability of regimes have become symbolically rather than directly threatening.

In fact, it is not Marx and the Marxist ideology which divides the people into classes and generates a class war, but capitalism itself is responsible for this division. What Marxist ideology did was to make this distinction more explicit in order to generate the inevitable course of history by provoking class conflict (Ollman, 1968; Quinney, 1980; Giddens and Held, 1988). In fact communism is a version of materialism rather than being a direct alternative to capitalism. In other words, capitalism and communism are two different versions of materialism, the former creating classes, based on material wealth, and the latter declaring war based on already existing class divisions (Giddens and Held, 1988). So they are, in fact, two integral parts of materialism regardless of the way in which they are perceived as conflicting ideologies. While the former exploits labour, the latter, as a reaction to their exploitation, denies the legitimacy of capital. Both Islam and Marxism saw the deep class divisions in society as a problem which needs to be tackled. However, the remedies they offer differ dramatically. While Marxism aims for a classless society (Ollman, 1968; Gellner, 1991; Hoffman, 1991 and 1992), Islam on the other hand accepts social and economic difference within a society as inevitable and even, to some extent, necessary, and tries to reduce the negative impact of the gap between classes.

The concept of class conflict is something entirely alien to traditional Turkish-Islamic ideology, which is based on the idea of co-operation of all classes within society. "It [Islam] cannot, [ideally], accept legal, physical class, social, political, racial, national, territorial, genetic, or even economic contradictions, so its arms are wide-open to all creatures, regions and ages" (Unal, 1993, p.47). In contrast to Marxist ideology which argues that, "...the history of all hitherto existing society is the history of class struggles" (Marx and Engels, 1848, p.47), Turkish-Islamic ideology sees life as more co-operation and less conflict. Not only Marxist arguments, but Western materialism in general hold the view that life is a struggle rather than a co-operative effort (Giddens and Held, 1988).

> The materialists further believed that, for its very existence and benefit, each unit of creation must continuously compete against all other units of creation, thereby endorsing the theory of the 'survival of the fittest'. They interpret every event in creation as comprised of conflicts and struggles (Selcuk, 1994, p.75).

On the contrary, Turkish-Islamic ideology of co-operation includes social life as well as the natural world (*Zaman*, 1992; Selcuk, 1994, p.74-86).

Thus, the Turkish experience of social movements and political violence has differed fundamentally from the British experience, and the results have been paradoxical. In the Ottoman State, for example, the paradox has been the coexistence of a high level of civil conflict with the remarkable stability of a regime that has enjoyed sustained legitimacy. Missing also from the Ottoman State was the Western world's feudal legacy of deeply entrenched class division (Bardakci, 1995). Not only the Ottoman State but also other previously established Islamic states have always been multicultural and multiracial societies (Apaydin and Alister, 1994, p.8-11). However, the common cultural denominators of Islamic states and societies are shared perceptions and beliefs, not colour, ethnic or racial origin, language or universal class dynamics (Hobohm, 1986; Karaman, 1993, p.7).

The *Qur'an* taught in many verses that all human beings are descended from a single ancestor, that none has an intrinsic right of superiority over another, whatever his race or his nation or his social standing. These principles are applied both as laws and as social norms (Dahhak, 1993, p.47). This quotation from the sayings of the Prophet Muhammed makes this view more clear;

> You should know that no Arab is superior over a non-Arab and, no non-Arab is superior over any Arab, no white is superior over black and no black is superior over white. Superiority is by righteousness and God-fearing alone (Ibn Hanbal, Musnad, 411, cited in Dahhak, 1993, p.47 and Mawdudi, 1993, p.22).

Islam ideally rejects a society which is based on colour, race, economic or social superiority (Karaman, 1993: 7). It does not envisage a completely classless society in an economic sense (Bardakci, 1995), however, it accepts the differentiation of human beings as natural in areas such as economic, physical, knowledge and ability as a fact, but this division is not the primary factor for the division of society into classes (Karaman, 1993, p.11). However, there are those who argue that inequality is not merely a matter of individual abilities and aptitudes; it is above all a social fact (Beteille, 1969). The opportunities an individual has and even his abilities are in part governed by his position in society. While many have talked about 'classless' societies these ideas have found very little support in historical experience.

Islam tries to keep the balance firstly by accepting the existence of divisions in society and secondly, aims to regulate this inevitable social fact. The rich and the poor, for example, are considered an integral part of a whole. In fact, all classes constitute an integral part of a whole which is the society and there is no conception of a society which has no poor or rich. This is not because the rich need the poor in order to exploit them, but is seen as an inevitable consequence of a free society which will exhibit these various groupings. Not only economic and material relationships in the society, but all human interactions are governed by this rule. The rich need the poor as much as the poor need the rich. In order to prevent this mutual need from resulting in negative exploitation, instead of trying to protect one from another after declaring war between the classes, a number of legitimate channels have been established by religion (Kutub, 1981 and 1982; Udeh, 1990), in order to minimise the potential harm of such divisions.

In confirmation of this assertion, Ilhan Bardakci (1995) a contemporary historian specialising in Ottoman history, argues that the gap between the classes in Ottoman history was not as wide as in the Western world. This was because the state's role in its dealings with divisional interests has been a just one. The Ottoman state was generally successful in fulfilling the basic requirements of its subjects including its non-Muslim citizens. The quotation from Orhan Beg, the second Sultan of the Ottoman State, "If destitution will pester to my people, it should first be hosted in my mansion" (cited in Bardakci, 1995), is a good example of the nature of relationships between the rulers and their subjects and also demonstrates how much interest the rulers show to the material well-being of their subjects. Bardakci further maintains that as this interest on the part of the state and the rulers for the subjects gradually faded away there resulted the erosion of traditionally held obedience to the rulers. This was demonstrated not only by political but also economic and socially motivated crowd events. Bardakci (1995) also cites two examples from early Ottoman history which clearly shows that social considerations were taken into account in punishing certain crimes, which the judges believed to be caused by maladjustment of the existing social and political arrangements of those times.

One of the aims of the Islamic state is to interfere in and to regulate the material inequalities of social groups. Changes in the individual and subsequently in the state of society are regarded as a necessary consequence of human nature, which has an innate inclination for change - be it improvement or decline (*The Light*, 1980 and 1981). It is also believed that a progressive and gradual change in social relations is a human phenomenon. In other words social change is not only an inevitable consequence of human life but is also a necessary consequence of human progress. Although human beings are not the only social creatures, they are the only one capable of modifying their social lives. This is done by various means rather than introducing a sharp-shock response by denying or destroying the existing social groups or any other long established arrangements. What has been said so far implies that any social change, according to an Islamic point of view, must be the result of a gradual and evolutionary progress rather than being a sudden and revolutionary one.

A number of religious obligations introduced by Islam aim to reduce or gradually modify the gap between existing social groups in favour of the weak. For instance, when certain crimes or sins are committed, the perpetrator is required to comply with certain punishments such as the freeing of a servant (Mawdudi, 1993, p.20) or feeding a certain amount of needy and hungry.

> Emancipation of a slave was also the legally required expiation for certain sins or failures in religious duties, for example, the breaking of an oath or the breaking of a fast: a good deed to balance or wipe out a lapse (Dahhak, 1993, p.50).

Slavery, which once created a whole social class, was not something introduced by Islam but was largely a by-product of wars between nations, the conquered peoples becoming the slaves of their conquerors. Islam had to tackle this long established institution as well as other social evils (Mawdudi, 1993, p.20; Hannan, 1994, p.87-95). The response of Islam to slavery has as with other social problems, been gradual rather than revolutionary. In Islam it is overwhelmingly the case that being a slave was a temporary condition. Unlike Western civilisation, slavery was not passed down, generation after generation in a deepening spiral of degradation and despair, with no hope for the slaves to escape their condition or their status (Dahhak, 1993, p.52; Norman, 1994, p.35). Islam aims to emancipate the slaves gradually while equipping them with all kinds of opportunities to be useful members of the community as farmers, artisans, teachers, scholars, and commanders, governors and ministers or even prime ministers.

The interests of the poor and lower classes have been secured by religious obligations rather than being left to the mercy of the ruling classes. The *Qur'an* declares that the poor have a right in the wealth of the rich (*Qur'an* 51:19 and 70:24-25; Ahmad, 1991, p.33). While Islam introduces a number of obligatory and voluntary economic obligations to the rich in favour of the poor, the Prophet Muhammed also aims to prevent the poor from exploitation by commanding the prompt payment of workers in his saying which states "Give the hireling his wages before his sweat dries" (Tirmizi, 1991, Vol. I p. 638). Furthermore, Islamic jurists are of the view that in ordinary circumstances private property rights are to be treated as inviolable. However, in compelling circumstances, individual ownership of particular kinds of property or productive assets can be subject to limitations in the larger public interest (Ahmad, 1991, p.34).

In fact, Islam emerged as a 'lower class' movement when it was introduced by the prophet. In Western thought the state has a negative connotation as being the instrument of systematic oppression of lower classes, but in Islamic thought, the state is regarded as the protector of the lower classes. Therefore, as a number of authors and academics have pointed out, the Islamic state is or should be 'the just state' (Ozdenoren, quoted in Gocer, 1993; Hatemi, 1993; Karaman, 1993; Huseyin, 1993a and 1993b; Unal, 1993, p.84). Again, the concept of the word *just* might have some negative connotations in Western thought, since it generally implies the severe punishment of criminals, who are mainly drawn from the lower classes. On the contrary, in Islamic thought 'the just state' does not only mean the state punishes the criminals severely, but also means the state prevents injustices and protects the weak from oppression and exploitation by the strong. In short, the Islamic state is only a means rather than being an end in delivering justice (Ozdenoren, quoted in Gocer, 1993, p.22).

Turkish-Islamic ideology aims to improve a society based on mutual aid and benefit instead of separating the society into classes and then trying to prevent them from exploiting each other. In addition society is united in some common values and norms. It is these values and norms which do not allow the creation of classes based on wealth. Of course, in Turkish terminology there are the poor and the rich and many other sub-groups between these groups, but these groups are not regarded as classes, in the same manner as they are in the West. However, in practice, whether this works outside of Islamic theory is another matter. There has always been some exploitative rich as well as rebellious poor, but the essential idea is that relationships are governed according to a classless society. This can be stated by saying that there is one class which includes all the classes from the richest to the poorest. This ideal is not easily realised or maintained and moreover, it is not a self-governed system. Rather, in order to maintain this mutual relationship and to keep the bridge between the poor and the rich, a number of religiously oriented measures have been taken. Well before the establishment of alternative approaches to traditional conservative ideology in the West, Islam has introduced a number of materially oriented obligations on the rich for the poor which are akin to those suggested by Western liberals and radicals (Kutub, 1981 and 1982).

Moreover, the notion of the 'welfare state', which today has been adopted by many Western countries, was originated by Muslims and dates back to the early days of Islam (Sah, 1967, p.248). This was not applied in the same way as it has been in the West which drifts the poor into a passive position of expecting the state to fulfil their essential needs. Rather, in Turkish-Islamic ideology, the intervention of the state into the relationships between the poor and the rich are positive and directed to make the poor productive and to prevent the rich from becoming unreasonably rich. Material relationships are slightly modified by the state in order to prevent the creation of two extreme poles; the richest and the poorest (Kutub, 1981 and 1982). All material relationships are regulated according to this essential rule.

The people have the liberty to find fault with the most prominent among the Muslims when they go astray, and have the right to be outspoken in all matters. In the early days of Islam, for example, the state's income was collected in various ways, and distributed by the state to its citizens in proportion to their needs. In one instance, the Caliph Omer (591-644) was questioned, during a Friday sermon, by an ordinary member of his subjects about the distribution of the goods from the states depot; which was then called *Beytu'l-Mal*, (Public Treasury) (Mawdudi, 1980, p.120). He was questioned because the person thought that the Caliph had taken more than his normal due which was supposed to be equal to that of an ordinary citizen. The Caliph responded in order to convince him that he had not taken more than his due and the extra piece was given to him by his own son. The ruler is bound to account for the income and expenditure of the *Public Treasury* and the subjects have every right to ask him for a full accounting (Unal, 1993, p.87). Again, it is documented that during the reign of Caliph Omer and Ottoman State not only the Muslims but all the citizens including all other religions benefited from the distribution of the state's income (Sah, 1967, p.248-249; Mawdudi, 1980; Akgunduz, 1993a-b).

In conclusion, while Islam does not divide society into distinct classes, it tries to defuse the possible tensions which may arise from material imbalance, by various economic obligations. It also emphasises voluntary spending for the welfare of the poor and needy not only to banish poverty but also to promote social cohesion and harmony (Ahmad, 1991, p.43). The following verse from the *Holy Qur'an* cautions that lack of such spending can lead to a society's ruination. "Spend your wealth for the cause of Allah, and make not your own hands contribute to [your] destruction..." (*Qur'an* 2:195). According to Islamic teachings, it is an obligation of all persons of means to spend a part of their wealth for the welfare of the poor and needy (Ahmad, 1991, p.42). Furthermore, the Islamic system incorporates several institutional devices to foster voluntary spending for the welfare of the poor. These economic obligations and voluntary spendings are aimed to prevent people from suffering absolute poverty as well as experiencing the decadence and irresponsibility of extreme richness.

In other words, the main idea is to bring all classes materially close to each other, by improving the overall quality of life and economic conditions. So far it seems that capitalism has not reached the stage of securing the interest of all without favouring a particular class. This might have been one of the reasons why communism flourished within the Western capitalist nations where class divisions were and still are more sharp and visible. Since Islam did not allow the creation of materially oriented distinct classes, communism, which is based on the class struggle could not find any ground in Eastern ideology (Sismanov, 1990). It is for this reason that the establishment of socialism in some Muslim countries such as Iraq, Syria and Libya has not been the result of crowd movements arising from class division. The division of classes in Muslim countries was not very visible and so severe as to provoke a class oriented struggle amongst different groups. The overthrow of previous regimes, therefore, in countries such as Syria and Iraq have been throughout military coups conducted by a tiny minority, rather than being a result of popular class movement. However, in Marxist terms this may be because the masses are subject to false consciousness and hegemonic control. In Marxist terms religion comes under this heading and Marx is famously credited with terming religion as "the opium of the people" (Marx, 1970, p.131).

Certain crimes, defined as a product of Western political ideology in general, and England and Wales in particular, have been mostly associated with class divisions and so the arguments about the role of the police as a neutral institution has always been a centre of controversy. Particular crimes are tolerated, or even praised, by certain political perspectives such as various left groups, as a legitimate means of struggle with an unjust society and its front line representatives i.e. the police and in some cases the army.

However, the radicals have made some crucial mistakes on two points. The first is while they rightly see crime as a reaction to an unjust society, they have failed to understand that the reaction to a just cause must necessarily be itself just. Violent crime or even theft, may not be as just as the radicals would imagine. It is for this reason that some radicals, such as Lea and Young (1984), argue that both conventional and left idealist interpretations of crime are superficial. The second point is, unlike the extreme radical view, it is suggested that crime is antisocial. The majority of working class crime, far from being a prefigurative revolt or redistribution of wealth, is directed against other members of the working-class (Lea and Young, 1984, Platt and Takagi, 1981). This shows that unlike the popular view held by left idealists, working-class crime really is a problem for the working-class (Matthews and Young, 1992, p.72). As Pearce (1976) has put it "Crime in the streets is a real problem for working-class communities" (p.17).

Platt and Takagi (1981) have also argued that crime is primarily an intra-class and intra-racial problem. It is not always a struggle between the strong and the weak or the rich and the poor, rather the working-class community itself suffers immensely from the criminals in its midst. They maintain that, white women are most likely to be raped by white men; young black men are most likely to be robbed or mugged by other young black men; and the working class families are most likely to have their home vandalised or broken into by strangers living only a few blocks away.

The left realists do not deny the impact of crimes of the powerful or indeed of the perfectly legal social problems created by the capitalism. The point they stress is that the working-classes are victims of crime from all directions; that one sort of crime tends to compound another, as one social problem does another; crime is a potent symbol of the antisocial nature of capitalism and is the most immediate way in which people experience other problems, such as unemployment or competitive individualism (Lea and Young, 1984).

Even if we accept crime as a legitimate means of struggle, both in the East and West, the left realist argument has proved that the loser of this war is and has always been the working-classes and the poor (Platt and Takagi, 1981). This implies that no form of crime and violence is as rational as some have argued. It does not yield the expected result, because it is not considered and deliberately organised according to the interests of working classes, rather it is an individually motivated and isolated act. Therefore, the rise in crime rates does not necessarily reflect the successes of the lower class in their war against the state and the ruling class. It may herald the failure of materialism and capitalist society, but does not necessarily reflect the successes of its rivals. If crime wins the war neither the lower classes nor the upper classes will benefit from it.

In addition to that, crime, as some radicals, as well as some religious groups, (*The Watchtower*, 1993, p.3) have argued, may be the inevitable result of capitalist society, but it does not imply that the workings of capitalist society are based on the production of crime; crime is not deliberately produced by the capitalist system. Rather it is universally accepted that peace between all classes is one of the most important conditions sought by capitalism. Therefore, crime may be an inevitable consequence of a materially based capitalist society, (*The Watchtower,* 1993, p.3) but not its deliberate production. In this respect, the failure of communism was not only the failure of itself, rather it was the defeat of materialism which placed priority on material needs indirectly while intentionally ignoring non-material aspects of human life. For this very reason the failure of state communism in Eastern Europe and Russia should not be perceived as the success of its rival, capitalism.

The State and Police

There has always been a mutually inclusive relationship between the nature of a police system, its practices and the state to which it belongs. The practices of a particular policing system mirrors the nature of a regime to some extent (Lofthouse, 1993a and 1993b). This relation becomes more visible especially in certain areas such as political oppositions involving crowd activities. It must be noted that while harsh methods used in suppressing political or other crowds reflects the nature of a particular regime, it does not necessarily lead to the conclusion that those countries which control crowds with seemingly less oppressive methods are not oppressive in other ways. It is, therefore, necessary to begin by exploring existing perceptions of the state and its links with the police in two cultures and their implications upon public order policing practices.

In the conventional conservative model, the role of the police, within the criminal justice system, is seen as attempting to 'solve' the problem of crime. They are faced with a problem and they do their best to deal with it within the limits of the law, with choices of action based on the pragmatic possibilities of resources and forensic science. Radicals, however, believe that the behaviour of the police is at base materially determined: following the logic of capital interests and serving the ruling classes rather than protecting the universal interest.

What is more, the definition of crime which is made by the law does not always reflect the universal interests of society. To espouse the idea of the rule of law would be to accept the image of law as a neutral arbiter which is above political conflict and remote from the control of particular groups or classes. It assumes that, "...the legislature represents the common will, the executive acts in the common interest, the law is a neutral referee that is administered 'without fear or favour' for the common good" (Wacks, 1987, p.181). However, Marxists reject this 'consensus' model of society and the idea that the law can be a neutral body of rules which guarantees the rights of all.

Marxist theory has traditionally held the view that "...the state is explicitly conceived as a repressive apparatus" (Althusser, 1971, p.131 and Gramsci, 1971, p.215; Lenin, 1969, p.11) and "...it represents particular class interests and primarily those of that class which control it" (King, 1987, p.29). King further maintains that this control is basically maintained by force as "Intrinsic to the notion of the State is that of coercion. If the State is rules (and practices) then they need to be secured and enforced. The State's 'apparatuses' fulfil this role" (King 1987: 18). This view is basically derived from the Marxian view (Marx, 1970, p.50) on state apparatuses such as the judiciary administration, police and the army which is that:

> ...representatives of the state, and their task is to administer the state against civil society rather than being representatives of a civil society which administers its own universal interests in them and through them (cited in King 1987, p.20, Marx, 1975, p.111).

The interests of the ruling classes are enforced upon the working class under the disguise of law and order. In the light of Marxist argument it is indeed difficult to uphold the argument that the law is a neutral set of rules to which all are subject. The inequalities of the law were highlighted by Anatole France who once said, "The law in its majestic equality, forbids the rich as well as the poor to sleep under bridges, to beg in the streets, and to steal bread" (Anatole France, Le Lys Rouge 1894, cited in Benyon and Bourn, 1986, p.15; Reiner, 1992, p.3). The following quotation, taken from Lea and Young (1984) reflects the view which left realists radicals hold about the state and its front line representatives.

> We reject the notion of conventional criminology that the state is a neutral institution acting in the universal interests of the population against, in this instance, 'the crime problem'. At the present moment the British state represents very largely ruling-class interests (Lea and Young, 1984, p.103).

Another left spectrum, the left idealists, hold slightly more extreme views about the state and its functions. This view is evident in a passage taken from a hand out distributed during a recent Bloody Sunday march:

> The main function of the police is to defend the system that breeds racism and fascism. They are not neutral upholders of democratic rights and will use any means necessary to prevent the growth of a militant movement that threatens the authority of the state (*Revolutionary Fighter,* January 29 1994).

For them, the state is the direct instrument of the ruling class and the source of all social problems such as exploitation, poverty and racism. They maintain that not only the police but also various institutions - whether ideological (like education and the mass media) or directly repressive (such as the police and judicial system) exist in order to maintain capitalism (Gramsci, 1971). It is for this reason that radicals see crime, or at least some crimes, as proto-revolutionary activities, primitive and individualistic, perhaps, but praiseworthy all the same. Theft, for example is perceived a redistribution of income (Lea and Young, 1984; Honderich 1976 and 1989). They believe that the criminal, not the honest person, has the superior consciousness: he or she has seen through the foolishness of the 'straight' world. For them to be well conditioned to the existing norms and values is to be well deceived.

One of the dramatic differences, revealed in this investigation is that the perception of the state as a neutral institution differs dramatically in the two countries. In Turkish culture the concept of the state has a rather different meaning. It is considered as an abstract concept having positive connotations. It is considered as apart from the government and the present political arrangements. Today, therefore, the present Turkish state is accepted as legitimate by the majority of its people not because they have acquired this consensus by their present practices in certain areas, rather it is a borrowed consensus which has its origins in religion and history.

The legitimacy of the police has also been based on the acceptance of the state as a neutral and legitimate institution; the legitimacy of the police is proven by its being the apparatus of the state. In other words, the more loyal the police are to state and its interests the more it is accepted as legitimate. In fact, it is a commonly held view that one of the primary roles and functions of the police is as an arm of the state protecting it from the 'enemies within'. Marxists such as A. Gramsci (1971), L. Althusser (1971) and broadly Marxist modern thinkers such as S. Hall (1979 and 1987a-b), T. Jefferson (1987 and 1990), G. Northam (1989) and P. Scraton

(1987) have united, in line with early Marxists, in the view that the police have been and are the apparatus of the state and serve the interest of the ruling class.

The place of the police in the state structure throughout the history of both countries has been one of belonging to the state. The nature of policing practices particularly in relation to public order related problems which most often involve political opposition in the form of mass crowd activities, has been indicative of the nature of the state.

It is commonly argued that in England and Wales, the police is a neutral institution serving the interests of all having no direct connection with the power-holding elites (Inan, 1993, p.39-40). This is a notion which has very often been challenged by many eminent radical scholars such as Bowden (1970 and 1978) and Bunyan (1977). Observations of this research, in line with other recent studies in the field (Aydin, 1994) have led to the conclusion that, despite its apparent decentralised structure and local accountability, the police are deployable as agents of central authority such as illustrated by their role in the miners' strikes of the 1980s (Kahn et al. 1983; Geary, 1985; Wiles, 1985; Scraton, 1985; Morgan, 1987; Weinberger, 1991). In certain areas centralisation has already been completed and been in operation for many years (Cerrah, 1991) such as Police National Computer (PNC) and intelligence gathering and dissemination institutions currently developing nationally the National Criminal Intelligence Services (NCIS) (Benyon, 1994b, p.60) and within EU European Police, (Europol). What is more, during large crowd events such as the miners' strikes and the inner city riots during the same period under the mutual aid arrangement (Waddington, 1994b, p.20) which is co-ordinated by a centralised unit operated by ACPO (Association of Chiefs of Police Officers), the police can become, at least temporarily, a centralised police force. Furthermore, recent arguments have shown that there is a strong commitment in the present government towards a centralised police force and it is planned to accomplish this through various stages, albeit by retaining a fiction of local accountability to aid legitimacy.

The most striking point revealed in this research is that, while in Britain the direct link between the state and the police is regarded as an indicator of police bias, in Turkey the relations between the state and the police is regarded as an indication that the police are a neutral institution serving all rather than power-holding elites. The legitimacy of the state in Turkey is rarely questioned, therefore its direct link with the police raises the legitimacy of the police rather than decreasing it. This does not stem from a lack of information about the nature of the present Turkish state and the legitimacy of its practice, nor does it reflects the consensus of all to the state's practices. Rather this perception is the continuation of a deep-rooted religious and historical perception about the police, which has only relatively recently been challenged by radical groups.

In Turkey crowd activities in the past involving political grievances have usually targeted certain key figures in the government rather than the system as a whole. Most crowd movements during the Ottoman state ended with the removal of individuals from office, who had become targets of grievances (Ocak, 1980; Sener, 1990; Kassam, 1993a-b). Even those who were engaged in violence did not regard their action as an uprising against the state and justified their actions by removing certain key figures who were seen to be destroying and misusing the state - an institution to which the dissenters have no objection.

After dealing with the contrasting perceptions held in both countries about the police and its relations with the police, the argument will now move on to considerations of use of violence for political aims. The effect of the nature of the state upon public order policing practices will be examined in later chapters.

Political Violence

There has been a significant increase in tolerance towards politically oriented crimes committed both individually and collectively. A number of contemporary social scientists have even justified politically motivated acts of violence (Ball-Rokeach, 1972; Graham, 1972). It is believed that in many cases the adoption of political violence, either in the form of individual criminality or collective crime, as a weapon of political struggle arises out of the impossibility of conducting an effective struggle by open political means.

Before giving an account of conflicting arguments on the legitimacy of political violence, it is appropriate to define the term political violence. Graham and Gurr (1969, p.86) define politically violent events "...as those involving an attack on an official or group of officials for any reason or an attack on an individual or group of individuals for political or social reasons. Thus an attempt on the life of a Congressmen would be considered a politically violent event even though the reason for the attack may have been purely personal". A more precise definition was made by Honderich (1976), who roughly defines political violence as a considerable or destroying use of force against persons or things, a use of force prohibited by law, directed to a change in the policies, personal or system of the government, and hence also directed to changes in the existence of individuals in the society and perhaps other societies (Nieburg, 1968, p.18, 1972; Meier, 1968; Bwy, 1968; McDonagh, 1978, p.9; Johnson, 1993).

In Turkish-Islamic criminology, the distinction between political crimes and ordinary crimes has been made more explicit. Unlike Western ideologies, not all criminal activities which are directed against politicians and officials, or have political connotations, are regarded as political crimes. There are two main reasons for this. Firstly, in Turkey and neighbouring countries, particularly during the Ottoman State, disobedience to the state and its representatives was mainly derived from political dissent rather than economic inequalities of the social system. However, it is possible to argue that the element of material conditions cannot completely be divorced from the pursuit of political power. Therefore it might be more appropriate to argue that crowd oppositions during the Ottoman Empire were more political with a less significant material element.

As will be elaborated in the coming chapter, the state intervenes in the economic and social spheres and regulates the economic inequalities of social classes. The state's intervention into the economic arena, ideally, does not favour any class against another, but aims to bridge the gap between the poor and the rich. The state, in Turkish thought, has a different role and function; the state exists to serve the people, rather than people existing to serve the state.

With regard to the social and economic classes, since Turkish ideology, which has been greatly influenced by Islam, refuses any sort of class distinction between human beings, one of the aims of the state is the economic welfare of the whole society. This was achieved to a greater extent in the early years of Islam and during a period of the Ottoman State (Kettani, 1979, p.13-14; Esposito, 1992, p.45-46; Mawdudi, 1993; Bennett, 1993 and 1994; Apaydin and Alister, 1994, p.8-11). This is because Islam is not only a religion to practise in mosques but rather a way of life which regulates and rules all aspects of society. Islam also imposes economic obligations on the rich for the poor and society is defined as a whole, no individual having superiority over another. There are rich and the poor, but they do not create a class based on the ownership of economic means, because the society is not established on the basis of material superiority or the ownership of goods (Kutub, 1981, p.185-199 and 1982).

Secondly, the experience of politically oriented crimes predates the rise in materially oriented crimes. Accordingly, in Turkey, the introduction of laws and regulations concerning political crimes has priority over Western ideology and criminology. Western thought was more intolerant towards political crimes, particularly before the articulation of modern political philosophy following the French Revolution (Udeh,

1990). Contrary to the West, which punished political crimes more severely than ordinary crimes, Eastern ideology introduced a number of preconditions which first of all limit the definition of political crimes in favour of its perpetrators, and secondly gives a number of legitimate rights to the perpetrators of politically motivated violent activities. Prof. Abdulkadir Udeh (1990), who was himself the victim of a political execution during Nasir's time in Egypt, in his four volume book written in Arabic and translated into Turkish, distinguishes political crimes from ordinary crimes. He sets certain conditions and argues that not all crimes committed towards a state official can be regarded as political crimes even though the perpetrator might have political motivations. Unless it has the following conditions these crimes are regarded as ordinary crimes and the perpetrators will be treated as ordinary criminals (Udeh, 1990, p.101).

Firstly, the commitment of a particular act must be directed towards the overthrow of the present government or include the disobedience of its commands in an 'open' and 'violent' way. Secondly, political criminals must make efforts to legitimise their action in order to be recognised as such. In other words, not all indiscriminate violent acts, which may kill or injure innocent civilians are regarded as political violence. Thirdly, activists must target key figures, who are, to some extent, responsible for the present system; in addition they must exercise their peaceful opposition against the rulers by a legitimate means. Fourthly, political criminals who fulfil the above mentioned conditions must have the power to carry out their ends and they must also be in a position to introduce an alternative system to the existing political arrangements. This implies that if an organisation or group of people do not have the power to change the existing system or if they do not have a wide public consensus, their action is still regarded as ordinary crime and punished accordingly.

Finally, if political criminals fulfil the aforementioned four conditions and manifest their opposition by using physical force, their action is now termed an 'uprising' and the perpetrator will be punished accordingly. If their violent struggle against the state and its agencies is lost they will be punished as political criminals, which means their punishment will be less severe compared with ordinary criminals (Udeh, 1990, p.101-108). John Hoffman, a contemporary political theorist, has argued that "...there is a case for political violence but only as an integral part of the case for getting rid of violence itself" (Hoffman, 1994, p.1) and this seems to be a re-articulation of Udeh's argument.

Political violence characteristically involves the infliction of harm on people who are not directly responsible for the state of affairs that the violence is meant to change. Often the victims will be ordinary members of the public; even if they happen to be politicians or captains of industry, they will only be responsible to a very limited degree for the poverty, inequality, oppression and so on that the violence seeks to relieve. Since the state is represented by individuals, politically violent acts are directed at the individuals rather than abstract institutions such as the state, the police and so on. On the other hand, in any state it is possible to distinguish the key personnel responsible for maintaining and directing a system of oppression as those who normally control the police state through the instrument of the police and security services. All such personnel, but particularly those most directly involved in state terrorism as directors or agents, are valid objects of attack. The other main targets of these kind of attacks are buildings and property. Police stations and army barracks are self-identified prime targets both symbolically and as centres of coercion. Since they house the direct agents of repression there is little need for concern if the attacks on property injure the occupants.

Whatever the underlying causes of political violence, since it inflicts injuries upon innocent people, it is still somehow problematic to justify such acts, on the basis of its relatively justifiable ends. So far no political perspective has offered a universally acceptable view. For instance, according to liberals, political violence is not tolerable in liberal democratic societies; provided that such a regime makes efforts to protect the rights of all citizens, including minority groups, and allows each person a fair chance of voicing their political views and interests, violence cannot be sustained as a legitimate tactic.

A Justice of the US Supreme Court, Abe Fortas (1968) for example, defines the limits and scope of lawful civil disobedience in his book, *Concerning Dissent And Civil Disobedience*, as an alternative to violence (Fortas, 1968; Sharp, 1972; Hare, 1972; Schwartz, 1972). Fortas tells how non-violent dissent can successfully achieve revolutionary goals within the law, institutions, and traditions of democratic society. He concludes that, "Ultimately, the basic means of protest under our system is the ballot box: the right to organise and join with others to elect new officials to enact and administer the law" (Fortas, 1968, p.25). This implies that at least some acts of violence are permitted within non-democratic regimes.

> The liberal attitude to violence has already been distinguished from the Tolstoyan view that no act of violence is ever justified, whatever its consequences. The liberal view, by contrast, allows that violence may be permissible in a dictatorship and other oppressive regimes when it is used to defend human rights, provoke liberal reforms, and achieve other such desirable objectives (Miller, 1974, p.406).

Miller summarises the Tolstoyan view that '...all acts of violence are morally prohibited whatever their consequences'. Miller argue that "this view makes no distinction between violence in liberal democracies and violence in regimes of other kinds, and implies that it can never be right to engage in violence to safeguard innocent life" (Miller, 1984, p.402). Miller concludes that "at the other end of the spectrum stands what might be called the Sorel-Fanun-Sartre view, namely, that in certain circumstances acts of violence may be therapeutic: they may help to liberate the person who performs them from the intellectual and emotional constraints of a repressive society (op. cit. p. 402).

A similar approach was introduced in a book called *Mecelle* prepared by a law commission of the Ottoman state, and edited by Berki (1982) at the turn of this century. The *Mecelle* begins with one hundred general rules concerning the application of law to specific events, and articles 25-30 legitimise the use of force for a particular purpose if it is believed and considered that by using this force a greater abuse of force will be prevented. This implies that the use of force must be decided with careful consideration. This approach, which to some extent legitimises the use of force by certain groups against the state, avoids the hypocritical view of a liberal approach. The radicals, rightly, refuse the liberal view by asking why violence against the state can be regarded any differently from violence perpetrated by the state, be it in the form of police brutality, warfare or support for oppressive regimes abroad (Hoffman, 1994).

A more subtle approach asks why violence should be singled out for condemnation when other phenomenon such as poverty or economic inequality may have equally harmful effects on human beings? The Marxist concept of violence accuses the state of using violence, and justifies counter violence on this basis.

> We have been told that policemen, landlords, employers, shopkeepers, and indeed whole social classes and the state itself, engage in violence as a matter of course. The fundamental suggestion, which has a considerable history, is not that policemen use more than the force allowed by their powers, that landlords send thugs, or that the state engages in war and will use its army against revolution. Rather, it is that policemen, landlords and the state, in what most people regard as their peaceful conduct, are engaging in violence (Honderich, 1976, p.97).

Both the liberal and radical views see political violence as instrumental. "Violence is by nature instrumental; like all means, it always stands in need of guidance and justification through the end it pursues" (Arendt, 1970, p.51).

Much has been written and said for and against the use and justification of political violence (Feierabend, Feierabend and Gurr, 1972; Hibbs, 1973; Honderich, 1976; McDonagh, 1978; Hoffman, 1988b; Honderich, 1989; Parekh, 1990; Salmi, 1993; Hoffman, 1994), but a universally accepted answer to this complex problem has not been found. Not only the liberal approach which permits political violence under oppressive regimes but not in so-called democratic regimes, but also Marxist perspectives do not tolerate violence when it threatens their own regimes.

However, many thinkers find the Western approach to political crime as hypocritical in nature. As Malcom X insistently stated in his speeches:

> I do not advocate violence. In fact the violence that exists in the United States is the violence that Negro in America has been a victim of, and I have never advocated our people going out and initiation any acts of aggression against whites indiscriminately (Malcolm X, cited in Clark, 1992, p.37).

> We're for peace. But the people that we're up against are so violent, you can't be peaceful when you are dealing with them (op. cit. p. 150).

> I've never advocated violence, but I do believe in protecting ourselves from those who want to harm us (op. cit. p. 183).

Although, Malcolm X repeatedly stated that he was not in favour of violence, he justified the use of violence as self defence and also regarded violence as a means of communication with those who deploy violence themselves. "The only demonstration that they pay attention to are the ones that contain the seeds of violence" (Malcolm X, cited in Clark, 1992, p.244).

> ...if you and I would just realise that once we learn to talk the language that they understand, they will then get the point. You can't ever reach a man if you don't speak his language. If a man speaks the language of brute force, you can't come to him with peace....There'll be some dialogue, some communication, and some understanding will be developed (Malcolm X, cited in Clark, 1992, p.87).

Moreover, the difference in the attitudes of Western democracies and particularly of the media towards two similar recent crowd movements in Algeria and Russia, have highlighted the fact that the Western approaches to collective violence, even to peaceful crowd activities, are hypocritical in essence. "Liberalism promises rights in theory but, at least initially, declines to extend these rights to everybody..." (Hoffman, 1994, p.18). As Hoffman clearly articulated "...liberal states have never really practised what they preach" (Hoffman, 1994, p.17).

For instance, the crowd movements in Russia enjoyed the support of the Western media and states, despite the fact that the extent of the popularity of these crowds was open to speculation and had no clear electoral support. On the other hand, in Algeria, a political party which had the support of eighty per cent of its population, was suppressed by an oppressive army with the help and encouragement of Western states and media. The West and France, in particular, has historical as well as current material and colonial interests in Algeria, played a large part in this political suppression (Mortimer, 1991; Pidcock, 1993, p.1).

The conclusion from the Algerian experience is, however, more relevant to the nature of Western states and their possible reaction towards political crowds when they impose a real danger by introducing radical changes within their own established systems. Those countries which tolerate political opposition in the form of mass crowd movements do it not because they are genuinely tolerant to real opposition but because they feel that their regime can accommodate this kind of political opposition within the system. In other words, crowds in less oppressive regimes may impose certain problems to daily life and to the authorities, but may not always pose a serious threat to the system itself. In fact, tolerance to crowd movements serves as a safety-valve for the regime and diffuses the tension which builds up over a period of time. The so-called democratic regimes tolerate and will continue to tolerate such events as long as these events serves as a safety valve, without imposing a serious danger to the existing regimes.

> When the rules of the game produce results unacceptable to the regime, just as happened in Algeria, the regime itself does not hesitate to revolt against the rules it designed itself" (Tamimi, 1994, p.4).

As Tamimi (1994) clearly stated above when crowds pose a real danger to the existing structure the response of so-called democratic regimes will not be less oppressive than those of so-called oppressive regimes. In fact the response to the Algerian crowd typifies the Western democratic response to crowds. The response to a similar political challenge, however remote it is, in a Western country will not be any different from the response the Algerian crowd had to face.

This reminds us that not only apparently oppressive regimes but all regimes including the most democratic ones are more or less oppressive but the way in which they oppress or control the population may differ. Radical authors such as Bowden (1970 and 1978) and Bunyan (1977) have pointed out the role of the state and its agents, the police and army, in their dealing with crowd events and protecting the interests of the ruling class (Hall, 1987; Scraton, 1978; Lofthouse, 1993a and 1993b).

In reality, the concept of 'oppression' is a rather relative term. Every country may be more or less oppressive in some respects compared with others. For instance, when the British state is compared to the US it may be seen as oppressive in its dealing with the problems in Northern Ireland. Since the US has no similar problem it may be seen to be more tolerant than the UK. However, when the two countries' police organisations are compared, in general, the US may be seen to be more oppressive than the UK. As a second example, a country such as Turkey may be regarded as oppressive, compared with Western democracies, but not when compared with neighbouring countries such as Iraq, Iran and Syria. Even Western democracies in general may be oppressive in their dealings with their particular problems compared one to another.

The most severe oppression is experienced in countries where there is a transition from one system to another, especially if this transition is imposed forcefully or when the state resists a natural and peaceful transition. In fact, all societies experience some sort of transition, change or evolution. The words 'change' and 'evolution' have less negative and violent connotations compared with the word 'revolution'. They mean mostly orderly and gradual change rather than sudden and dramatic change. Revolution is defined as "...a wholesale change in the governing of a nation, in the political and to some extent the social, economic, cultural complex of habits and institutions a people lived under" (Brinton, 1965, p.3). Revolutions are rapid and sudden changes which take place in a society, either from democracy to a non-democratic regime or from a non-democratic regime to democracy. When this transition is challenged and prevented from taking place by the state or any particular group, violent confrontation takes place. This was the case, for instance, in Algeria, where eighty per cent of the voters had chosen Islam as their democratic choice (Pidcock, 1993, p.1).

Western responses towards two similar crowd movements, the Russian and Algerian, have given rise to doubts about the reliability and universality of Western ideology towards political violence. First of all, these two incidents have shown that the Western liberal approach towards political violence is hypocritical in nature as it does not offer a universally acceptable definition of political violence. It is still not clear why the crowd movements in Algeria, which represented an overwhelming majority of eighty per cent, should be regarded as anti-democratic, and therefore, condemned. It has also proved that the so-called democracies are not less tolerant towards a real opposition compared with so-called totalitarian regimes, when they are threatened even in democratic and legitimate ways. These events have illustrated that today's crowd events are not isolated incidents at a national level. Today's societies are so tightly knit, in terms of world economic organisation, communication networks, transnational capital and labour movements that a particular crowd movement cannot be considered as an isolated and private concern of a particular country. Therefore, crowd movements have international dimensions and this must be taken into consideration in order to achieve a political end. This leads to the conclusion that there is a need to take account of what Smelser calls 'structural conduciveness' at an international level. A crowd movement may fail even though it has the support of the majority of the public, unless it has international approval, which can be seen to constitute 'structural conduciveness' at an international level.

An important point revealed by the examination of early Islamic history is that contrary to the commonly held view, the right to oppose authorities and protest peacefully is not peculiar to Western democracies. Islamic political systems are full of examples of peaceful opposition, and the response they receive from the authorities has not been as severe as many would imagine (Ocak, 1980; Sener, 1990; Agirakca, 1992). For instance, when the fourth Caliph of Islam Ali (598-661) faced political opposition from a group called 'Harigees', he did not interfere or use any force as long as they did not engage in violence (Armagan, 1987; Daftary, 1992, p.32-91). Even though the dissenters, the harigees, were openly declaring their intention of killing the Caliph (Mawdudi, 1980, p.121), they were allowed to hold public meetings and had access to all facilities which were available to other parties. For example, they were allowed to come to the mosque, which was functioning as parliament, in order to express their opinion.

The right to oppose the authorities and demonstrate peacefully is not uniquely peculiar to Western democracies. The acceptance and tolerance of peaceful political opposition in practical terms in Turkish-Islamic political history dates back to its early days. The Turkish Constitution of 1982, which is not Islamic but secular, bears a similar article in relation to the right to protest (T. C. Constitution Article 34). This states that "...all public meetings and demonstrations are allowed, without prior application for permission, provided that they should be carried out peacefully".

Since Islam rejects any social division based on material or racial superiority the functions of Islamic states aim to reduce the material deficiencies of the people. On the one hand, it introduces a number of material obligations to the rich for the poor; on the other, it helps the poor to attain a certain level and become active and productive rather than relying on state benefit. Therefore, if a group of people have any grievances within the boundaries of these limits, and if they and their opposition fulfil the conditions outlined above, crowd violence is regarded as socially meaningful. In their conflict against the state dissenters have certain obligations and if they fail to achieve their goal, they win certain rights which means punishment will be relatively less severe compared to ordinary criminals (Udeh, 1990). This approach implies that if an opposition fulfils these conditions, that it has the consensus of the people and this legitimises crowd violence to some extent. The state and its functions are legitimate as long as it has the approval of the general public. When it loses this approval and consensus, the political opposition gains legitimacy as it is assumed that it is based on the consensus of the general public.

Summary

Not surprisingly, the Western political perspectives particularly the conservative approaches towards the state, class and political violence are similar to the response to individual criminality. Human beings are criminal in nature and there can be no justification for their collective violence. Collective violence is the amalgamation of individual criminality without having any social meaning or justification. On the contrary, the conservative practices in areas where inner-city disturbances were experienced were in clear contradiction with conservative ideology. For instance, Lord Scarman's inquiry identified unemployment as one of the primary causes of the discontent in the area of Moss Side which sparked off the troubles there. As a result of his report, £1.4m was pumped into the area for training and job creation schemes (Miller and Warren, 1993, p.24). Despite their denial of unemployment and deprivation as the cause of inner city riots their response has been more or less based on attempting to address material deprivation and inequality.

In contrast to Western conservatism, Eastern conservatism admits the possible negative influence of economic and social arrangements and accordingly takes a number of preventive measures. For instance, it draws the boundaries of poverty in order not to tolerate crimes caused by so-called 'relative deprivation'. The state and its agents are responsible for crimes which are committed by those who are below the poverty line. This rejects the justification of any crime based on relative deprivation.

Within this chapter the role of institutionalised factors such as class, the state, and its agents, the police, have been compared in two nations. It has concluded that the perceptions of the ruled about their state and its agents has a crucial importance in the response to particular events. However, as the present so-called Islamic regimes are far from fulfilling the requirements of their people the violence they experience "...is a reaction to the violence of despotic states" (Tamimi, 1994, p.3). Therefore, one can easily conclude that their legitimacy is questionable not only in terms of Western values and norms but also Islamic law (Hussain, 1994; Appendix 2; Tamimi, 1995, Hussain, 1995).

As this point needs more clarification, the next chapter compares Turkish-Islamic and Western conservatism in relation to human nature and crime in general, and collective violence in particular.

5 Towards Construction of a Combined Factors Approach

Introduction

> Societies have the criminals which they deserve (A. Lacassagne, cited in J. V. Ginneken, 1992, p.113).

The previous chapter dealt with various issues related to the state, class and the police which, according to the theory of this book, can be termed *institutional* factors. The theory argues that the nature of the state and the role it plays in the interactions between the social and economic classes is vitally important in the creation of dissident crowds and the nature of the police response to crowd events. The theory also reveals in the previous chapter that the existing perceptions of the state and its agencies vary from one country to another. In support of the thesis of this book, the following account will deal with issues arising from the failings of institutional factors. It is also argued that these failings are always associated and combined with constitutional factors. These will be explored in more detail in the following chapter.

Before applying our model, the Combined Factors Approach, to individual crime and collective violence, the commonly identified causes of crime in general and collective violence in particular, have been reduced to two broad categories. These are 'materially oriented grievances' (socio-economic), which are mainly derived from the inconsistencies of economic, political and social arrangements in a given society. The effects of these factors on the individual manifest themselves in a rather different form, mostly associated with some legitimising notions (Stevenson, 1992, p.310) and non-material abstract concepts and ideas. Again, these are reduced into one category, Constitutional Factors, embracing many non-material factors such as the biological and psychological.

The reason why this classification has been introduced is that while socio-economic and political factors are external and malleable, socio-psychological and biological factors are not created by society. They are acquired by the individual at birth and upgraded/degraded by environment and social settings. Although the environment and social settings influence the latter to some extent, their influence on non-material factors is limited.

Therefore, the discussion on the coming pages, in line with this assumption, will rotate around the causes of crime and collective violence. Firstly, the link between poverty, deprivation and crime will be examined. Secondly, some non-materially oriented grievances such as the lack of political representation and relative insecurity will be analysed as examples of the manifestation of the failings of social settings in association with non-material factors.

The discussion will then move on to the main argument which sees the origins of individual crime as well as collective violence as the result of maladjustment at the institutional and constitutional levels. Finally, the model for explaining crime and collective violence is introduced. The research concludes that human behaviour cannot merely be the result of either social or psychological factors, rather it is both. To stress one factor as the source of human behaviour is inadequate and arguing which of these influences comes first, becomes a 'chicken and egg' debate. Rather than one causing the other they are mutually inclusive and inter-related.

Causes of Crime and Disorder

There is no universal theory of the causes of crime and collective violence and it is unlikely that one can be constructed. Many explanations have been advanced (Berkowitz, 1962; Arendt, 1970; Bersani, 1970; Tutt, 1976; Campbell, 1976 and Kahan, 1976) but all have been criticised. Conventional theories traditionally argue that since crime is concentrated in the lower classes, it is caused by poverty or by personal and social characteristics believed to be associated statistically with poverty, including feeble-mindedness, psychopathic deviations, slum neighbourhoods, and deteriorated families (Mannheim, 1955; Fink, 1962; Mannheim, 1965a and 1965b; Wolfgang and Weiner, 1982; Samenow, 1984). It is also suggested that crime is caused by baby booms, permissive parents, brutal parents, incompetent schools, racial discrimination, lenient judges, the decline of organised religion, televised violence, drug addiction and drinking (Marsh and Kibby, 1992), inner city unemployment, or the capitalist system.

Some have argued that crimes are committed by those who have nothing to lose. It has also been argued that the capitalist system, which has nothing to offer to 'losers', is responsible for some materially oriented crimes. The individual has to have economic or professional success in order to influence society or gain its respect, recognition or protection.

Society does little to accommodate those individuals who are 'losers' and offers few opportunities for the lower classes to break from the vicious circle in which they are trapped. The individual may struggle to achieve a desired status and through ambition, succeed. On the other hand, the individual may resort to flight into an imaginary world, in which case he becomes psychopathic.

However, detailed analyses of these theories reveals that there is no single explanation for crime and it is not feasible to construct a universally applicable crime theory based on only one of these factors. For example, it is hard to imagine that both permissive and brutal parents produce the same kinds of criminals, though it is conceivable that each may contribute to a different kind of criminality. Many children may attend 'bad' schools, but only a small minority become serious criminals. Capitalism may contribute to crime, but the connections seem to be rather complicated, since while high crime rates can be found in socialist as well as capitalist nations, some capitalist nations, such as Japan and Switzerland, have very little crime. Poverty is even considered as a protecting factor rather than being a contributing factor for some social problems such as suicide (Durkheim, 1952, p.245).

The argument of this book is that the conception and explanations of crime and violence which have just been summarised are misleading and incorrect; that crime is, in fact, not closely correlated with poverty and/or with the psychopathic and sociopathic conditions associated with poverty, and that an adequate explanation of criminal behaviour must proceed along quite different lines, namely combining both 'constitutional' and 'institutional' factors in human behaviour.

Social problems are also caused by a multitude of factors and cannot be reduced to a single explanation. As social problems 'crime' and 'disorder' are caused by factors ranging from materially orientated grievances such as poverty, deprivation, unemployment and so on, to non-materially orientated factors such as human nature and psychological motives (Clinard, 1964; Davies, 1971; Renatus and Artzt, 1973). Crime and violence appear to stem from such a tight-knit weave of both 'biological' and 'environmental' influences that the dominance of any single discipline in explaining collective violence cannot be justified (Glueck and Glueck, 1962; Storr, 1968; Swanson, 1976). To define crime and collective violence only as the result of *constitutional* factors, i.e. human nature, without referring to its social causes, *institutional* factors, is as meaningless as defining crime in terms only of material causes such as poverty and deprivation.

It has convincingly revealed that taking into account only environmental and social factors is insufficient, and there is a need to understand more about the nature of violence and in particular of aggression, which requires cross-disciplinary effort. Consequently, a non-secular account of crime and criminality will be given and it is hoped that this will, at least, contribute to a better understanding of the current approaches to crime, violence and disorder.

Human Nature, Crime and Disorder

Any attempt to explore the inner dynamics of crowd activities and violence will inevitably lead us to the issue of human nature and crime. The analysis of this book has led to the belief that there is a link between the understanding of human nature and approaches to crime and collective violence. If one believes that human beings are naturally well behaved and good, one will expect that the problem of order can be easily managed; if one believes them to be naturally evil and disorderly, one will expect the provision of order to require extraordinary measures; if one believes human nature to be infinitely plastic, one will assume that the problem of order can be solved entirely by plan and that we may pick and choose freely among all possible plans.

Recently, there have been fierce debates on the role and influence of human nature on both individual and collective violent crimes. The debates came to a climax in February 1993 with the abduction and killing of two year old James Bulger, by two ten year old boys in Liverpool (Leicester Mercury, 17 February 1993). Following the tragic incident, the then Home Secretary of the Conservative Government, Kenneth Clarke launched a moral crusade against rising crime and in particular against young criminals. He put the blame on family, society and human nature and demanded more severe punishment for young offenders. The Church, whilst simultaneously blaming the Government for failing to provide a moral unity around commonly held values and norms, also supported the 'back to basics' campaign. The Clergy blamed not only the Government, but the whole of society including the family and even the Church itself for failing to provide religious, moral and social restraints for young offenders. Conversely, certain sections of the media and several politicians blamed the Church for failing to provide moral leadership. The main opposition parties focused on the material and social conditions of society, ignoring the moral and non-material aspects of violent crimes. Neither the Liberal nor the Labour party openly denied the role of the criminality of human nature while they opposed the Government's plans for tough measures and severe punishments for young offenders.

Apart from liberal and radical politicians, an overwhelming majority of academics (Benyon, 1993b and 1994a) insist on material factors and social conditions, in explaining crime, particularly delinquent and teenage crimes. This materialistic approach dominates academic wisdom to such a degree that they attempt to explain all crimes by these means, denying the existence of non-material factors. The advocates of radical and liberal approaches to crime tend to deny the accuracy and scientific value of non-material explanations. Perhaps academic wisdom has gone too far in attempting to explain all crimes in a material context. It seems as if their insistence is a reaction to the conservative approaches, which places too much emphasis on individual human nature and moral restraints. Therefore, the liberal and radical approaches tend to be a reaction to extreme conservative ideas rather than being a new approach to crime and violence.

It is perhaps easier to explain violence committed by adults with material factors and social conditions, such as unemployment, bad housing, relative deprivation and so on. However, it is problematic to explain the murder of a two-year-old by two ten-year-old boys, who were not directly experiencing the disadvantage of bad social conditions. Therefore, the rise in crime among the young in the early 1990s, culminating in the James Bulger case, has forced social scientists to focus on the influence of human nature on crime. Our examination will rotate around the establishment of conservatism on the basis of religious beliefs and includes various scientific arguments for and against the influence of human nature. Since this section is about the comparison of two religions, Islam and Christianity, it is inevitable that it will include the influence of these religions on the existing political arguments surrounding the field.

Despite the Christian perspective on crime, which is mostly influenced and shaped by the *Bible*, the Islamic sources, the *Qur'an* and the *Sunnah* (sayings and deeds of the Prophet Muhammed), do not refer to human nature as the source of criminality. The quotation below from the *Bible* is a clear example of this contradiction:

> Never again will I curse the ground because of man, even though every inclination of his heart is evil from childhood (Genesis, 8:21).

According to the Christian creed the criminality of human nature dates back to Adam and Eve when they disobeyed God's order not to eat of the forbidden fruit of knowledge (Genesis, 2 and 3). Therefore, it is believed, in Christianity, that "The sin of Adam is inherited by all the children of Adam; and so all human beings are born sinful" (Unal, 1992, p.44). Unal (1992) asserts that the concept of original sin was imported into Christianity by Saul [Paul], while Jesus and the disciple James himself insisted upon actions and the law. Unal argues that like other borrowed Christian beliefs, the doctrine of 'inherited sin' also finds no support in the words of Jesus or of the prophets who had come before him. What is more, it is clearly expressed in Jesus's words that all children are innocent and pure, and not born in sin (Unal, 1992, p.44-45). In support to this view, in his book, *Christianity versus Truth,* Unal (1992, p.45) quotes the following verse from *Bible*.

> Let the little children come to me, and do not hinder them, for the kingdom of God belong to such as these. I tell you the truth, anyone who will not receive the kingdom of God like a little child will never enter it (Mark, 10:14-15).

Contrary to the prevailing Christian belief, Islam considers human beings as the most exalted species among God's creation. The *Holy Qur'an* states that "We have indeed created man in the best of moulds" (*Qur'an* 95:4; *The Light* 1980, p.3). Human beings are created by God in a naturally good and pure state, free from sin. This is called the state of *fitrah.* The following translation taken from the commentary of the *Holy Qur'an,* by Yusuf 'Ali (1989) clarifies this view.

> He [Allah] created man virtuous and pure: he gave him intelligence and knowledge; he surrounded him with all sorts of instruments of His grace and mercy. If, in spite of all this, man distorts his own will and goes against Allah's Will...It is only when he has made his own sight blind and changed his own nature or soul away from the beautiful mould in which Allah formed it (Yusuf Ali, 1989, p.589).

In addition to a number of verses in the *Holy Qur'an* the essential innocence of human beings is stated by the Prophet Muhammed that. "All are born as innocent" (Munawi, 1972, Vol. 5 p.33). A new-born baby, for instance, is totally innocent and does not bear the sin or guilt of parents or ancestors. Babies begin with a clean slate. While on the one hand the *Holy Qur'an* rejects inherited criminality, on the other it places responsibility on the individual. No one has the burden of crime at birth, nor has the responsibility of their forefathers' crime: "...no bearer of burdens can bear the burden of another" (*Qur'an* 13:15). Everyone will be held accountable for their own deeds and actions, dictated by free will. Besides this supposed innocence, it is assumed that each individual has the capability of doing good and evil deeds (*Qur'an,* 6:160 and 164; 40:58; 17:15; 27:92; 90:18 and 19).

In line with the Islamic perspective on criminality and the associated innocence of human nature, some modern Turkish scholars such as T. F. Unal (1992 and 1993) and W. Yildiz (1994) have argued that there are two reasons why human nature should be regarded as essentially innocent and good. Firstly, why should we assume that human nature is essentially criminal on the basis of its relatively few criminal elements, when those elements in society are still relatively rare compared to the decent ones? On the basis of the majority of the law-abiding and respectful citizens it can equally be argued that human nature is essentially good. Secondly, not just the actions of the decent elements of society, but also the majority of the actions of the so-called criminal elements of the society are in fact peaceful and innocent, sometimes even praiseworthy. What is more, when evil acts are examined in proportion to decent acts and deeds, crimes committed by so-called criminals seem to be less significant in proportion to their routine and peaceful activities.

In addition the *Holy Qur'an* also stresses the importance of the immediate environment, the family, in shaping an individual's decisions and behaviour. In another hadith, the Prophet states that, "Each child is born in a natural state of goodness [it is called, in Islam, the fitrah]. It is only his parents that later turn him into a Jew, a Christian or a Magian" (Hamid, 1989, p.21). The term *parents* in the above translation has the wider meaning of environment and all social institutions. Again, the religions named were the ones best known at the time of the Prophet, but it refers to any religion or world view which takes a person away from his natural position (Hamid, 1989). The inherent qualities of man cannot be changed forcibly, but man can improve his inherent qualities.

Islam assumes that human beings were created with an in-built moral sense which recognises true and good and false and evil. On the other hand, although God created mankind in a naturally good state, the 'fitrah', He also created the capacity or power to do both good and evil. The individual is granted freedom of will together with a power of choice and inclination. In consequence of his use of this real freedom of will and choice, he earns good or evil, reward and punishment. "What comes to an individual results from the choices and actions of that individual, and this is in accordance with the law of cause and effect that God has decreed for all His creation" (Dahhak, 1993, p.147 and 169).

There are numerous verses in the *Holy Qur'an* which states that responsibility lies with the individual whether the act he commits is good or evil. However, the following verse may suffice to make *Qur'an's* point clear enough.

> Who receiveth guidance, receiveth it for his own benefit: who goeth astray doth so to his own loss: No bearer of burdens can bear the burden of another (*Qur'an*, 17:15).

Islam frequently refers to human nature as being capable of doing evil deeds as well as good ones (*Qur'an*, 6:160 and 164; 40:58; 17:15; 27:92;90:18 and 19). It regards human nature as a raw material, in some sense like minerals to be worked upon, to be purified and refined. Therefore, Islam puts the blame for transgression on the immediate environment, parents and families. It is the insufficiency of the immediate environment, such as parents, family, peer groups or the distant environment such as social conditions, religious organisations, educational institutions and the media, which turns the raw material, into evil. Either they fail to provide the necessary conditions to upgrade the good side of the human nature or they provide bad examples and lead the individual into evil.

However, Islam does not completely deny the existence of inherited criminal or evil tendencies or inclinations in the individual (Dahhak, 1993, p.143-144), but it places emphasis on institutional factors, (economic, political and social), in amplifying or eradicating these feelings. However, Islam's acceptance of innate attributes and traits is far from being similar to that of "Lombroso's belief that criminals posses an innate, primitive predisposition to crime" (Denno, 1990, p.1). Over a century ago Cesare Lombroso, an Italian physician, suggested that some individuals were 'born' criminals with distinct physical features that he believed characterised primitive men, such as sloping foreheads, long arms, and flat feet. However, he was refuted 40 years later by Goring (Denno, 1990, p.8). Islam completely denies the notion of the inherited criminality of human beings. Regarding the influence of innate attributes, traits or tendencies it is believed that they can be eradicated or at least controlled by the proper functioning of institutionalised factors such as good education and healthy environment.

Islamic ideology radically differs from its Western counterparts in its understanding of human nature, therefore, the response they provide to crime and disorder will inevitably be different, despite their nominal similarities. In contrast to Western conservatism which argues that "...human beings are not naturally good and law-abiding" (Oerton, 1968, p.26), Turkish-Islamic conservatism believes that human nature is a raw material, capable of doing good as well as evil. Western conservatism mainly places the blame on so called criminal or violent individuals rather than dividing the blame into two; society and the individual.

> Generally speaking, an offender has a criminal personality not because something has changed him from good to bad, but because something has stopped him changing from bad to good (Oerton, 1968, p.26).

In contrast, Christian theology posits inherited guilt and sin and therefore speaks of necessary constraints, or 'orders' against sin, including obedience to the legal authorities. Western conservatism believes that human nature is essentially criminal unless we control it, while Islamic ideology argues that human nature is, essentially, innocent unless we spoil it. The only common point is they both see a relationship between crime and human nature but in a different context. This apparently insignificant difference becomes crucial when considering punishments meted out in both cultures. While the former denies the influence of social conditions and introduces severe punishment for criminals, the latter divides the blame between both *constitutional* factors such as human nature and *institutional* factors such as economic, political and social arrangements.

Islam, therefore, unlike Christianity, focuses on material and environmental factors, besides acknowledging the possible negative role and influence of human nature. It also presupposes that the social and material environment has a significant influence in the shaping of human nature. Although D. R. W. Wood asserts that like Islam, Christianity ought to take into consideration the material and environmental factors (1995), he fails to provide any verses referring to his assertion. In the *Bible*, there seems to be more emphasis on criminality stemming from within human beings (Genesis, 8:21 and Romans, 7:17-25), and less, if any, references to external factors. On the other hand, Reverend Clinton Bennett (1994), a lecturer in the Study of Religions, Westminster College, Oxford, clearly stated that on the point of being innocent at birth, Islam appears to be more clear and feasible than Christianity. Furthermore, the Western liberal approach to crime seems to indicate a similar line with Islam:

> The liberal approach tends to see economic, social and cultural deprivation as the major causes of crime and disorder, with people behaving in this way either because they are deprived of material goods and status or because they learn it as they grow up. These explanations tend to assert that behaviour is largely conditioned by environmental factors such as family background, material conditions, housing, educational opportunities, cultural experiences and the influence of the mass media (Benyon, 1993, p.10).

Like Western liberals and radicals, Islamic ideology acknowledges a correlation between the basic material needs of the individual and crime

(Rahim, 1993), while denying the relative deprivation and the effect of want on human nature as acceptable excuses for crime. In one hadith, the prophet equates destitution and unbelief, [Kade'l faqru en yekune kufran], "Poverty is near to being in infidelity" (Tabrizi, 1991, Vol. II. p.1049). It implies that poverty is as much hated as infidelity, as in some people "it [poverty] can be an occasion for inward distress and rancour and ingratitude towards God, which is a root of unbelief" (Dahhak, 1993, p.163). For this reason, in Islam, the material and social conditions of society have always been taken into account before enforcing the penal law, in the punishment of certain property crimes. According to this consideration, either the punishment is reduced or not given at all (Zeydan, 1985; Udeh, 1990).

Punishment is not given in order to punish human nature, instead the criminal is considered to be a victim of social conditions as well as his/her own free will. By taking into account the social conditions of society, Western liberals and radicals follow the Islamic tradition, but what they fail to realise is that not all crimes are committed under the influence of social conditions. It is problematic to explain all crimes by liberal and radical approaches. It is difficult, for instance, to blame the prevailing social conditions such as unemployment, bad housing and so on as the cause of 'white-collar' crimes (Geiss, 1970; Sutherland, 1970; Pearce, 1976; Palmer and Humphrey, 1990a-b; Croal, 1992). An approach which acknowledges the selfishness and greed of human nature might be more appropriate in explaining this kind of crime, besides taking into account the structural insufficiencies of the society, such as lack of legal and social control, which allows certain people to be able to commit these crimes. Nearly everyone would agree that some forms of wrongdoing cannot be prevented other than by inner checks. No system of social control relying only on coercive measures to control such behaviour would have much success. As Durkheim (1950, p.248) has stated 'Physical restraint would be ineffective; hearts cannot be touched by physico-chemical forces'. He also further stresses the necessity of external control on human behaviour:

> To achieve any other result, the passions first must be limited. Only then they can be harmonised with the faculties and satisfied. But since the individual has no way of limiting them, this must be done by some force exterior to him. A regulative force must play the same role for moral needs which the organism plays for physical needs (Durkheim, 1952, p.248).

Therefore, at least certain crimes might have been committed by people whose decision to commit these acts is dominated by *constitutional* factors such as human nature rather than *institutional* factors such as political arrangements and social and economic settings. Consequently, consideration should be given to human nature approaches, at least in dealing with certain type of crimes.

Islamic thought tries to distinguish between the influence of human nature and social conditions by drawing the boundaries of poverty (Mawsili, 1975, p.100). It offers a set of rules which defines the limits of material influences, and severely punishes those crimes committed outside this boundary. For instance, poverty and wealth is not a subjective matter left to the individual to decide. What is more, no one has the right to justify taking another's property, according to their relative deprivation, which is based on subjective and personal justifications. If a person is below the poverty line, which is drawn by Islam (Mawsili, 1975, p.100), it is the responsibility of the state to provide his basic needs.

The Islamic state gives priority to justice rather than law and order (Taymiya, 1992, p.125-133). It attempts to deliver justice in many areas such as social justice, political justice and economic justice (Ahmed, 1991, p.15-23). The application of penal law ideally comes after the state has fulfilled its role in delivering justice in other areas. The state has to tolerate certain crimes if it has failed to provide justice in other areas. In its ideal form, if the state has failed to provide social and economic justice for its citizens, it has no right to punish the 'criminal' for such crimes. For this reason, during the reign of the second Caliph of Islam, Omer (591-644), who is famous for his strict and uncompromising application of Islamic Law, certain property crimes committed during a severe famine were pardoned (Cawziyye, 1969, p.13-14; Zeydan, 1985, p.194-195; Udeh, 1990).

Socio-Economic Grievances

Grievances which are caused by material deprivation are more visible and tangible than those which are caused by non material ones. But as the model of crime and collective violence proposed in this book illustrates, material and non-material grievances are inter-related, both causing and affecting each other. On the other hand, while most grievances stem from material deprivation, they are mostly associated with abstract concepts such as 'social justice', 'freedom' and 'equality'. Poverty and deprivation, which will be examined in the following account, are only two of a number of materially oriented grievances.

Poverty and Deprivation

In a rapidly changing world, definitions of poverty based on relative standards will be constantly changing. What is 'necessary' for a decent standard of living is a matter of social definition which may change over time. In England the level of income at which SB (Social Benefit) is received is widely accepted as a crude and basic measure of the 'poverty line', that point below which people may be said to be 'in poverty' (Bilton et al. 1987; Haralambos and Holborn, 1990; Denscombe, 1994). With regard to Turkey poverty is seen in terms of absolute rather than relative deprivation. This derives mainly from the Islamic definition of poverty which takes the absolute necessities as the basis of poverty. As will be seen in the following account, in the early Islamic era and throughout Islamic history absolute deprivation was generally accepted as mitigation for certain crimes committed by those who were experiencing absolute deprivation.

After this introductory explanation, the perception of crime and collective violence in respect to poverty and deprivation will be compared and contrasted from Turkish and English political perspectives. The argument will rotate around three established broad views. Apart from these, some eminent and relatively recent crowd violence theories such as *subcultural* and *relative deprivation* theories will be considered.

In Western thought the conservative view regards collective violence as 'rare', 'needless', without purpose and irrational. In this view, any form of crime and collective violence "...occurs because of a lack of conditioning into values: the criminal, whether because of evil (in the conventional model) or lack of parental training (in the welfare model), lacks virtues which keep us all honest and upright" (Lea and Young, 1984, p.95). This indicates that crime is simply anti-social behaviour involving people who lack values. It assumes that the existing structures are adequate, and that there can be no justification or necessity for violent agitation. The state is, according to this view, a neutral institution that protects the universal interests of all against problems such as crime and violence of any kind. This view, which is based on controversial notions such as the criminality of human nature, lack of parental control and educational qualities, implicitly and explicitly denies the social and economic aspect of the problem. In concentrating on the invisible factors of crime, it fails to see the role and influence of environmental and social factors.

Not only the 'conservatives' but also some radicals (Lea and Young, 1984; Wilson, 1985; Waddington et al. 1989) have rejected the simple relationship between crime and poverty. For them there are a number of causes for crime, and poverty is only one of them. However, their explanation does not go beyond suggesting that material needs should be satisfied. Consideration shall also be given to the assertion that traditional Turkish-Islamic thought, which counterparts more or less Western conservatism, does not see crime as the only result of the lack of non-material qualities.

The difference between Turkish-Islamic and Western thought on crime and violence manifests itself at two levels. In the narrow sense, in the West some crimes such as drunkenness, possession of drugs, prostitution, pornography, and the like, are regarded as victimless crimes (Tame, 1991). On the other hand, Turkish-Islamic criminology rejects the definition and concept of victimless crimes. This stems from the assumption that all crimes, directly or indirectly, affect either the criminal himself or the environment and future generations. Islamic criminology regards the individual as the foundation stone of society and does not allow individuals to harm themselves in any way. On this basis, during the early days of the Ottoman State, not only were intoxicating liquids and drugs prohibited, but even over-roasted coffee since it was believed to be a health hazard.

No one has the right to expose himself to unnecessary risk and danger (Hoffman, 1988a). Therefore, suicide, which is the greatest danger to the individual if it is attempted, has been regarded as one of the cardinal sins in Islam, and any individual attempting suicide was punished if the attempt was unsuccessful. This is based on the assumption that no one is completely the owner of their own body and, therefore, no one has the right to harm his body nor to end his existence. There are reciprocal obligations between society and the individual.

There is no need to elaborate on how a person who damages his health mentally or physically, also causes damage to the general economy, family, the environment and future generations. In abstract terms, according to Islamic criminology, no one is free to harm themselves, therefore, there is no victimless crime. The differences in the definition of 'crime' and 'criminal', with regard to so-called victimless crimes, stems from differences in the understanding of the concept of freedom. Since Turkish-Islamic ideology does not accept absolute and limitless freedom, the so-called victimless crimes of the West are not regarded as personal.

The individual is not completely free to act even on his body, let alone on another's body or property. The disposition of one's own body is limited and controlled. In addition the individual is subject to environmental and social factors in their activities. In fact, the individual is in constant conflict with their inner desires and the forces of social and environmental factors. Therefore, an act of crime committed by an individual is the product of both his inner desires and external factors.

In a broad sense, Turkish-Islamic criminology accepts the influence of the social and material environment on crime, in line with Western ideology. Tame (1991) exhibits a very similar approach when he remarks that, "...while not denying that individuals are influenced by social 'forces' and the social environment, nothing can remove freedom of will" (Tame, 1991, p.131). He quotes Bidinotto saying that, "...to excuse criminals because of poor social environments leaves unexplained the crimes of those from good environments. And the sociological excuse is an insult to millions of others from the poor backgrounds, who have not turned to crime" (Bidinotto, 1989, p.6, quoted in Tame, 1991, p.131). It will be shown on the following pages that while Turkish-Islamic criminology stresses individual criminality, it also adds weight to social and environmental factors. The most striking point is that unlike some Western criminological thought it does not accept relative deprivation as an acceptable excuse for crime. On the other hand, historical evidence shows that absolute deprivation, which is defined by Islam, has been taken into consideration in the punishment of certain crimes.

With regard to criticism of Western traditional conservatism on crime and violence, the first and the most severe criticism comes from the radicals, an approach which varies considerably, since there are a number of sub-groups under this category. The radical perspective regards crime and violence as purposeful, structured and politically meaningful and collective violence is seen as a normal, legitimate and effective means of protest by groups who have no other opportunities and who are experiencing real deprivation and injustice (Lang and Lang, 1968, p.11-13; McCord and Howard, 1968, p.24-27; Tomlinson, 1968; Benyon and Solomos, 1987; Pugh, 1990).

While conventional crime theories focus on poverty crimes, which are mainly committed by lower classes, they exhibit an inconsistency in their dealings with white-collar crimes. As conventional theories of crime and collective violence are mostly based on crimes committed by lower classes, they are far from being universal. Therefore, it is hoped that the model introduced within this research will be an explanation of crimes committed by the middle class and upper classes as well as the lower classes.

White-collar crimes are those carried out by middle and upper-class persons, 'respectable' citizens, in the course of their occupations, usually in a commercial environmental. Edwin H. Sutherland, who coined the term 'white-collar crime' (Geiss, 1970, p.171) defines it as committed "...by a person of high socio-economic status who violates the laws designed to regulate his occupational activities and principally refers to business managers and executives" (op.cit. 171).

Conventional crime theories offer no explanation, for example, of middle-class and upper class crime. If crime is disproportionately committed by lower-class persons, as conventional crime theorists argue, because they find their lack of schooling and job opportunities a barrier to realising legitimate aspirations, then people with adequate schooling and reasonable job prospects should not commit crime, yet they do. It is clear that most violators are middle or upper-class and have had little or no contact with the criminal subculture. The theories that criminal behaviour in general is due either to poverty or to the psychopathic and sociopathic conditions associated with poverty are invalid for a number of reasons. For example, the generalisation that criminality is closely associated with poverty obviously does not apply to white-collar criminals. With a small number of exceptions, they do not live in abject poverty, were not brought up in slums or broken families, and are not weak-minded or psychopathic. They were seldom problem children in their early years and did not appear in juvenile courts. "The proposition, derived from the data used by the conventional criminologists, that 'the criminal of today was the problem child of yesterday' is seldom true of white-collar criminal" (Sutherland, 1970, p.32-33).

The financial and moral cost of white-collar crimes is far greater than poverty related crimes committed by lower-classes. Indeed, the cost of white-collar crimes is probably several times greater than the cost of all crimes which are customarily regarded as 'the crime problem'. An executive of a big company, for example, can embezzle as much as the annual loss from many burglaries and robberies. Although burglaries or robberies in excess of a million pounds are practically unheard of, several million pounds embezzled is small fry among white-collar criminals. While there are no adequate measurements available, common forms of property crime, e.g. robbery, burglary, larceny and auto theft, cause relatively less financial damage compared to the cost of white-collar crimes. Furthermore, white-collar crimes cost the society dearly in terms of the erosion of moral values. They violate trust and therefore create distrust, which lowers social morale and produces institutional and social disorganisation on a large scale.

As the Combined Factors Model includes crimes committed by both well off and deprived people, we agree with Sutherland's (1970) conclusion on the point that "...a description of white-collar criminality in general terms will be also a description of the criminality of the lower class. The respects in which the crimes of the two classes differ are the incidentals rather than the essentials of criminality" (Sutherland, 1970, p.31). On the other hand, Merton introduces three reasons for white collar crimes, which discredit conventional crime theories. It also supports the argument of this book which attempts to introduce an explanation for crimes committed by both lower and upper classes.

> ...middle and upper-class violators tend to be fearful of losing the means to ensure continued success goals, or they are actually losing success goals attained earlier and need more effective means to counteract that, or they desire success goals beyond those already achieved and seek additional means to attain them (cited in Palmer and Humphrey, 1990b, p.140).

Poverty is only one of the many causes which may cause an individual to drift into crime. In the previous account, it has been shown that poverty is not necessarily and inevitably linked with crime and therefore the lower classes are not the only suspects. There are many other factors which need to be taken into consideration in dealing with crime problems. What is more, the existence of white-collar crime on a large scale (Mannheim, 1965a and 1965b; Bersani, 1970; Pearce, 1976; Box, 1988; Croall, 1992), has also discredited conventional crime theories and has led the researcher to search for alternative explanations for the crimes committed by the affluent as well as the deprived.

In recent years, in their explanations of the causes of riots sociologists and social psychologists have turned to the concept of relative deprivation, developed originally by Stouffer et al. (1949). Today, this has become one of the most popular theories of crime and crowd violence (Gurr, 1968, 1970, 1972 and 1989). The central idea is that the root cause of rebellion lies in people's feelings of frustration, discontent and despair.

> Relative deprivation is not whatever the outside observer thinks people ought to be dissatisfied with, however; it is a state of mind that can be defined as a discrepancy between people's expectations about the goods and conditions of life to which they are justifiable entitled, on the one hand, and on the other their value capabilities - what they perceive to be their chances for getting and keeping those goods and conditions (Gurr, 1968, p.51).

This development is an acceptance of the fact that a satisfactory explanation of crime and violence must include a psychological dimension. Social and economic accounts were alone insufficient in explaining crime and violence. As D. Waddington has rightly pointed out there was no direct correspondence between economic hardship and public disorder. "The relationship was mediated by a felt sense of relative deprivation rather than absolute hardship" (Waddington et al., 1989, p.9). As indicated earlier, this is one of the significant differences between Western ideology and Turkish-Islamic ideology, which refuses to regard relative deprivation as an acceptable excuse for any crime.

As the term implies, deprivation is a rather relative concept. What is wealth for some may be poverty for others. Unless the boundaries of poverty are drawn, anyone may feel themselves relatively deprived when compared to others. As Lea and Young (1984) have stated, relative deprivation can occur in employed people as well as in the unemployed, since deprivation is dependent on subjectively experienced discontent. According to this assumption not only poor or middle class people, but even upper-class people may feel deprived compared to the relatively well off and therefore will commit economic crimes (Bersani, 1970; Sutherland, 1970; Geiss, 1970; Box, 1988; Palmer and Humphrey, 1990a-b). This can be regarded as one of the main causes of white collar crime. This again draws our attention to the greed and selfishness of human nature. As "...deprivation and other key variables such as legitimacy are fundamentally social-psychological, relating to expectations, evaluations, or temporal comparisons that can only be manifest within individuals" (Rule, 1988, p.212). This leads us to the conclusion that relative deprivation theory, which is apparently based on the social meaningfulness of crimes, comes indirectly to the conclusion of traditional conservative views of crime and violence. Lea and Young (1984) insist that discontent is a product of relative not absolute deprivation and they try to explain how this discontent arises on the basis of human psychology. The quotation below makes it clear how they see the relationship between relative deprivation and crime.

> It is not absolute poverty, but poverty experienced as unfair (relative deprivation when compared to someone else) that creates discontent; and discontent where there is no political solution leads to crime. The equation is simple: relative deprivation equals discontent; discontent plus lack of political solution equals crime (Lea and Young, 1984, p.88).

It seems that while Lea and Young try to demonstrate how relative deprivation leads to crime, they contradict their own argument, which sees crime and violence as socially meaningful without referring to its biological and psychological roots. This is because the theory of relative deprivation is based upon how each individual person feels about himself compared to others. In abstract terms, the concept of relative deprivation is the product of individual comparison and decision based on individual feelings and views. Whether this decision is accurate is another matter and is completely dependent on subjective comparison and personal judgement. The CFA combines the individual's and society's role, and openly denies the accuracy of Marxian definition of relative deprivation which sees the relative deprivation as the result of society without referring to the individual at all.

> Our desires and pleasures spring from society; we measure them therefore, by society and not by the objects which serve for their satisfaction. Because they are of a social nature, they are of a relative nature. (Karl Marx and Friedrich Engels, Wage Labour and Capital, cited in Gurr, 1970, p.22).

Lea and Young (1984) maintain that "...discontent occurs when comparisons between comparable groups are made which suggest that unnecessary injustices are occurring". An explanation is still required as to why a so-called deprived group chooses relatively well-off people as comparable groups rather than choosing relatively poor people. For instance, if those ethnic minorities who feel themselves relatively deprived compared with the host communities had chosen their own people in their own countries, the outcome of their judgement would be entirely different.

In addition, if crimes committed due to relative deprivation are to be tolerated, this may lead to the toleration of white collar crimes which are committed from similar motivations. As long as we do not accept the criminality of human nature we will have to find a logical and socially meaningful explanation of white collar crimes (Sutherland, 1970; Geiss, 1970; Palmer and Humphrey, 1990a-b). These crimes can be explained by an approach similar to those of relative deprivation. Many members of the 'upper class', when making comparisons, see themselves in the context of their own social and economic environment and, thus ignore people who are not at their own level. According to the relative deprivation theory they are expected to commit crimes. They may justify their action according to the subcultures to which they belong. They do not have to compare themselves with the relatively poor; similarly ethnic minorities do not compare themselves with people in their own countries.

If we tolerate or justify the crimes committed by the unemployed and the working classes, according to the same theory, we will have to justify and tolerate the crimes committed by the upper classes. As boundaries of poverty are drawn by the sacred law, the 'Shari'a' (Mawsili, 1975, p.100) Islamic criminology will not tolerate crimes committed by those who are subject to relative deprivation. If a person, for example, possesses, apart from his basic needs such as accommodation, transport and household effects, an amount of 85 grams of gold, or the equivalent in the form of money, estimated in December 1994 to be £700, that person is not classified as 'poor' and not eligible for receiving welfare funds. A crime committed by such a person, therefore, is regarded as inexcusable and needs to be punished. What is more, some of the causes of crime, such as alcohol consumption and using drugs, are both 'sin' and 'crime' according to Islamic criminology, let alone being a rationalization for crime.

Unlike the conventional conservative viewpoint on crime, which regards the criminal as flawed and lacking human values and cognition, the radicals (left idealists), argue that "...crime occurs not because of lack of value but simply because of lack of material goods: economic deprivation drives people into crime" (Lea and Young, 1984, p.95). The radicals are correct when they see crime as a reaction to an unjust society. However, this reaction does not always stem from absolute deprivation. It is evident that not only absolute poverty but any degradation of the economic or social status of the individual will inevitably result in some degree of maladjustment and lead to crime. Society leads the individual to expect certain material standards and a certain level of social status. That standard may be far above that which is actually necessary to maintain life and animal comfort. Once the standard is established, any decline from it maladjusts the individual and causes them to strive to re-attain that to which they believe themselves to be entitled. This is called relative deprivation theory.

Finally, let us consider the view held by liberals on crime and violence. In fact, the liberal perspective does not depart significantly from the radical and conservative perspectives. They see violence as inevitable under certain conditions such as high unemployment and widespread social disadvantage. One of the differences between the liberals and radicals is that, while the radicals argue that the discontent which stems from poverty is an inevitable result of the capitalist system the liberals believe that the system can be adjusted without making fundamental changes in society. On the other hand, they share a view similar to conservatism in trying to find the solution within the system itself.

Political and Socio Psychological Grievances

Western societies have, to a large extent, been transformed from religious oriented societies to secular ones at the expense of the destruction of religious beliefs and values. Le Bon (1969) has stated that two fundamental factors were at the base of this transformation. "The first is the destruction of those religious, political, and social beliefs in which all the elements of our civilisation are rooted" (Le Bon, 1969, p.14). Despite this transformation, individuals and indeed communities, still have some inherited social and moral values which can become a source of discontent when they are dissatisfied with the existing political and social arrangements.

Lack of Political Representation and Relative Insecurity

Having indicated, in the previous discussions, commonly held causes of crime and violence, it is necessary to note that grievances leading to discontent and violence are not always materially oriented. This is partly because not all members of a capitalist society vouchsafe capitalist values and norms. Non-material grievances may remain as a source of discontent and lead to crime and violence, unless these are met by existing channels. It was evident in the Salman Rushdie case, for instance, that the Asian Muslim community in Britain were willing to engage in violent disorder which they would not consider for material grievances. This can be partly explained by a lack of political representation and discrimination and partly by the relative insecurity felt by all ethnic minorities. The disorder related with the Salman Rushdie affair, therefore, can be explained, by both, 'subcultural' and 'relative insecurity' theories similar to relative deprivation.

Relative insecurity is an inevitable result of diverse and multicultural societies. Some sections of society will feel themselves relatively deprived and less secure compared with mainstream society. In recent years a number of studies and research projects have been undertaken by various institutions concerning the problems of ethnic minorities from various aspects (Cole, 1989; Benyon et al., 1991; 1992a; 1992b and 1993a). However, I have been unable to record any research or questionnaire which includes questions related to the felt insecurity of ethnic minorities. The only relevant question included in the questionnaire was, "Do you intend to return or move to the Caribbean or Africa to live?" which was obviously insufficient to include any sense of insecurity (Benyon et al. 1991). Lack of political representation and relative insecurity are given as examples of non-material grievances, not because they are purely non-material, having no connection with social, political and economic arrangements, but because it is easier to understand them when they are examined in association with psychological factors. In fact, non-material grievances become sources of discontent when they are associated both with human factors and with social settings. They cannot be a source of discontent when they are taken as isolated factors.

Lack of political representation is one of the failings of social settings which leads to the marginalisation of certain groups. "The failure of government policies may affect people's identity with the polity, their view of the legitimacy of its rules and agents and their voluntary consent to its actions" (Benyon, 1993b, p.18). Therefore, not only certain ethnic groups but also some sections of the host community may be politically marginalised and under-represented. Their basic material needs might be met by the existing social arrangements but their failure to have access to the same political institutions as the indigenous population increases a sense of discontent. Political under-representation is examined under the title of non-material grievances not because it has nothing to do with social and political arrangements, but because it is a rather abstract concept when compared with other sources of discontent such as poverty and material deprivation and its influence on an individual is less direct.

Lack of political representation can be taken at two levels. In the wider sense, the state deprives certain groups from access to power and decision-making processes. These groups in a multiracial society, can be various ethnic groups and this discrimination can be historical and systematic. A very limited number of people of ethnic origin may gain access to political institutions but their effect on the whole structure is minor. In the narrow sense, not only ethnically marginalised groups but also politically and culturally marginalised groups may be eliminated from political institutions. The continuous discrimination of ethnic and politically and culturally marginalised groups leads, therefore, to the creation of their own norms and values and this can be a source of discontent and conflict in society.

The transformation which took place in Western societies was not, of course, welcomed by all sections of society. Not only the immigrant groups but even some sections of the host community have failed to adapt to this transformation to the extent that capitalism requires. This results in the maintaining of original cultures and a resistance of the dominant culture. As a result a conflict arises between the dominant culture and significant subcultures. The notion of 'Britishness' for instance has failed to embrace all the ethnic or newly generated subcultures in British society. The notion of 'Britishness' was, in fact, introduced in order to offer all citizens, regardless of their origin, race, colour and religion, exactly the same rights and freedoms which the host community already have, and enjoy. In practice, it has failed to provide equal protection to all classes and ethnic groups. This is a potential danger for all multi racial societies. When 'national identity' does not provide equal right and protection, 'communal identity' gains priority over the former and might lead to alienation. The Salman Rushdie case has shown how a conflict can arise when some fellow citizens place their religious loyalty higher that the basic obligations of citizenship. However, this is so not because certain groups have strong communal and religious identities which prevents them from integrating within mainstream society, but because the mainstream society is not ready to grant them rights which they themselves enjoy.

In practice British citizenship does not offer all British citizens the same rights and freedoms. In the Salman Rushdie case the Muslim community felt that British law did not protect their religion from insult, since the existing law of blasphemy only protects the Anglican Church (Parekh, 1989, p.45).

British Muslims resented the fact that British law, far from being satisfactory, overtly discriminated against other religions by excluding them from the protection of the laws of blasphemy. In contrast to this unequal protection provided by the law, Islam has provided a universal protection to all religions and beliefs. In one verse the *Qur'an* prohibits the prophet, and indeed all his followers, to abuse or insult, verbally or physically, any other beliefs, religions and their prophets as well as their followers. The verse states that, "Revile not ye those whom they call upon besides Allah, lest they out of spite revile Allah in their ignorance" (*Qur'an*, 6:108).

In line with this verse the Muslim communities maintained an atmosphere of tolerance to all non-Muslims. Particularly during the reign of the second Caliph of Islam, Omer, all non-Muslims and ethic groups enjoyed a great deal of freedom in their religious practices (Sah, 1967, p.277-249). Their life was regarded as sacred and their places of worship were protected as well as the mosques (Mawdudi, 1993, p.12-13). Non Islamic groups enjoyed the same rights and freedom as Muslim society, provided that they paid the 'cizye', equivalent of a special tax payable by non-Muslims for their protection and granting of rights (Apaydin and Alister, 1994, p.11).

On the other hand, although the modern Turkish state is not very comfortable, since its inception, with the Islamic movements in Turkey, yet the present secular Turkish Penal Law (Turkish Penal Law Article 175, cited in Alikasifoglu and Dogu, 1987, p.222-223; Durmaz, 1989, p.297-298; Icel and Yenisey, 1990, p.759) includes an article which introduces a universal protection to all religions, holy scriptures and prophets, and violation of this article is a criminal offence.

Non-Muslims enjoyed a religious tolerance under the rule of the Ottoman State, and the Jewish community, in Istanbul in 1992, commemorated the 500th anniversary of their migration from Spain where they escaped execution (Apaydin and Alister, 1994). The flexible policy of Turks toward Orthodox Christians (Unal, 1993, p.150; Apaydin and Alister, 1994) and other religious minorities was often well received by the subject populations: "This live-and-let-live policy was in striking contrast to the fanatical bigotry of Christian states at the time. Balkan peasants in Mehmet's times used to say, 'Better the turban of the Turk than the tiara of the Pope' " (Goldschmidt, 1988, p.132, cited in Esposito, 1992). The following quotation taken from J. L. Esposito's (1992), despite the book's rather anti-Islamic title, *The Islamic Threat*, is a clear example of the religious tolerance enjoyed by all minorities within the Ottoman State.

> The king of the Turks, who rules over a great part of Europe, safeguards the rites of religion as well as any prince in this world. Yet, he constrains no one, but on the contrary permits everyone to live as his conscience dictates. What is more, even in his seraglio at Pera he permits the practice of four diverse religions, that of the Jews, the Christians according to the Roman rite, and according to the Greek rite, and that of Islam (Coles, 1968, p.146-147, cited in Esposito 1992).

This religious tolerance does not uniquely belong to Turks. In the early Arab conquests, ethnic and religious minorities enjoyed great tolerance and were not entirely excluded from mainstream society. This stems from the very nature of Islam which commands religious tolerance in the following verse. "Let there be no compulsion in religion: truth stands out clear from error" (*Qur'an* 2:256). There is no obligation in religion. Despite the influence of the Western world, which experienced religious oriented internal and external wars in mediaeval times when Christianity was more powerful and influential, the Turks became more tolerant to other beliefs and values when the Islamic influence was more profound in their lives.

Despite the intolerant and uncompromising image of Islam, most Muslims are, in fact, tolerant and respectful towards other beliefs and values and in turn expect to enjoy the same degree of tolerance and acceptance from the community in which they live. In fact this negative image is partly the result of Western misunderstanding and prejudices which have historical roots and partly the misrepresentation of Islam by some Muslim nations and certain groups (Esposito, 1992; Halliday, 1993; Bennett, 1993; Hussain, 1994).

The expectations of tolerance and acceptance of the immigrant communities in general and Muslims in particular, which stems from their own values and beliefs, are coupled with an unwillingness to adapt to the values and norms of mainstream society. These groups preferred to retain their own cultural values and norms as much as possible, while at the same time, enjoying the rights which mainstream society offered them. In the end, all ethnic minorities kept their cultural values and norms, while the newly established subcultures generated new values and norms.

Of course, there would be no problem as long as there was no conflict between these cultures. It was not always possible to keep the balance in the legal aspect and this resulted very frequently in violent confrontation between the people who belong to the subcultures and the police as the representatives of mainstream society. Therefore, it might be more appropriate to examine some violent acts in a subcultural context rather than trying to see the problem stemming from the criminality of human nature. The same theory was applied by Lea and Young (1984) in explaining materially oriented crimes and violence. They have argued that, a riot "...is not a situation where a mob of people have taken leave of their senses, but a response understandable in terms of the subculture concerned" (Lea and Young, 1984, p.77).

Subcultural theorists, instead of viewing deviant behaviour as pathological, irrational or lacking in meaning, interpret it as a socially evolving activity with a definite, meaningful rationality. It must be noted that in the Salman Rushdie affair, neither the conservatives, liberals nor the radicals, who are supposed to be advocates of subcultural theory, considered violence committed by the Muslim community in the subcultural context. This failure and the lack of understanding on the part of official bodies generated the feeling that the Salman Rushdie case was a deliberately organised plot against the beliefs of Muslims for international political considerations (Appignanesi and Maitland, 1989; Ahsan and Kidawi, 1993).

While British Muslims felt that they were a target of a planned attack, they were also blamed by all sections of society, from the media to official bodies, for violating one of the most fundamental human rights; freedom of expression and speech. The insult and violations of Islam in Salman Rushdie's book were hardly considered. Iqbal Sacranie, joint convenor of the UK Action Committee on Islamic Affairs, summed up the resentments and feelings of British Muslims when the Prime Minister John Major met Salman Rushdie. "We have two million citizens in this country who have no legal remedy against Rushdie's gratuitous abuse and yet the Prime Minister seems to be concerned with the rights of one individual" (Sacranie, 1993).

It has become evident that it is not always possible to reconcile two different cultures in such sensitive areas. This was not only a conflict between right and wrong, but a conflict between two cultures based upon entirely different values and norms. The rights of free expression, without any limitation, established according to Western values and norms is not accepted by Islamic culture. Since subcultural theory attempts to place the behaviour of people in the context of their subculture, it was perfectly possible to rationalise the reaction of the Muslim community when examined in the context of their subculture.

The following quotation, taken from Lea and Young (1984) affords an excellent example how this theory can be applied to a particular situation;

> It [the subcultural theory] does not explain human action in terms of the propensity of particular individual....Rather, it suggests that individuals can only be understood in terms of the subcultures of which they are a part (Lea and Young, 1984, p.83).

The surprising point is that one such attempt is apparent in a passage from Le Bon in which he argues that, "The mental constitution of crowds is not to be learnt merely by a study of their crimes, any more than that of an individual by a mere description of his vices" (Le Bon, 1969, p.19). This implies that rationality of individual and collective violence cannot be analysed by merely examining the act of violence itself but it has to be examined in its subcultural context. Ultimately, we may still not justify acts of violence, committed by sub-culturally motivated individuals or crowds, but we can understand the rationale behind these acts of violence, from the point of view of the perpetrators.

What contemporary crowd theorists failed to see is that there are more non-material than material causes for discontent. The causes of disorder, which Smelser describes as strain, may arise from the lack of non-material as well as material demands. Smelser (1962) rightly regards deprivation as the most frequent source of strain which gives rise to hostile outbursts, which for him can be real or threatened, absolute or relative. Neither Smelser nor any other contemporary crowd theorists have emphasised the importance of abstract social values (e.g. religious freedom, social acceptance etc.) as grievances. They failed to acknowledge that in relatively more developed countries non-material demands gain priority compared with material grievances. If the individual is denied these social values the desire to obtain the same status as those who already possess them is created. For instance, not only the first immigrant generation but even the second generation who were born in Britain feel insecure in comparison with the host community.

This has been one of the reasons why if the police stops a member of an ethnic minority group they feel discriminated against by the police. This is a feeling which can be called relative insecurity similar to relative deprivation. Whatever economic condition affects minorities, they still feel insecure because they belong to a minority group, rather than to the host community. Moreover, events such as the Salman Rushdie affair give a clear message to ethnic minorities that they do not have the same protection the law provides the host society. Relative insecurity does not always stem from direct discrimination. Since the main source of this feeling is from within ethnic minorities themselves, even if the host community treat them in the same way as they treat each other, the possibility of having this feeling still remains.

Immigrant communities know perfectly well that they are comparatively more comfortable in the host country, but they compare themselves with the host community rather than with a similar peer group in their own countries. The researcher's personal contact with the Muslim community, in Leicester, over a period of four years, has revealed that they live in constant fear and uncertainty about their future. Even some members of minority groups believe that there is always the possibility of one day being forced to go back to their native countries. It seems as if the members of ethnic minority groups live in a constant fear of repatriation. The fear of repatriation belongs not only to the first generation, but also the second and third generations seems to inherit this fear, despite the fact they are taught at schools that they have the equal rights as the rest of the society.

An extreme version of this simmering discontent can be seen in Bosnia, where community divisions have erupted into full-scale war. Another example is Germany, where rights of citizenship have been awarded to ethnic minorities but where this citizenship is largely ignored by the dominant culture. The Turkish community in Germany are subject to frequent attacks similar to the situation in the UK, where British Asians are targeted for abuse and violence.

This insecurity is not to be understood in its narrow sense, as a physical threat to their lives. The majority feel much more secure in terms of a physical threat than in their own countries. It is an emotional and cultural security that is lacking one can only feel in his/her own country. What is more, there has been a real increase in the number of racial attacks on members of ethnic minorities in major European states, such as Germany, France and England (Francis and Matthews, 1993; HMSO, 1993; Karim, 1993; Elamin, 1993; Jones, 1993; Winstone, 1993; Leech, 1995).

Neither the improvement of political and social conditions nor economic conditions can provide any feeling of security and it seems very difficult, if not impossible, to eradicate this feeling. Moreover, as Malise Ruthven remarked following the Salman Rushdie case, "...in Britain relations between the Muslim and host communities have been set back, possibly by a decade or more" (Appignanesi and Maitland, 1989 p.160-161; Ahsan and Kidawi, 1993, p.244). This can only be a source of regret.

What is more, frequent racially motivated attacks on members of ethnic minority groups, (*Police Review*, 1993;Volume 101, Number 5234: 7; *Trends*, 1994, Vol. 5, Issue 6; Bunglawala, 1994; Joseph and Hannon, 1994; Rabia, 1994) has a detrimental effect on the integration of ethnic minorities into 'Britishness'. "The climate of racist violence has steadily risen, and there were an estimated 140, 000 attacks on black and Asian people last year [1993]" (*Workers News*, 19 March, 1994).

Multi-racial societies, such as the UK and USA, are bound together with a unifying concept, common standards or at least some mutual material benefits. These concepts can be 'Britishness', for a UK citizen, or being a noble 'American citizen' for an American. These unifying concepts will serve their purpose as long as they provide 'something' to their members. When these concepts fail to serve their purpose, other concepts and identities, such as Welsh, Scottish, or Muslim, Hindu or Christian becomes more dominant and leads to alienation from the ruling ideology. When communal identity dominates the national identity, those who have a strong communal identity do not feel themselves as secure as the host community. This inevitably leads to 'relative insecurity' when coupled with institutionalised racism, and erupts as crowd violence following racially oriented attacks, (*Police Review*, Vol. 101, Number 5234, 1993, p.7), from what is considered to be the host community. This does not lead to the conclusion that the unifying concept, a national identity, should eliminate minority identities.

Historical evidences show that it is perfectly possible to maintain a unifying identity, which binds all citizens, while maintaining communal identities. In fact, communal identities are not the result of multi-racial society; even one nation societies might have various communal identities in terms of religion, sect or even political ideology. As in the case of Ottoman State, the unifying concept may embrace all communal identities and religious identities. The state falls apart when this concept fails to function.

Relative insecurity is not only strengthened by uninstitutionalised individual attacks. The existing political arrangements may, deliberately or unintentionally, create the institutionalised exclusion of certain groups. As Waddington et al. (1989, p.160-161) has pointed out, "...where a group can express its dissent through established channels within the framework of parliamentary democracy, the political system will appear as in principle amenable to change and influence. The opposite case is that of 'marginality', where the group is, or feels, effectively disenfranchised, under-represented by the system". This was the case when British Muslims, in the early stages of the Salman Rushdie affair, tried to find a political and peaceful solution.

> Muslim leaders did not translate the offensive passages in Urdu or Arabic for fear of provoking violent reactions among their followers. They quietly pursued the matter with the publishers, members of Parliament, the attorney- general and the Prime Minister. Many of them did not at this stage ask for a ban on the book...(Parekh, 1989, p.44).

Though Muslims were intensely frustrated and angry, and though isolated individuals spoke of violence, no Muslims threatened Rushdie's or his wife's life, or even threw a stone at him or his house - something any one of the thousands of hot-heads could have easily done at a time when he was unguarded and vulnerable. Neither Salman Rushdie nor the publishers took them seriously enough to engage in a dialogue with them (Parekh, 1989, p.44). Their plea was unheard and they felt politically mariginalised and under-represented against what they saw as a well planned and organised attack on their religion. Muslims saw the British state as an immutable and hostile institution; an institution over which they had no control or influence (Waddington et al., 1989, p.161). They saw violence as the only means by which they could achieve their ends and defend their beliefs.

As E. Mortimer (1991, p.11) has put it "...in the Western perception of such incidents, violence by Muslims is always magnified, violence against Muslims ignored and downplayed". The British Press was just as dismissive and "...almost the entire British Press got emotionally unhinged and lost its balance" (Parekh, 1989, p.45). They mocked the Muslims, accused them of 'intolerance', and wondered if a tolerant society should tolerate the intolerant. They were called 'barbarians', 'uncivilised' and 'fanatics'. The book-burning incident, which took place in 14 January 1989, led to a torrent of denunciation.

> Hardly anyone appreciated that the burning of The Satanic Verses was more an act of impatience than of tolerance, and that it bore no resemblance to the Nazi burning of libraries and persecution of intellectuals. No one cared to point out either that a few months earlier several Labour members of Parliament had burnt a copy of the new immigration rules outside the House of Commons without raising so much as a murmur of protest (Parekh, 1989, p.44-45).

The Muslim community was also accused of ignorance for failing to apply critical faculties to the text itself. However, the power of the written word in shaping ideological forces is well-known. A British Prime Minister, William Gladstone, once held the *Qur'an* in his hand and said: "So long as there is this book, there will be no peace in the world"

(Zakaria, 1991, p.59; Bennett, 1993). From an Islamic viewpoint, of course, Gladstone was merely using the text, the *Qur'an* symbolically to illustrate the power of Islam which could not be brought under Colonial power. Gladstone admitted that he had not read the *Qur'an*, but it represented, as did Rushdie's work, an intrinsic and threatening cultural value. It was an awareness of these religious and cultural values inherent in Rushdie's work that so enraged the Muslim Community, who also recognised the power of the written word.

What is more, Gladstone's remarks were echoed in the Islamic world in a slightly different form creating anger and hatred as many Muslims believed Gladstone saying that 'As long as this book [holding the *Qur'an* in his hand in the House of Commons] remains in the hands of Muslims we will never be able to dominate them'.

Prejudices do not die, they thrive on hostility and affect the judgement of even the best people. What the Salman Rushdie case has once more demonstrated is that creating a sensitive and compassionate community based on mutual respect and concern is a collective task requiring the efforts of not just the politicians but of all individuals within society especially academic establishments and creative writers. It must also be acknowledged that the cultural schism is too wide to narrow and that tolerance is the best hope.

Summary

Within this chapter 'poverty' and 'deprivation' have been examined under the subtitle of socio-economic grievances and it has been concluded that they are not and cannot be the primary cause of crime and collective violence unless individual and subjective considerations are taken into account. The effects of political and social arrangements for example are usually to be understood with the individuals' own biological, psychological and cultural specificities. Failings of political and social settings, which will be called as *institutional* factors, might create grievances, such as 'lack of political representation' and this leads to 'relative insecurity'. These are not easy to understand without taking into account the non material aspects of the individual which will be called *constitutional* factors.

The following chapter will be devoted to explaining the complex interactions between the individual's own specificities and the role of external factors on the individual. The model, which will be called the Combined Factors Approach, will explain collective violence as well as individual crime as a direct result of these combined factors.

6 Combined Factors Approach and Crime and Disorder

Introduction

> ...deprivation and other key variables such as legitimacy are fundamentally social-psychological, relation to expectations, evaluations, or temporal comparisons that can only be manifested within individuals (Rule, 1988, p.212).

In the previous chapters various types of crowd have been examined (chapter two and three) and it was concluded that the behaviour of crowd participants is influenced by and constitutes two integral parts: the physical components (chapter three) i.e. the crowd itself and the police and agents of social control as a counter crowd. The leaders or leadership is a factor which determines the kind of action which both crowds will take. The psychological components of crowd behaviour have been examined through concepts such as 'suggestibility', 'rationality' and the 'collective mind'. These theories and concepts, which were put forward mainly by classical crowd theorists, have been handled with caution by the modern crowd theorists as they indirectly, if not directly, imply the refusal of the importance of the social context.

The research has also discovered a direct and crucial relationship between the nature of the state and some of its institutions such as the police and the army (chapter four). The interactions between crowds and these institutions also draws attention to the problem of political violence and related social issues.

This research argues that disorder and crime are an end product of multitudes of factors, and are not explicable by a single cause nor can its causes be easily generalised. In order to demonstrate this argument, poverty and deprivation have been used as an example and it is shown that these are not, and cannot be, the cause of crime in general nor of collective disorder in particular. Crime is the end product of failings in areas which not only affect the physical human body but also the non-material side of human beings. In chapter five, lack of political representation and relative deprivation were given as examples of this. In addition, the researcher has also coined a new concept, 'relative insecurity', which seems to be a more tangible way of considering the operation of the CFA model on crowd events involving ethnic minorities (chapter five). As the following account will demonstrate this cannot be understood without taking *constitutional* factors into consideration (chapter six).

In line with this argument, the research has introduced its own approach to crime and disorder which incorporates the two integral parts of human behaviour. The remainder of this chapter is a detailed account of the CFA model. However, before moving on to the details of the model, it must again be stressed that this research, rather than introducing a new and complete model of disorder, aims to draw the attention of future researchers to the need to take into account a multiplicity of factors. The model, as an alternative to the existing theories in the field, seems to be very immature as it is not applied to all the events which took place within the research period. However, one observation is used as a case study in order to give an idea how the model can be applied to crowd events. The implication of the model to public order policing practices is more visible in chapter seven in which the model is applied to public order policing.

Combined Factors Approach

The Combined Factors Approach model tries to explain crime and disorder in terms of a lack of material and non-material basic needs. It argues that it is not the lack of or maladjustment of only one of these two elements but rather the combination of these two integral parts which leads to crime and disorder. Most modern criminological theories, particularly the radical and liberal approaches, have focused on social factors, while conventional theories give priority to 'criminal nature' type explanations. Current examinations of the effect of biological and social differences on crime produce a dilemma, namely the long-standing controversy between environmental (nurture) and biological (nature) orientations in the social sciences. The questions raised by this dilemma are: are we 'blank slates' ultimately defined by social and cultural forces, or are we genetically predetermined organisms with prescribed roles to play? Is our behaviour malleable and perfectible or is it constrained and resistant to change? Are we inherently gentle and altruistic, or are we aggressive, even violent beings, barely civilised by our culture? More specifically, are the criminals in our society 'born' or 'made', a product of their biology or of their environment?

Constitutional factors are the source of non-materially oriented grievances. Although they are subject to modifications by environmental and social factors, non-material grievances mainly derive from constitutional factors. On the other hand, any maladjustment or injustices in social and political arrangements create materially oriented grievances such as poverty and deprivation. However, it must be acknowledged that the distinction between non-material and material grievances are largely invisible as they are usually interrelated in complicated ways.

All the observations carried out have concluded that to explain collective action as merely the outcome of social settings is an inadequate explanation of the mobilisation of masses and their violence. Rather, crowd behaviour, as with individual behaviour, is subject to various external and internal factors which operate at different stages. For instance, the formation of crowds is caused primarily by social factors while the behaviour of crowd participants and crowds at interactional levels is more determined by biological and psychological than social factors. These two factors, which will be defined as constitutional and institutional, work in combination at all stages of crowd behaviour. However, the influence of these factors may gain priority over one another at certain stages.

Taking one aspect from a particular crowd event and attempting to explain it by using only one factor only raises more questions. For example, how do we explain a crowd movement which does not involve violence, while a similar crowd or even a smaller crowd causes serious violent disorder? If the violence in crowded settings was caused by environmental and social factors, we would expect to experience violent confrontation at all crowd events which take place in the same environment and social setting. Similarly, if we assume the removal of 'biological and psychological' influences on crowd behaviour, we will encounter the same problem in explaining crowd violence. Disorder at situational level is more a result of immediate factors rather than being a result of the long term relationship between two groups, that is the police and the crowd.

The CFA model, as the name implies, combines *constitutional* (biological and psychological) and *institutional* (Environmental and Social) factors in the production of individual crime and collective disorder. This model, which attempts to explain the inner workings of human behaviour, is universal and inclusive and therefore covers 'deviant' behaviour as well as 'normal' and 'acceptable' behaviours. However, this model is not simply an amalgamation of existing crime and disorder theories. Rather it is a unique way of approaching the problem of crime and disorder by incorporating the previously introduced perspectives.

It has become clear from the previous chapter that political perspectives in England and Wales, which have been broadly classified as *conservative*, *liberal* and *radical*, mostly explain crime and disorder as the outcome of material grievances. Even the conservative spectrum, which is supposed to perceive crime and disorder as the result of non-material qualities such as lack of parental control and educational attainments, tries to solve the problem of crime by offering materially oriented solutions such as the development of equal opportunities to compete in society in the anticipation that a just distribution of wealth will naturally occur. By doing this, they have been indirectly accepting the materially oriented explanation offered by the liberals and radicals. Since all of these explanations rotate around material factors it is more appropriate to classify them as materialistic approaches.

While the conservatives see crime and disorder as a manifestation of behaviour which is psychologically generated, they paradoxically offer materially oriented solutions, which do not relate to the root cause of the violence. Conservative arguments seem to be placing the blame on the individual, while most, to varying degrees, acknowledge the effects of environment. Contrary to the conservative argument the view that crime and disorder is caused by social forces and that the individual is not entirely to blame for their behaviour is still widespread. The liberals and the radicals seem to be focused on the material side of grievances, mostly ignoring the non-material. Riots, according to the liberals, reflect a socially defined situation while the radicals regard riots as politically motivated struggles.

Although these political perspectives dismiss the conservative argument which is based on human nature and psychology, they try to explain the immediate causes of disorder by focusing on psychological explanations. Theories generated by radicals, such as political marginalisation, relative deprivation, and subcultural theories seem to be all subject to the psychological state of individuals. They are highly subjective and heavily dependent on human psychology (chapter five).

To summarise, observations have led to the conclusion that crowd behaviour is not, and cannot be entirely determined by social factors. Even the most materially oriented crowd behaviour involves some non-material factors which will be defined in the forthcoming pages as *constitutional* factors. These include variations in the psychological state of an individual under certain circumstances as well as certain innate drives and traits which are acquired at birth (Glueck and Glueck, 1962; Berkowitz, 1968; Unal, 1993, p.92). Strong evidence has been found showing that even in crowd events, caused by absolute deprivation, the role of human nature explanations such as 'greed' and 'selfishness' were noticeable as well. After outlining the CFA model, which aims to provide an insight to the origins of crime and disorder, it will be applied to a case study which is the 'destruction of Squatter's Houses' in Izmir, Turkey (observation 12).

Constitutional Factors (Biological and Psychological)

Various explanations have been advanced in order to explore the genesis of human behaviour. It was assumed that nature or nurture controlled particular behaviours. Later, attention was drawn to the 'contributions' of genes and experience. Now it is clear that these factors are intertwined in complex ways. On the other hand, many social scientists either deny the importance of non material factors altogether, or argue that they are at best only marginally involved in human behaviour.

The CFA model, however, argues that collective behaviour, as all other forms of human behaviour is shaped by two kinds of reinforcers; primary and secondary, or immediate and remote (figure 6.2). A primary reinforcer derives its strength from *constitutional* factors, an innate drive or trait, such as hunger, sexual appetite or aggression; a secondary reinforcer derives its strength from the social and physical environment by learning. These are broadened in the model and presented as *constitutional* factors, which constitutes and affects 'free will' in choosing which action an individual will take, and *institutional* factors, which have a crucial role in shaping 'free will' and affect individuals' responses in decision-making (Unal, 1993, p.92).

Constitutional factors are a composite of innate drives, feelings, beliefs, and values. Although beliefs and values may be seen as a product of social institutions such as the family and religion, their effect on individual behaviour is usually observed to be associated with rather subjective and psychological forms. It is plausible to classify them under two main areas: biology and psychology. They are open to influence and are shaped by various external factors such as the environment and social arrangements. In other words, constitutional factors can be modified, to a certain extent, by institutional factors. Institutional factors include all the social institutions which are relevant to the material necessities of human beings, from basic needs such as food, accommodation and clothes, to status and wealth and so on. Those institutions range from the smallest social unit, the family, to the wider social environment i.e. schools, religious institutions, the media, the state and its control agencies.

There is no need here to elaborate that human beings have a number of in-built feelings and emotions. Therefore, the CFA model presupposes the existence of innate drives and individual traits such as 'aggression' and 'cowardice' as primary reinforcers as it is not feasible to argue that all human feelings are entirely acquired after birth from the environment and social settings (chapter five).

The CFA also accepts individual variations in those innate traits. An individual, for example, may display tendencies towards aggressive or cowardly behaviour. This tendency may be modified by events (figure 6.1). Those individual innate traits and social settings interact to affect human behaviour. A given trait, for example, may magnify or reduce the effect of some social adversity; the magnification or reduction may be additive or multiplicative. On the other hand, the extent and degree of influence these in-built and innate attributes and individual traits have on crime will perhaps remain a mystery, as the existing studies and theories are unable to explain all the complex interactions.

Regarding the specific topic of the research, the concept of 'aggression' has a particular significance (Berkowitz, 1968, p.14-17). Numerous hypotheses have been advanced to explain human aggression and although many have been subsequently discounted by scientific authorities, some persist in specialist fields and/or popular writing. Aggression is often simplistically described as "...the fighting instinct in beast and man which is directed against members of the same species" (Lorenz, 1972, p.ix). One of Freud's psychoanalytical claims about aggression was that such behaviour was a consequence of redirected thanatos (death wish) that could otherwise lead to suicide. Lorenz, who was certainly much influenced by Freud, developed the view that there was an intrinsic drive for aggression which was part of the genetic endowment (Lorenz, 1972; Brain, 1990, p.26). His view was that aggression was part of our animal inheritance and that the activities involved helped to make social groups more cohesive. Lorenz also suggested that formalised competition (e.g. the Olympic games) could be a means of containing the negative consequences of these activities (Brain, 1990, p.35). There are also other views such as Gurr's assertion that aggression results from relative deprivation (Gurr, 1968).

The word 'aggression' has rather negative connotations, and has usually been associated with violence and the use of force. In contrast to the commonly held view Unal (1993a, p.22-30) and Unal (1993b, p.8-9, 64 and 156) regard aggression as an extreme form of an innate drive which he calls the 'power of passion and anger', which is presented as a rather neutral attribute which can be positively as well as negatively used. Figure 6.1 which is inspired by this perspective illustrates how the 'power of anger and passion' may be manifest in individuals from one extreme to another. For Unal, aggression itself is not an individual innate drive, rather it is an extreme form of another drive which may be manifested at various levels under differing circumstances. For example, when aggression is used as a counter force it might be called self-defence and praised, rather than being regarded as negative behaviour.

It is also asserted that aggression necessarily involves arousal (Meier, 1968, p.36). Arousal is a psychological term applied to evidence of internal changes including alterations in heart-rate, respiration and the distribution of blood in the tissues. Oerton (1968, p.28) argues that, "...the two most basic and important drives with which we are born are in fact the drives of 'sex' and 'aggression' ". Here, he uses the word 'drives' to mean the emotional forces which move people to act in a particular way. It is necessary to finally note, however, that 'aggression', like any other behavioural concept, is influenced by diverse factors, which are difficult, if not impossible, to disentangle (Berkowitz, 1968). These factors have been reduced into two main categories for purposes of this thesis; these are environmental and social factors and they will be examined in detail in the following pages.

Institutional Factors (Environmental and Social)

Institutional factors cover all non-constitutional factors ranging from the immediate environment the family, neighbourhood, school and the media to the physical environment and climate. However, there are other situational and environmental factors found to be related to aggression and violence such as heat, noise and architectural design. Some early sociologists have drawn our attention to the possible influence of climate and season, and particularly heat, on human behaviour (Lombroso, 1968; Ibn Khaldun, 1987; Lacassagne, cited in Ginneken, 1992). As these factors seem less useful as predictors of violence for individuals they will not be discussed in detail. However, the influence of the physical environment cannot entirely be dismissed as the layout of the streets and lack of open spaces and recreational facilities are acknowledged, by some contemporary social scientists, as contributory factors to certain crimes committed by young people (Newman, 1973; Clarke, 1978; Gurr, 1980; Wolfgang and Weiner, 1982, p.308-310). Waddington et al. (1989, p.165), for instance, argue that "Space can of itself be more or less conducive to disorder, since it structures the room for manoeuvre for protestors and police". They further argue that:

> Planning may structure the *situation* of the protest. Physical layout, specific space which is being contested, and the visibility and symbolism of targets may all vary in each situation but remain constant as crucial factors (Waddington et al., 1989, p.169).

However, it has been argued that the influence of social factors exceeds that of environmental factors and physical design (Clarke, 1978, p.43). 'Anonymity', which is an inevitable consequence of city life, may also have some contributory effects. However, this theory places a special emphasis on immediate and institutionalised factors such as the family, religion, schools and the media, without entirely denying or overestimating the possible influence of the physical environment.

The primary reinforcers of human behaviour, *constitutional* factors, are greatly influenced by the secondary reinforcers, *institutional* factors: the environment, society and its institutions, the family, religion, the media and various aspects of the educational and training process. Social settings or the environment do not create aggressive individuals but may magnify or reduce the aggressiveness of an individual. Society, by the institutions it produces and the values it sustains, may also affect the extent to which families and communities are able and willing to inculcate a conscience, and instil a concern for others among its members that make an orderly society possible. Society also, either directly or through the agency of one of its organs, plays a moderating or modifying role among its members and groups, "...for it is the only moral power superior to the individual, the authority of which he accepts" (Durkheim, 1952, p.249).

The society and social environment, ranging from the closest environment, the family, to the wider environment and all social institutions, particularly the media, may play an important role in the shaping of these existing innate traits. However, society's role is limited rather than being the main creative force of an individual's characteristics. As the most powerful and highest state institution the government plays a substantial role in the shaping of smaller institutions. As Benyon (1994a, p.1) has clearly stated "One of the principle objectives of good government is to achieve and maintain civil order". This clearly requires the state to intervene into relationships between different social and economic classes. "Structural conflicts are always [supposedly] mediated through the state, in its role as moderator of sectional interests" (Waddington et al. 1989, p.159). However, Hoffman, (1992, p.22) argues that states emerge because people cannot resolve conflicts of interest simply through informal pressures. Hoffman deploys Bull's definition of the state as "...an institution which seeks to promote order in a disorderly way" (Hoffman, 1992, p.11). It has been further demonstrated in the previous chapter that the controversial role of the state has a profound influence in certain crowd events such as the Miners' Strikes of the eighties and the anti Poll-Tax demonstrations of the late eighties and early nineties.

Since individuals in society are subject to varying degrees of modification, the degree or the quality of action may vary between good and evil, in much the same way as individuals vary. For instance, each human being has the 'power of anger and passion', which is one of the innate drives involved in the commission of violent crimes. However, its manifestation may vary between individuals depending on the influence of their immediate and remote environment. The 'aggressive' drive, for instance, may occur very rarely in some individuals and frequently in others; it may appear suddenly, in response to events and blow over almost as quickly. Figure 6.1 demonstrates the power of 'anger and passion' manifested in various degrees ranging from one extreme, 'cowardice', to the other, 'aggression'. Between these two extremes there is 'valour', which is supposed to be the ideal state of this feeling in an individual.

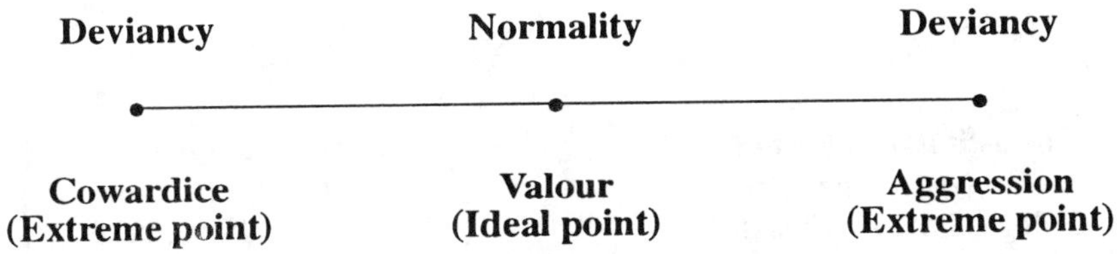

Figure 6.1: Illustrates how an innate drive such as 'power of anger and passions', manifests itself in various degrees and forms in one individual.

The argument of this model is that crime and disorder appear to stem from a combination of both *constitutional* (primary-biological and psychological) and *institutional* (secondary- environmental and social) influences on human behaviour. Accordingly, there is a social behaviour that develops in intimate settings out of complex interactions of constitutional and institutional factors, and this influences how individuals choose between the consequences of alternative behaviours. However, the model incorporates the *primary* (biological and psychological) factors with caution, as the model includes innate drives and genetic factors, without embracing a view of the so-called criminal as an atavistic savage or any other sort of biological anomaly. Although this model argues that much behaviour, including crowd behaviour and disorder, is affected by innate drives, this does not mean that violent acts committed in crowded settings are committed by 'born violent individuals' with uncontrollable, antisocial drives.

Not only collective action but all forms of human action, including crime and disorder, must be considered in the light of these mutually inclusive and combined factors. Therefore, crime and disorder as with normal social and peaceful behaviour, are the end product of this complex process. This implies that even the most materially oriented crime, theft, has something to do with other factors and motives, and cannot be a direct result of poverty or relative deprivation, which are mostly regarded as failings at an institutional level. According to this view as each human action is the product of two combined elements and is made by using 'free will', each individual is responsible for his or her actions and these actions have a basis in rationality (Unal, 1993, p.61). However, to rationalise a particular action does not necessarily make it right or justifiable just because it is a product of the human mind.

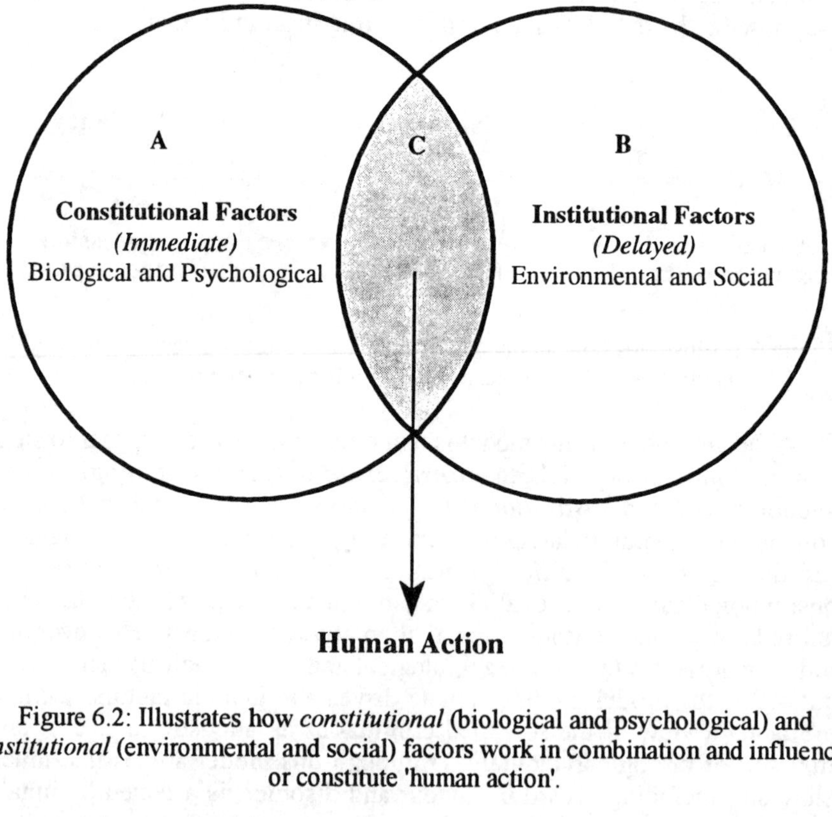

Figure 6.2: Illustrates how *constitutional* (biological and psychological) and *institutional* (environmental and social) factors work in combination and influence or constitute 'human action'.

Figure 6.2 illustrates how these two factors constitute and affect human action on an individual basis. In the figure, the constitutional factors (biological and psychological) are circled as **A** and institutional factors (environmental and social) are circled as **B**. These two circles intersect at point **C**, which is where human action derives. It is argued, in the CFA theory, that from this area it is equally possible to produce good or evil actions. It is up to each individual to decide what action they will take by using their free will. Although each individual is capable of choosing good or evil, the decision they make is heavily influenced by institutional factors; the environment and social settings.

Crowd behaviour and disorder can be seen as a wide manifestation of this feeling in more complex ways than individual violence. An individually committed violent act may be motivated by one or two dominant elements, but since the crowd is made up of a large number of individuals their violent actions may be influenced by numerous motives. This raises doubts about the radical view of the rationality of crowd violence.

As the term implies, collective behaviour and disorder are guided and motivated by various kinds of beliefs, feelings, assessments of the situation, wishes and expectations. Therefore, besides examining the material grievances which drift the crowd into violent action, it is important to explore the social, psychological and non-material states of each individual in the crowd. Since each individual's psychological state is closely related to his social and material environment, to examine crowd violence from the combined factors model does not completely deny the social import of crowd violence. This is something which both conventional and contemporary Western crowd theorists have failed to acknowledge.

While early crowd theorists over-emphasised the psychological aspects of crowd behaviour, contemporary theorists have concentrated on the social aspects of crowd violence, by oversimplifying non-material factors. Perhaps, the time has come for present-day social scientists to restore the balance, a task which is still far from being completed. However, the Combined Factors Approach model is eclectic, drawing from different and sometimes opposing schools of thought. It incorporates both genetic predisposition (internal factors) and social learning (external factors) and considers the influence of both primary (delayed) and secondary (immediate) factors. An individual act as well as collective action is sometimes best understood as a reaction to immediate circumstances and at other times as an expression of enduring behavioural disposition; both sorts of explanations have a place in the model. On this point it must admitted that it is not the intention of this study to undertake such a task, since this research will go no further than provoking future studies in this field.

Combined Factors Approach and Crime and Disorder

Not only crime and disorder but every human behaviour has its origin in a multiplicity of causes, often intertwined and confused, each of which we must, in obedience to the necessity of science, investigate singly. This multiplicity is generally the rule with collective disorder, to which one can almost never assign a single cause unrelated to the others. In line with this assumption, CFA model primarily reduces all possible causes of crime and disorder into two broad categories: *constitutional* and *institutional*. The effects of these mutually inclusive and combined factors on crime and disorder have been examined as a process towards a behaviour which some might call 'deviant and criminal' which others perceive as 'normal and meaningful'.

Finding a phrase which is not normatively committed posed difficulty as the terms *normal* and *deviant* behaviour, *vicious circle of crime* and *normal social behaviour* all have value laden connotations which pose difficulties to the researcher. In the following account, however, the process begins with the CFA model's figure (Figure 6.2) and it is assumed that the model works at all stages of this process. It has been left to the reader to name the end product of this process in line with his/her preferences.

Figure 6.3 which starts with the CFA model and consists of six stages, is an illustration of how this model works at various stages of a process towards crime and disorder. The model is applied to two types of materially orientated crimes; 'poverty related crimes' and 'white collar crimes'. The research argues that both the 'haves' and the 'have-nots' are subject to the CFA model; however, the end product of this process is not the same as the existing structural, social and political arrangements which are in favour of the strong and at the expense of the weak.

This model does not introduce a definite and definitive set of stages and expect all crowd events to follow these stages. What it suggests is that all stages, introduced by this model or any other, involve the combination of the broad factors at all stages. A crowd event, for example, might include a stage which may not be illustrated in this figure, or a stage which is illustrated in this figure might be missing in a crowd event. For instance, since not all crowd activities involve marginal groups and subcultures, the stage which refers to marginalisation may be missing from a particular crowd action. However, it is asserted that at all stages of a crowd movement, starting from underlying causes and mobilising factors to interactional level, crowd behaviour is always subject to two kinds of determinants and these are the inner dynamics of the crowd behaviour. Its manifestation may vary between countries and cultures. Smelser's (1962) and Waddington et al.'s (1989) model provides some viable explanations of this variation in the occurrence of violence under certain circumstances.

This research attempts to apply the CFA model to events portrayed by the media and the police as public order events. It also refers to white-collar crimes which do not attract popular attention nor become so-called public order events. In the observations, 23 events out of 33 have been identified as involving political and social motivations. The research has also identified that not only overtly contentious crowd events but also so-called peaceful events, such as the two mourning crowds of the late Turkish president Turgut Ozal and the Notting Hill Carnivals, have social, political and social motives. Regarding the so-called 'issue-less' leisure and entertainment crowds, the research has found no evidence referring to overt materially based political motives and factors. Therefore, the research's findings indirectly confirmed the studies carried out by Williams et al. (1986, 1987, 1988) and Dunning (1990), Dunning et al. (1986, 1990 and 1992) who argue that football violence has sociological and historical roots in the development of a specific recreational culture somewhat detached from a strict materialist base.

One common characteristic which the research has identified in relation to socially and politically motivated and contentious crowds events is that their participants are usually derived from the economically, politically and socially marginalised sections of society. The following six stages, in which the CFA model will be applied, the process towards to possible collective confrontation and disorder will be analysed. A special emphasis will be placed on white-collar criminals in order to show why they do not participate in disorder.

Stage one The process (Figure 6.3) begins with the CFA model (Figure 6.2) which demonstrates how *constitutional* (biological and psychological) and *institutional* (environmental and social) factors work in combination and can lead to deviant/normal behaviour. Stage one includes two combined elements, internal motives and external factors and the existence and workings of these two imaginary intersecting circles is assumed at all stages of this process.

A combination of material factors, which refer to social arrangements, and non material factors, which are related to individual, works at an individual level. For example, an individual does not participate in a crowd event, violent or otherwise, just because they are genetically and inherently violent. Participation is mainly determined as a result of unjust social settings and a perception of these arrangements. In other words, participation is determined, to some extent, by social arrangements and falls within the scope of sociology rather than psychology. This implies that crowds are not made up of psychologically motivated individuals, but socially deprived ones.

However, the research also asserts that the participation of an individual to a crowd and the nature of the act committed is very much influenced by the environment in which an individual has grown up and been nurtured. For example, a person who acquires religious beliefs and values from their immediate environment, (e.g. the family, religion, and education), may refrain from crime, although they may be relatively poor. On the other hand, a relatively rich person, who has money and status, belonging to the upper classes of society, may commit crimes because they lack non-material qualities and restraints. This demonstrates that contrary to popular belief, which attempts to explain crime as the simple result of lack of material or non-material necessities, these two elements are the integral parts of a whole. Lack of moral qualities may lead to crime and disorder when they are coupled with material inequalities and social injustice. The institutions which are responsible for this modification range from the immediate environment, the family and religion to the remote environment, society, education, the media and all other state institutions.

Stage two This stage refers to the state of the individuals who feel themselves deprived. This stage includes white-collar crime, as it sees the rich as well as the relatively deprived subject to a similar felt sense of poverty (chapter five). Any maladjustment or deprivation absolute or relative, of material and non-material needs, force or drift the individual to formulate an ideology which fits a way of life which they have to live rather than one which is chosen willingly. This is best stated in a Turkish proverb translated as; "If you do not live according to what you believe in, you might begin to believe as dictated by your living! " It indicates that the way in which each individual lives is determined by religious, secular and moral beliefs. If an individual fails to live according to their beliefs they then try to establish an ideology which fits their actual way of life and this is the basis of all subcultures which depart from dominant cultures. This assumption indicates that having been rejected by mainstream society for any number of given reasons, certain economically and socially marginalised groups, such as the Teddy Boys, New Age Travellers and the like, form their own subculture. The failure to have access to material and non-material necessities leads to deprivation, relative or absolute, and this results in the formation of a socially alien or deviant subculture.

Stage three The third stage of this model is about subcultures, which are in constant but indirect conflict with the dominant culture. The notions of 'lack of political representation' and 'relative security' (chapter five) are just two examples of the manifestation of economic and political marginalisation. The very existence and way of life of the politically, culturally, ethnically and sometimes religiously marginalised communities are considered as an opposition to dominant culture and mainstream society. Their demands, such as the attempts of the Muslim communities in the early stages of the Salman Rushdie case to solve the problem peacefully, are bound to fall on deaf ears and be considered not worthy of attention.

This stage also assumes that not only the so-called criminals but also the white-collar criminals belong to a subculture of their own. However, as they are not politically and economically marginalised they are accommodated by the existing social and political arrangements and their subculture is not considered as alien to the dominant culture. In fact, although the crime they commit is not accepted as normal even within their own subculture they remain as a part of their 'respectable' subculture as long as their crime is not noticed. And this is something which happens very rarely compared with the so-called ordinary criminals.

Stage four The undeclared but ongoing conflict between the marginalised subcultures and dominant cultures becomes more visible as the least powerful ones make some direct demands such as the Salman Rushdie case, or indirect demands by committing property crimes. Political and industrial demonstrations are a way of addressing the demands of the economically and politically marginalised in the form of collective action. However, property crimes committed by individuals can be seen as a more indirect expression of demands made of the existing arrangements. Even the perpetrators themselves may not be aware of the messages which can be taken from their acts (Berkowitz, 1968; Jenkins, 1968; Quarantelli and Dynes, 1968). As the individual criminal has no popular support or means of defence they are caught and convicted for the acts they commit.

On the other hand, despite the huge material cost and the moral damage caused by white-collar crimes, the numbers of the convicted white-collar criminals is still very minor (Sutherland, 1970; Geiss, 1970; Pearce, 1976; Palmer and Humphrey, 1990a-b; Croal, 1992). As the concealed conflict gradually becomes more overt and visible, it causes more discrimination, marginalisation and criminalisation (Hall, et al. 1987b; Keith, 1993, p.231-255) of the members of the sub-culture.

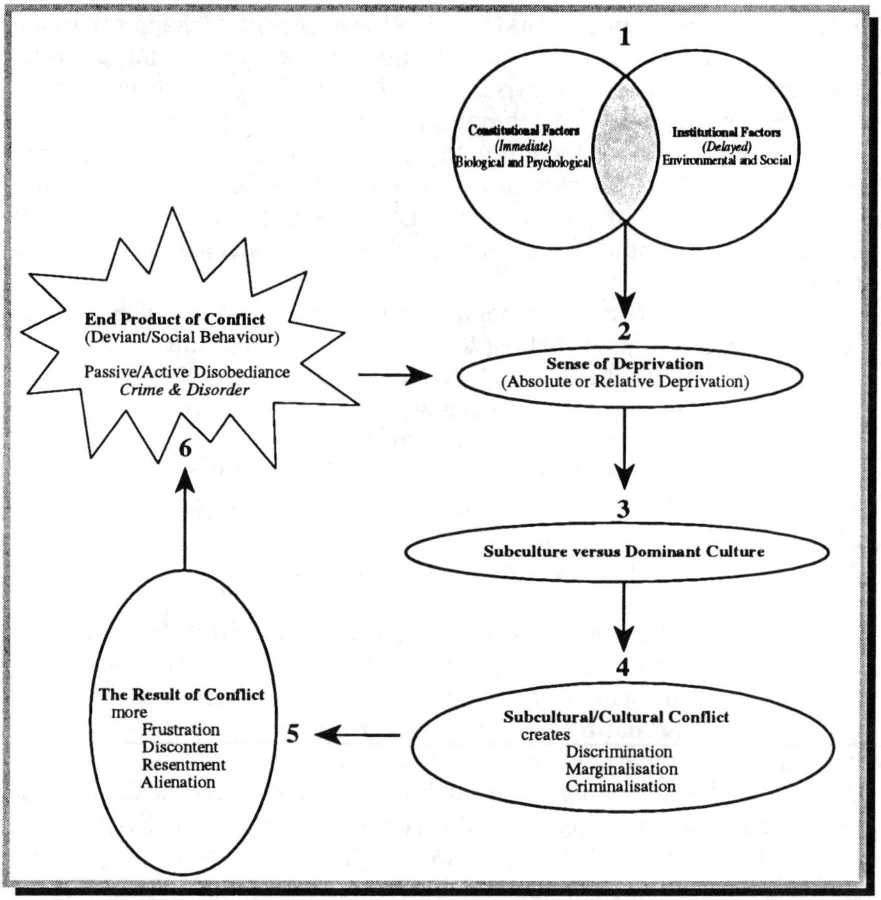

Figure 6.3: Illustrates the workings of the CFA at various stages of a given crowd event.

The state and its law enforcement agencies are very much in favour of the dominant ruling class of which the white-collar criminal is a part. In the light of Marxist argument it is indeed difficult to uphold the argument that the law is a neutral set of rules to which all are subject. The quotation from Anatole France that "The law in its majestic equality, forbids the rich as well as the poor to sleep under bridges, to beg in the streets, and to steal bread" (Anatole France, Le Lys Rouge, 1894, cited in Benyon and Bourn, 1989, p.15; Reiner, 1992, p.3), is worthy of quoting once more as it perfectly expresses the essential hypocritical and discriminative nature of the state and its institutions.

Stage five As the marginalised groups and individuals make direct or indirect demands from the existing political and economical arrangements, the nature of the state and its agencies becomes more rigid. As the conflict between the haves and the have-nots becomes more overt it produces more alienation, discontent and resentment.

Although the term marginalisation has often been deployed it would be misleading to regard the participants of all crowd events as marginalised and uprooted masses. The observations have revealed that most crowd activities, particularly political and industrial ones, attract solid working class citizens rather than uprooted masses. Their goals are rational, purposeful, and objective rather than irrational or anomic. In fact, it is rather difficult to deny the rationality and meaningfulness of large human gatherings since it is problematic to explain them by psychological motives without referring to a social and environmental context.

Stage six The last stage is the most overt product of this conflict; deviant behaviour or meaningful social behaviour is manifested in various forms, ranging from 'civil' and 'passive disobedience' to 'active crime' and 'disorder'. It is somehow problematic to define the end product of this circle. Therefore, the word 'product' has purposefully been chosen, deliberately avoiding the use of value laden concepts such as 'crime', 'criminal' or 'deviant' behaviour. As a universal concept for so-called crime has not been found yet, it is perhaps more appropriate to leave it open for the reader. What is crime and disorder for some may well be socially meaningful behaviour for others.

Figure 6.3, in confirmation of the first hypothesis of the research, asserts that at the final stages of the process, *constitutional* factors gain priority over *institutional* factors. The nature of crowd-police interaction is more subject to psychological determinants than sociological determinants. The import of constitutional factors can be acknowledged without entirely dismissing or undermining the role and import of the constitutional factors.

This figure, in confirmation of the second hypothesis, also reveals the essentially hypocritical nature of the state and its control agencies in their dealings with the acts committed by the weak and the strong. As demonstrated in figure 6.3 the criminalisation of acts or behaviour depends upon who commits them not the act itself. Consequently, participants of the riots and disorders mostly derive from economically and politically marginalised groups and communities. Although white-collar crimes victimise an important section of society directly and almost the whole of society indirectly, the perpetrators of these crimes are still rare compared to so-called ordinary criminals. White-collar people do not riot, not because they are less criminally inclined than the so-called riot participants, but because they have more concealed ways and means of committing crimes.

One important point revealed from the application of the CFA model to crowd events is that despite the fact that crowds are usually mobilised by economic, social and political motives, the actual occurrences of collective action and disorder are mostly associated with and legitimised by an abstract concept rather than being referred to overtly material profit or gain. This fact again demonstrates the validity of the CFA, which argues that not only in the first stages but also the last and contentious stage of collective action involves some non-material elements.

This research has found that crowd behaviour is mostly socially motivated rather than being psychologically derived. However, socially motivated acts are mostly associated with abstract concepts which have their origins within human beings; even the most materially oriented grievances erupt on the basis of abstract concepts rather than for a particular material gain. There is usually a need for a trigger incident, or a 'flash point' to spark off a riot. For instance, most of the inner city riots which have taken place in the United States and England in the last three decades, were triggered by an incident involving an unjust treatment of a young black by a white police officer. There would appear to be a direct relationship between the police and inner city riots. However, the reports (Scarman, 1983; Kerner Commission Report, 1968; Benyon, 1993) and studies which followed these riots have unanimously revealed that heavy handed police methods and dealings with a particular group are not and cannot be the only instigators of these events. This suggests widespread unjust treatment of a particular group by the dominant ideology. It is important to remember, however, that none of these events began as a reaction to existing social arrangements but in response to an isolated incident.

Human beings do not protest or riot just because they are hungry, but do so when others are unjustly satisfied while they were hungry. In the same way, crowds do not gather and demonstrate just because they were prevented from obtaining some material gains, but because they feel that they are treated unjustly by the system or the dominant groups. In the observations no evidence was found which suggests a direct relationship between poverty, absolute deprivation and disorder. Most grievances stem from a felt sense of injustice and are usually associated with an abstract and legitimising notion (chapter five). This applies not only to contemporary crowd events but also to historical events.

For example, in the last stage the conflict which, according to the argument of this model, is the result of failings in earlier stages, both material and non-material needs, justifies itself referring to some 'legitimising notions' (Waddington et al. (1989, p.8-9) quoted from Stevenson 1979, p.310) or an abstract concept such as *freedom*, *justice*, *equality* and so on. This demonstrates, according to the CFA model, that even in the final, 'interactional' level of a conflict, where human behaviour is guided more by *institutional* than *constitutional* factors, the behaviour of individuals as well as the crowd is still influenced by *constitutional* factors which are revealed in the form of legitimising abstract concepts and notions.

Injustices are not rare incidents and certain groups experience these all the time but injustice leads the mobilisation of masses, when it becomes visible and associated with an abstract concept. Crowds act for non-material causes more than material ones. Even the most materially oriented goals are usually associated with an abstract concept. Not only historical crowd movements such as the food riots of the eighteenth century (Benyon, 1987) but also contemporary crowd movements have always been associated with an abstract concept. Although the main reasons for riots have been unjust social arrangements, the crowds always seek an abstract concept, an idea, to justify their action. A crowd movement purely based on a material goal without an association with a non-material concept or idea is a rare event. It is for this reason that historically most of the successful mass movements which achieved the overthrow of totalitarian regimes, were mobilised by an abstract concept such as *freedom*, *equality* or *justice*.

A further example will be the crowd movements which took place in Russia in the name of abstract concepts such as freedom, equality and justice in early twentieth century. Although the revolution was sparked off and fuelled by the discontent which was based on material inequalities and injustices, the main factors which mobilised the masses were abstract. On the other hand, the same regime, which was established on the promise of providing equalities was overthrown after a period of less than a century in the name of the same abstract concepts: *freedom*, *equality* and *justice*. The lessons drawn from these experiences are that riots or crowd actions which are seemingly caused by social factors usually erupt in the name of non-material abstract concepts.

With regard to the behaviour of participants during a crowd event, psychological factors dominate sociological factors as the latter become less dominant and remote compared to the former. A crowd, which is made up of sociologically derived participants, acts under the influence of the present situation, what Waddington et al. (1989) call 'situational' factors. Sociological factors, which lead to gatherings of large numbers, become less dominant in the reasons for an individual joining a crowd, and the remote factors, what Wilson and Hernnestein (1986) call 'constitutional factors', become more apparent and influential (Berkowitz, 1968). Therefore, the behaviour of a crowd participant is mainly modified and shaped by situational factors. As the process gradually moves towards the interactional level, the behaviour of crowd participants in particular and the crowd in general becomes more psychologically determined. Therefore, at the final stage of this encounter a special importance should be placed upon *constitutional* (psychological) determinants without entirely ignoring the long term effects of the *institutional* factors.

During the occurrence of a crowd event, emotional concepts such as 'provocation' and 'intimidation' have a significance as they relate to types of policing practices, including tactics and equipment deployed. Consideration should be give to those concepts during the deployment of manpower and equipment in the form of a 'show of force'. Any mistreatment or overreaction in using these methods and tactics may lead to more visible forms of biological and psychological factors such as aggression and violence. The influence of the manner of the deployment of police and equipment upon constitutional factors and its possible consequences in causing disorder will be examined further in the following chapter.

Combination of Institutional and Constitutional Factors

The conclusions reached by this research have been utilised throughout the text rather than being collected under one main section. This is so for the reason that each chapter has its own specific conclusions, besides leading the research to a general conclusion. The implications of the general findings of the research is applied to public order policing practices in the following chapter.

Despite major differences in the characteristics of crowds and public order policing practices between the two countries the similarities found have afforded an opportunity to apply the CFA theory to the public order policing practices in both countries. The implications of the theory to public order policing practices will be incorporated into one chapter, dealing with both systems simultaneously.

Throughout this research observations were made, both in Turkey, England and Wales, at many crowd events (Appendix 1) which required the deployment of police public order units. After completing a number of observations the model of this research, the Combined Factors Approach, is outlined as a new approach, and observations were made in order to test whether observed events fitted the model. It is found that all observed crowd actions fit this model, which sees crowd behaviour as the result of failings or maladjustment at *institutional* and *constitutional* levels.

Demolition of 'Squatters Houses' in Izmir, Turkey

As the primary object of this study is to draw conclusions from observations in respect of public order policing practices in both countries, choosing an example and applying the model to this particular event will be satisfactory. The observation in question took place in 1992 in Izmir, Turkey, when over one hundred police officers were deployed to maintain peace during a demolition of squatters houses. Observations made during this event have led to the belief that the workings of the theory is valid for all the observations.

Before moving on to analysis of the observation it might be more appropriate to consider reasons why this example has been chosen. The first reason is that, the researcher was familiar with the social and economic situation of that particular area as he grew up in a similar area of the same city. Fifteen years ago he experienced and felt what those whose houses were being demolished were experiencing on that day. The second reason is that having experienced the same situation allowed him to explore the underlying causes of this event rather than focusing on apparent symptoms. Therefore, the observation of this event was relatively more complete compared to others. The researcher could also observe and understand both sides of the problem. As a person who lived in a similar area it was not difficult to understand local feelings and attitudes towards the police. Again, as a person who had worked in the police force as a uniformed police officer he was familiar with police perceptions of that particular situation. Although the Combined Factors Approach is universal and therefore must be applicable to all crowd events, the above mentioned reasons have made the workings of material (social) and non material (psychological) factors more visible for the researcher. The following account makes clear how the event involved the two factors of the CFA model.

The reason for the deployment of the police was to maintain peace and provide the security of the city council men to carry out the demolition. None of the basic services such as water supply, electricity and road, which were supposed to be provided before the construction of the houses were present. The rationale behind the demolition was that to provide these basic services after the construction of the houses would be very costly and difficult and this in itself necessitated the demolition of some of the houses. In fact the word 'house' is not the word to define these premises, because of their poor construction. Most of the so-called 'gecekondular' (squatters' houses) were built within a few days, by the people who are unable to stay in the rural areas because of the lack of job availability, and who were therefore forced to cities for economic and social reasons (Komur, 1992; Altayli, 1995; Turenc, 1995; Cem, 1995). From this respect the need to occupy a land and build a small hut for sheltering those who are in a desperate situation seems to be absolute deprivation.

However, as the CFA model maintains, even at this stage not all human activities are the result of absolute deprivation. For example, most of the dwellings were built by those who already occupied a neighbouring land a few years or moths ago and their presence subsequently recognised by the authorities as legitimate. One politician who was then the head of the opposition party, and now the President of Turkey, legitimised this type of housing by complimenting them as 'the flowers of our cities'. Big cities are surrounded by this type of housing site, which when viewed from the air, as politicians generally do, seem very attractive, like a flower garden surrounding the city. However, the life conditions in these slum areas are very poor and less picturesque.

Almost all political parties make similar promises which are barely possible to implement if they come to power. This type of promise and compliments, which curry favour with economically disadvantaged people prior to elections are not rare. Rather they are an integral part of corrupt political life in Turkey. The researcher had personally experienced similar things during his studentship of seven years when he was living in a different area of the same city.

This electioneering usually takes place prior to a general election when every political party is desperately in need of support from the working class communities. For example, it was widely acknowledged that one of the local mayoral candidates, who was elected as mayor during the destruction of the houses promised the people that if he was chosen as mayor he would legitimise these houses by giving them an ownership certificate called 'tapu'. After election it was he who gave the order for the dwellings to be demolished. By this time, many people from neighbouring sites, encouraged by empty promises, had moved to the site which was later demolished.

During the observation the researcher remained with the crowd and listened to their side of the story. Some of the arguments regarding the election promises were related to the researcher by the local residents during the observation. The researcher introduced himself as a research student from England, and people took him as a journalist. He was surrounded by people urging him to write their plea. Some of those whose houses were being demolished were complaining about the state saying that the state had provided accommodation for the Kurds who fled to Turkey during the mass execution of Kurds in Iraq in 1991-2. Others were referring to the influx of Turks from Bulgaria in the mid-eighties. In these two cases, the Turkish state had been seen to provide accommodation and social benefits for refugees while unjustly ignoring its native citizens. An old Kurdish lady was crying that 'Is it a fault to be a native citizen of this country'. On the other hand, some people who were observers rather than participants of the crowd, were telling quietly that in fact most of the people who built houses on the land already had other houses acquired a few years ago in the same way. It was again evident that at this event, which was caused to a great extent by absolute deprivation, the participants justified their act by referring to the sense of injustice and inequality.

Immediately after the demolition some of the people began moving their goods from demolished houses to their other houses. As an old resident of a similar area, the researcher admits that he tried to establish residence in two different parts of the city while he was a teenager and studying at a college. However, his last two attempts were unsuccessful as he had to leave for another city to continue higher education. His family still lives in a house in that area which was acquired in the same way, by occupying state owned land and building a slum on it before basic services were provided. The local government has now provided electricity, water, road and transport services to the area and the houses which were built 15-20 years ago are now recognised as legitimate and the owners of the houses will, hopefully, be given their official ownership certificate soon.

It is not easy to disentangle the constitutional factors from institutional ones. For instance, some members of that particular community acted in response to absolute deprivation which is mainly the result of failings at the institutional level. This is partly because the state failed to provide a desirable standard of living for country people and this led to the influx of people from villages to cities. In addition, political parties, far from providing city-based long term and stable housing facilities for those people, manipulated them for their short term political ends.

On the other hand, some members of that particular group, if not the majority, are not motivated by absolute deprivation. Their acts are to be explained more by relative deprivation, which is rather subjective. Therefore, even in this case, where the failings of institutional factors were quite visible, conservative arguments such as avarice cannot easily be dismissed. While some members of that community were suffering relative deprivation others were acting with sheer greed, to acquire a second house. In many cases people have squatted on a large site and after a while sold it to someone who cannot, or will not, build a slum house. In fact, the house which the researcher's family lives in now was acquired in this way. Of course the sale interaction was not legal or official, but was done informally, by 'gentleman's agreement'.

Demolition of illegally built houses is the result of misconduct and maladjustment at economic, social and political spheres which the CFA model sees as *institutional* factors. In recent years, police deployment during these demolitions has become a routine task for the police in major Turkish cities such as Istanbul, Ankara and Izmir. Although the houses built by economically deprived and marginalised people were regarded as illegal and their demolition constituted a public order problem, the same acts committed by the wealthy have been tolerated by existing political arrangements (Ozguven, 1995). In big cities especially in Istanbul there are certain areas which are occupied by the rich to build summer houses. Despite the high quality of their construction these houses are technically illegal and according to the law should be demolished in the same way. As these houses are mostly built on very valuable land overlooking the Bosphorous the construction of these houses is illegal environmentally too. Yet, the demolition of these houses is rare and what is more, if the destruction takes place it does not have as dramatic financial effect on the people who built these houses compared to the squatters' houses.

During the operation, questions were asked to find out how the residents felt about the police. It was discovered that there was no direct dissent against the police for the role they played during the demolition. They were perceived as 'Emir Kulu' (bound to obey orders) with no part in authoritarian decision-making. The main dissent was directed against the mayor for whom they voted a few months previously, believing that their houses would be saved from demolition. Some members of the crowd even suggested a demonstration in the city centre protesting against the mayor. An old lady was criticising the inhabitants for believing the mayor and building houses relying on his promises.

The police conduct during the demolition was surprisingly peaceful. The demolition was supposed to be carried out by city council officials and the reason for police presence was just to maintain the peace and prevent the crowd from intervening in the demolition. The demolition began at about 9 am when most of the men left home for work. This made the task easier by preventing clashes. However, some women protested and did not want to leave their houses, and some of them were taken to hospital for treatment for fainting. There was no attack on the police or the city council officials apart from a few attempts to throw stones by children. However, over-zealousness of a senior city council official, who was responsible for supervising the demolition, was perceived as provocative and almost sparked off a conflict.

Although the police presence might have been regarded as provocative in the Western context as they were fully armed and some of them were carrying shields, in fact there was no direct dissent towards the police. Two armoured police vehicles were also deployed which could have been perceived as provocative. However, the behaviour of individual police officers was quite restrained. During their deployment they seemed unhappy with what they were doing there. In fact, in the conversations with the rank and file officers, during the journey from the Public Order Unit to the site, almost all police officers made complaints about their deployment in an incident which was caused by the mistake of another institution.

Surprisingly, amongst the demolished houses one belonged to a city official who was working in the department responsible for the demolition of illegally constructed houses. He was not on duty on this day and his house was demolished along with the other houses. What is more, sometimes the police were the victim of the demolition as a house belonging to one of the chief inspectors, who was on duty on that day, was demolished a few weeks ago by the same unit. By way of a limited form of protest, during the lunch break some officers declined to have their lunch, which was provided by the City Council, in front of those whose houses were being demolished.

CFA and Modern Crowd Theories

It has been argued earlier that the CFA is a comprehensive model incorporating both the classical and modern crowd theories. Despite representing a unique approach to the problem of crime and disorder, it is greatly influenced by some comparatively recent crowd theories. In particular, these are Smelser's (1962) *Value Added Theory* and Waddington et al.'s (1989) *Flashpoints* model. In order to demonstrate the value of the CFA model amidst other theories these two theories have been chosen as constituent elements.

This research does not intend to introduce an entirely new and alternative crowd and disorder theory. In line with the first hypothesis it aims to draw attention to the need to examine the crowd behaviour from multitudes of factors and provide a multilayered account. Here, figure 6.3 illustrates the central theme of the research by combining *immediate* and *delayed* factors. This model, the research argues, can be applied not only to the observational examples carried out for this research, but also to other theories. For example, the CFA can be accommodated the Value Added Theory of Smelser (1962) and the Flashpoints model of Waddington et al. (1989), with only minor qualification. The existence and workings of the CFA model incorporate all stages of these models.

Inevitably, both modern and classical theories have played an important role in understanding disorderly crowds and shaping public order policing policies. Two modern theories which are the focus of this section have apparent similarities yet differ in nature when they are examined closely. One of the criticisms which can be directed to Smelser's model is that his theory, which starts seemingly as a well argued scientific argument, suddenly changes into a kind of 'public order manual' when it comes to advocate the 'short, sharp shock' theory of riot control. "When the authorities issue firm, unyielding and unbiased decisions in short order, the hostile outburst is dampened" (Smelser, 1962, p.265). Waddington et al. rightly finds Smelser's prescription for avoiding disorder more likely to cause it (Waddington et al. 1989, p.174).

On the other hand, the *Flashpoints* model, is perhaps the only modern theory, which "...combines reference to antecedent conditions (the 'tinder') with a highlighting of interpersonal interaction (the 'spark'), thus involving both psychological and sociological perspectives" (Waddington et al., 1989, p.2). However, despite this early acknowledgement, this work is mainly concerned with social factors paying less attention to psychological aspects of crowd dynamics. Importantly, the term *Flashpoint* implies a degree of 'spontaneity' in crowd behaviour.

The *Flashpoints* model is an accurate account of how and why disorder occurs in certain circumstances and it might be helpful in explaining many disorders which occur under similar conditions. However, it is problematic to accommodate all crowd events within this model as generalisations in crowd behaviour, as with many other social issues, raise many questions. M. Keith (1993) in *Race, Riots and Policing,* regards generalisations, by definition, as necessarily excluding the significance of the historically and geographically specific circumstances in which disorder is defined and appreciated (Keith, 1993, p.18). Yet the *Flashpoints* model tries to avoid making over specific generalisations at an early stage by classifying crowds events as 'issue oriented riots' and 'issue-less' (Waddington et al. 1989, p.16). However, a subtle response to Keith's concern about generalisations can be found in the *Flashpoints* model as it clearly states that, "Such a model should in principle be applicable to a whole range of situations, allowing differentiation between types of crowds yet remaining sensitive to the special features of any individual instance" (Waddington et al. 1989, p.156).

The second issue related to the *Flashpoints* model is the model's identification of events which are supposed to be the cause of violent confrontation. It can equally be argued, for example, that there may be many other incidents or interactions which might potentially be a flash point. They are called 'flashpoints' when they cause a violent confrontation otherwise they are seen as unremarkable incidents. As Waddington et al. (1989, p.3) themselves made it clear "...the crucial comparison needs to be with those events which superficially have all the attributes of a flashpoint but which never materialise as such". To clarify the difference between a flashpoint and an ordinary unremarkable event is obviously an area worthy of further study.

The Combined Factors Approach which is partly influenced and inspired by the *Flashpoints* model gives the details of the stages leading to the formation of a crowd. It also involves the crowd's interaction with various institutions of the establishment. Although the CFA model may imply a rise towards a violent confrontation, similar to that of the *Flashpoints* model, it does not regard the violence as an inevitable product of certain conditions and interactions. Depending on the nature of the social context, the cause protested against and the nature of the police response there is only a 'possibility' that the violence may break out at interactional level.

The main reservation that this research has about the *Flashpoints* model is the exact timing and expectation of disorder, an issue which social scientists are often pressed to comment on by policy makers. However, this is a point about which Waddington (1995) himself expressed his concerns not only in his published work (Waddington et al. 1989, p.177), but also at one of his latest presentations which took place at the CSPO, on 6 February 1995. Regarding the exact timing of the confrontation S. Hall (1987) seems to be quite right in his remarks that "No social scientist is able to say on this day or that day, at this hour or that hour, X or Y will trigger off social unrest" (Hall, 1987, p.48). The CFA does not assert that under certain and definite circumstances the violence will definitely occur. What it does is to define the stages of a process which leads to a possible confrontation. However, the occurrence of disorderly confrontation is very much dependent on the nature of the relationship between the crowd and the police at *interactional* level, a stage at which it is very difficult to identify what kind of behaviour will definitely lead to confrontation.

Although the initial intention of this research was not to apply the *Flashpoints* model to the observations, a close examination of CFA model shows a clear acknowledgement to the *Flashpoints* model. For example, the issues dealt with in chapter four of this book, such as 'the state', 'class', 'the police' and the 'political violence', clearly fall within the first three stages of the *Flashpoints* model, which identifies them as *Structural*, *Political/Ideological* and *Cultural*. Secondly, chapter seven includes issues which again fall within the last three stages of the Flashpoints model, *Contextual*, *Situational* and *Interactional*. The uniqueness of the CFA is that it combines *institutional* and *constitutional* factors at all stages of this process which cause a crowd to drift towards confrontation with the agents of social control, rather than seeing psychological imperatives playing a role only at the interactional level of the process.

Summary

In the third chapter of this book the internal dynamics of crowd behaviour have been examined and it was concluded that crowd behaviour and public order policing consists of two integral parts. The first part, the physical component of public order policing is made up of three physical elements: the crowd, its leaders or leadership and the police. The second part is mainly concerned with some crowd attributes which are mainly put forward by classic crowd theorists such as Le Bon and Tarde. These attributes include concepts such as 'irrationality', 'suggestibility', 'crowd mind' or 'collective mind' and 'collective disorder'. This book proposes that crowd behaviour is the result of two combined elements, mental and physical factors.

In line with this argument chapter six introduced a model of crime in general, and disorder in particular, as the combination of two factors on each individual. It was argued that neither individual crime nor disorder can be explained by a single factor. Crime and disorder are instead the result of maladjustment or failures to provide for the two basic needs of human beings, that is material and non-material (spiritual) needs. The Combined Factors Approach assumes that human behaviour is guided by both material and non-material factors.

After introducing a new theory on the genesis of human behaviour, the argument now moves on to the application of this theory on everyday policing practices. The next chapter will attempt to apply the CFA model into the existing arrangements. The application of the CFA on crime and disorder and its implications for public order policing practices would have two stages; that is long and short term implications. Short term implications are mainly concerned with the psychological elements of human behaviour at an interactional level, while long term arrangements are related to environmental and social causes of crowd behaviour. It is also stressed that the police response and arrangements in the short term might have long term derogatory effects on police and crowd relations.

7 Implications of the CFA on Public Order Policing Practices

Introduction

> No social scientist is able to say on this day or that day, at this hour or that hour, X or Y will trigger off social unrest, but it will follow, as night follows day, that such an excluded population with a deep sense of social injustice will sooner or later explode (S. Hall, in Benyon and Solomos, 1987, p.48).

The main theme and indeed one of the most important findings of this research is that crowd behaviour is caused and strongly influenced by *institutional* factors such as the state and its various agencies, particularly the police. *Institutional* factors play a dominant role in the formation of crowds at certain times and locations to express their dissent and opposition or their support and solidarity for a particular cause. However, these factors becomes less visible and dominant during the occurrence of actual crowd events, as remote factors such as biological and psychological conditions become more dominant. Accordingly, this research argues that during crowd events the behaviour of crowds, individual participants and even the police is more subject to psychological imperatives than to long-term social and political considerations.

The maladjustment of social and political arrangements, which cause the gathering of a particular crowd, are less visible and do not determine the outcome of events. Therefore, it is the argument of this research that the human element, which we call *constitutional* factors, should be taken into consideration during the policing of a given crowd without entirely dismissing the impact of *institutional* factors. The influence of institutional factors on the crowd and individuals during the policing of an event usually has long-term deteriorating effects.

Appropriate police conduct during a crowd event or in a particular area may not have a long-term positive effect on those prolonged and accumulated social problems which contribute to crime. However, bad policing practices may have long-term negative effects on the relationships between a particular community or group and the police. Therefore, police conduct during a crowd event is more relevant to the psychological state of crowd participants. This is because policing practices are, in the detection of individually committed crimes and collective violence, like treating the apparent symptoms rather than eradicating the underlying causes.

A particular policing practice is bound to be or perceived to be coercive and paramilitary unless it functions on behalf of a system which primarily sets out to meet the social, political and economic demands of its subjects. However, this does not imply that such a system will perfectly satisfy those demands or that there will be no opposition involving large numbers of people.

Essentially, such a system should respond to political or any other opposition with the deployment of the least sophisticated weaponry necessary to handle the events with sensitivity by taking into account not only the long-term social and political causes of the event but also short term socio-psychological aspects of crowd behaviour. This would create, at least, some positive influence on relationships between the police and a particular community even if it does little to solve the deep rooted causes of the underlying social problem. It would be too optimistic to expect to solve the problem, which is experienced by discontented people and has deep rooted causes, solely by good policing practices.

Observations of various stages of policing at crowd events have shown that as policing gradually moves towards an interactional level of psychologically oriented practices, such as a 'show of force', there are detrimental effects on the crowd such as 'provocation' or 'intimidation'.

Assembling Process

In line with the general theme of the Combined Factors Approach, the assembling process refers to long-term causes which lead to the formation of crowds at certain places or venues and at certain times as well as to short-term and apparent causes. While the short-term causes of the assembling process are mainly concerned with how a particular crowd gathers, the long-term causes deal with the reasons for individuals coming together to form a crowd at a particular place or time. The short-term causes of the assembling process might involve psychological reasons. However, it is insufficient to explain the gathering of a crowd using only short-term and psychological reasons; long-term effects of social, cultural and economic conditions must also be considered.

The combined factors approach (CFA) works at all stages of a crowd movement, starting from the assembling process to the interactional level and through to dispersal. But some of the factors gain priority over others at certain stages. For instance, while in the long-term assembling process it is not feasible to argue that the crowd gathering is the result of psychological motivation, it might be more appropriate to refer to the social causes of the gathering. On the other hand, it is not helpful to examine and explain crowd behaviour as well as individual behaviour at an interactional level with social causes. In the long-term assembling process, sociological factors determine the gathering of a crowd and at the interactional level, sociological factors are dominated and overwhelmed by psychological factors.

In terms of the assembling process, crowds can be grouped under two broad categories; 'organised' and 'spontaneous' crowds. In organised crowds, it is generally accepted that similar people tend to gather together. This might be the case to some extent, since the members of a crowd gathered at a particular place may share similar feelings and opinions. A number of recent crowd participant studies have shown that beside the general cause of the gathering, a number of individual motives can also be found. In abstract terms, there is usually at least a general idea or a common purpose or grievance which leads to a gathering at particular times and locations. Crowds are human groups which gather and unite around some common purposes and thanks to crowd, individual weakness might easily be turned into collective strength (Ginneken, 1992, p.167).

However, the existence of such a general cause does not make the crowd potentially dangerous. Unlike the arguments of conventional crowd theorists, the majority of crowd events occur without any serious violence. In these events the police may have to make some arrangements not only because the crowd imposes a danger to other people or the police but also because they may create danger to themselves.

Therefore, the police presence at large gatherings does not necessarily raise the violent expectations of a crowd. The majority of the police presence and the conduct of the police is designed to ensure the safety of the public rather than protecting non-participants from crowd violence. Past experience demonstrates that the crowd imposes more danger to itself than to others. To illustrate this, examples from this century in England will suffice: 173 persons were crushed to death and nearly a hundred injured, at a London tube station on 3rd March 1943, and 33 persons died and hundreds were injured at Bolton Wanderers football ground on 9th March 1946. Between 1902 and 1989, there have been five major disasters inside British football grounds and a total of 275 people were killed in those incidents. In the last incident, in Hillsborough, Sheffield, 95 people were killed (Moore, 1991, p.2; Dickie, 1993, p.89-98).

These and similar events in other countries indicate that there is always a need for organising and controlling a crowd (Smith and Dickie, 1993). The police are often responsible for the rationalisation of crowds and in such situations physical measures such as crush barriers may be employed or officers themselves may form temporary barriers in order to exercise control (Dickson, 1993; Rubes, 1993; Hopkins et al. 1993).

In addition to these routine tasks, in crowd events where there is an expectation of violence, the police have to make extra arrangements. These include the deployment of sufficient officers and the usage of sophisticated crowd control equipment. As indicated earlier, the most important point in public order policing is the way in which public order events are dealt with as this reflects the nature of the relationship between the state and the public. It is for this reason that the use of sophisticated riot equipment such as riot shields and CS gas in British cities has been criticised as a dramatic move towards an authoritarian state. Whatever the grievances of a frustrated crowd, be they material or ideological, the important point is the crowd's perceptions of its relationship to the state and its front line representatives, the police force. It is this perception which determines the outcome of encounters between the police and the public in politically motivated and volatile situations.

With regard to the second type of gathering, 'spontaneous' crowd events, the police have neither the time nor the opportunity to deploy ordinary preventive policing tactics. Since the nature of the crowd is already perceived as violent, there is no room for manoeuvre and ordinary methods are inadequate. Before moving on to the police response to spontaneous crowd events, it is appropriate to begin with a definition of 'spontaneous' events. Miller (1985, p.31) defines spontaneous events at two levels. The first and general meaning indicates that a spontaneous collective behaviour event is unexpected by the authorities, by spectators, and even by the participants themselves. Often such episodes seem to be triggered by an everyday routine happening such as the acquittal of the four officers accused of beating a black lorry driver, Rodney King, in Los Angeles in 1992, or the accidental shooting of a woman in 1985 during the Tottenham riots, London. However, Moore argues that both of the riots mentioned above were predictable and that preventive measures could have been taken (Moore, 1995). He further argues that the police were incompetent on both occasions and the only one of the 1985 riots in Britain which could be classified as spontaneous was Handsworth, Birmingham.

The second and the most exact meaning of the term spontaneous is 'occurring without external cause'. Applying this definition to collective behaviour is problematic. It is often taken to mean that spontaneous collective behaviour is caused solely by the internal cognitive states of participants: their individual attitudes, perceptions, and fears. This view is based on the literal meaning of the term spontaneous, complies with conventional crowd theories and implicitly denies the external causes of a riot. Subsequently, it denies the overall rationality of crowd action and places the blame on individuals' internal motives. However, a number of studies of spontaneous riots have proved that besides the immediate causes of spontaneous riots which are usually apparently insignificant incidents, deeper causes undoubtedly exist. It is clear that the concept of spontaneity is a relative rather than an absolute concept. All of the above suggests that violent crowd events, even seemingly the most spontaneous ones, can be reviewed as the result of a combination of causal factors.

It might be appropriate to use the term 'spontaneous' in order to deny the existence of pre-arrangements or plans behind these events. In Britain and the USA official reports on crowd violence have concluded that, '...the urban disorders...were not caused by, nor were they the consequence of, any organised plan or 'conspiracy' (The Kerner Commission Report, 1968; The Scarman Report, 1983). This conclusion does not imply an absence of an emergent organisation or leadership within the crowd members during the riots. The distribution of petrol bombs and selection of targets for attack and looting clearly show that during a riot the crowd may become organised and evolve a leadership (The Kerner Commission Report, 1968; The Scarman Report, 1983).

Pre-Event Arrangements

It was indicated in the previous chapters that one of the positive changes in police perception is that the police no longer view the crowd as politically threatening. Today crowd control has become a routine task for the police and a majority of these events do not impose serious public order problems. Despite the general belief that a crowd is potentially violent, most large gatherings do succeed in assembling and dispersing peacefully and without a violent incident.

However, not only so-called potentially violent crowd events but even the most peaceful crowds have a potential for danger. It is for this reason that studies of collective behaviour are not only concerned with potentially violent crowds. It is because of this potential danger that a number of extensive studies of the characteristics of crowds have been carried out in recent years by police as well as scientists (Rubes, 1993; Sime, 1993; Dickson, 1993; Berlonghi, 1993).

Long-Term Arrangements

Pre-event arrangements are mostly made on the basis of judgements which are inevitably preconditioned by past experiences (Waddington, 1994b). The nature of a crowd and its sheer size is also important within the context of a particular incident, although the police handling of crowd events mainly involves short term arrangements. However, it also requires the development of strategies which need long term planning and training. These include the establishment of Police Support Units (PSUs) for deployment at large events and the training of those officers who are responsible for the governing and commanding of these units (Moore, 1986). The training of senior police officers (Moore, 1985) responsible for the conduct of these units also needs long term consideration.

This need has led the police to the conclusion that they require advance warning of a potential incident so that arrangements can be made to have sufficient officers available to deal with whatever emergency might develop at the scene. Those responsible for the safety of the crowd and the police must be able to observe the behaviour of a crowd while an event is taking place and to make timely decisions for effective action. For this reason, in recent years 'crowd management' has become an important part of police officers' training.

Remote factors, such as the social and political causes of a violent crowd situation are, operationally and practically, a luxury which no senior police officer can afford. It is like having a discussion about whether a cancer patient, whose illness has been caused by smoking, deserves medical treatment, while the patient is on the operating table.

But the policy of public order policing and the training of relevant units must take into consideration the remote factors of a riot situation as well as considering its possible negative impact on police and public relations in the future. It might be a luxury for the police to look back when responding to a riot situation, but it is necessary, both operationally and practically, to take into account the long term effects of public order policing.

Public order training and first hand experience One of the problems facing the police when dealing with public order events is the deployment of adequately trained personnel (Moore, 1986). The dilemma the police have is two-fold. The first is that as a police officer with first hand public order experience gradually rises through the ranks, he becomes remote from the practical experience gained from past assignments.

First hand practical experience in public order events, particularly those involving violent clashes, is vital. However, to acquire first hand experience is problematic as incidents involving violent confrontation are still relatively rare compared with routine police work. First hand experience is very important not only for rank and file officers but also for senior officers who are responsible for the deployment of their personnel. Certain areas in some cities might experience high level confrontations once or twice in a decade and so the units and officers operating in these areas might well be relatively trained and experienced compared with others. However, in case of a spontaneous violent outbreak it is virtually impossible to deploy these experienced officers for operational and practical reasons.

Secondly, it is likely that in the case of a spontaneous violent outbreak, the officer in charge will, at best, be one whose experience is limited to theoretical and classroom based training. This fact was repeatedly stated during the public order courses which the researcher attended in the UK (Appendix 2). Many senior officers complained that they lacked first hand practical experience. As Moore (1986, p.95) points out "Experience is, therefore, or so it has been suggested, the highest form of study". To give the same level of practical and theoretical training for all officers who might be involved in public order events is very costly and has a low priority given the incidence of violent crowd events.

The nature of police work and training gradually shifts from practical to managerial and political skills as officers are promoted. Senior officers are more concerned with the managerial side of public order problems rather than the application and implementation of public order tactics at ground level. At the courses the researcher attended he has discovered that during the deployment of a PSU at an event, Gold Command is responsible for providing managerial skills, liaison with other agencies such as the fire and ambulance services, and making arrangements with neighbouring police forces through mutual aid agreements. Despite Gold Command's limited role in the implementation of public order tactics on the ground, the senior officer is responsible and accountable for the activities of officers who have little or no experience.

In England and Wales, lower ranking police officers receive a certain amount of public order training but in Turkey the training of such officers is left to the vagaries of daily experience (Appendix 2) and this trial and error method sometimes had quite serious consequences. Only a small percentage of police officers receive an initial training which consists of learning certain basic skills such as how to handle shields and other equipment and the use of truncheons for defensive and offensive purposes. The researcher was informed, on one occasion, by one of his ex-colleagues and personal friends that he was appointed as an experienced tutor officer for a newly arrived officer on the second day of his first assignment to that unit (interview, 9).

Ground level commanders should be familiar with the political and social consequences of their work. Training on the regulation of a peaceful crowd or the dispersal of a violent crowd is not sufficient as mistakes made during the dispersal stage might have long term negative effects on relationships between the police and that particular group or community (Metropolitan Police Notting Hill Carnival, 1993a-b). The role of ground level commanders is much more complex and requires more theoretical information and expertise than their seniors. They are required to be in control of two crowds; the police, and the crowd which the police are supposed to be policing. The commanders need to understand not only the psychology of the crowd but also the psychology of the officers under their command. For this reason in recent years the number of police officers within a PSU serial has been reduced to 6 officers in order to allow sergeants to supervise their officers better.

The implications of CFA model on ground level public order policing practices is that senior police officers should be familiar with the nature of the work which their officers are expected to implement. They might be more occupied with the political and managerial side of their work, but lack of information about the nature of public order policing may prevent them from fully comprehending the problem which they have to deal with.

Short-Term Arrangements

Short term arrangements involve strategies which have become routine through the years such as pre-arrangement of the route of the march or the venue of the crowd event and the control of pedestrians and vehicles. Although these seem to be minor issues, any disagreement or misunderstanding of these simple procedures may be a source of trouble at a later stage. However, the most important point raised by these issues is the problem of communication and negotiation at various stages of crowd events (Waddington, 1994b, p.69-104). Therefore, the following pages concentrate on various aspects of formal and informal communication between the crowd and the police.

Communication One of the important factors which determines the outcome of crowd events is the communication, or lack of it, between the police and the crowd leaders and organisers. The level and nature of communication is so important that it must be maintained at each stage of a public order event: pre-event arrangements, during the course of a crowd event, and if violence does occur, after the violent confrontation. In the early stages of an organised and potentially violent public order event, communication with the organisers reduces the tension to some extent. Lack of communication between the organisers and the police may raise the tension even at the most peaceful events. Therefore, the police are generally willing to negotiate in principle, since this makes their job potentially easier. Maintaining communication between the two sides has more importance during politically motivated volatile crowd events. One of the biggest recent public order events, the Poll-Tax demonstration and riots in Trafalgar Square, London, in 1990, has again reminded the police that, "...communication between police and the public has to be improved" (Metropolitan Police, 1991, p.14). It is believed that the communication between the two sides may help to reduce the occurrence of unexpected violent behaviour.

> Clearly the communication processes which take place during the actual incident assume crucial importance. Who says what to whom in which form may determine whether conflict escalates or is defused, as well as being a means by which collective understandings and interpretations of events are formulated and disseminated (Waddington et al. 1989, p.12).

During a demonstration the police should feel confident in their expectations of restraint by crowd members and, equally, that those organising the crowd event should be able to anticipate similar moderation from the police. Such mutual trust is usually achieved through prior and joint planning and establishing a communication link between the police and event organisers (Waddington, 1994b). However, communication becomes difficult during crowd events from a practical point of view and if violence does occur, communication is reduced to the minimum level.

With regard to the communication between individuals in volatile crowd events, the police have an important decision to make. It is this interpersonal communication which mostly has a detrimental effect on and determines the outcome of the crowd event. A lack of information between the crowd members and the police creates, as conventional crowd theories suggest, the 'social contagion' which leads, as H. Blumer (1975) has suggested, to the formation of 'emergent norms'. The lack of information and communication between the crowd and the regulating and controlling bodies leads the crowds to act according to the information generated by the crowd itself. Therefore, much of the police effort has been directed to the prevention of this vicious information circle. This can be achieved either by preventing communication between crowd members or by providing one way alternative communication via a Public Address System (PAS) controlled by the organisers or the police.

In fact, communication is considered at two stages: *long term* (formal) and *short term*, (informal) communication. Long term communication refers to the relationship between the police and a particular community or a group of people. This relates to communication before the immediate assembling of the crowd. The existence or lack of long-term informal communication between the police and certain groups is as important as immediate or short-term communication. Again, this is more related to the nature of the state and its agencies and the practices affecting a particular community. In line with the CFA model, long-term communication falls within the scope of *institutional* factors and requires multi agency efforts to improve it.

With regard to public order policing practices during a violent or potentially violent confrontation, inter-personal communication has two aspects. In the first sense, inter-personal means to have face to face positive contact with the members of a crowd. This can be simply a smiling face and talking amicably with members of the crowd.

Communication in an ordinary sense, during violent, potentially violent or even peaceful events, is very important and this is usually achieved via public address systems. These are mostly provided not only at closed venues such as football grounds, underground stations and concert halls, but also at open air venues, demonstrations and carnivals. Communication is important, not only for making announcements such as lost property or children or warning people against possible structural or accidental dangers such as collapse of a wall or a fire, but also for minimising possible dangers which might be caused by the misunderstanding and misinterpretation of particular acts.

Both of these complementary types of communication are necessary during the policing or regulation of a crowd. When the police rely only on the second type of communication, and if this is coupled with a lack of long-term communication, there is always a possibility of rumour and the misunderstanding of trivial incidents. The incident which sparked off the 1981 Brixton riot is a good example of showing the inadequacies of interpersonal communication unless it is fed by long-term communication between the police and a group of people. The Brixton riot was sparked off when a police officer's action was misinterpreted while he tried to help an injured young black man.

Immediate communication during a crowd event is provided by and maintained via personal contact and by the deployment of various means of communication. However, long-term communication, as the name implies, is provided by more general means of disseminating information such as the media. The media portrays certain images about certain groups and communities and convey its messages through routine reporting. This accumulation of information is backed up by a concentration of reporting during an event. The following is a more detailed account of the role played by the media.

Anti-BNP March of 16 October 1993 and the Media The police pre-planning of crowd events is mainly based on previous experience and perceptions. The arrangements are, therefore, sometimes made on the basis of a perceived threat rather than an actual threat. An attentive study of this apparently simple procedure reveals that pre-planning, which is apparently based on police perceptions and experiences of past events is also influenced by other institutions. For example, media coverage of crowd events reinforces existing police perceptions, which might already be biased. It also legitimates the heavy handling by police of crowd events by concentrating on relatively minor incidents. As Hall (1976) and Hall et al. (1987b) have made clear, media concentration on certain issues at certain times may create a moral panic and mobilise the police on perceived rather than actual threats.

Similar media coverage of a mass demonstration, which took place in London, on 16 October 1993, was observed. The demonstration was organised by the Anti Nazi League (ANL), Youth Against Racism in Europe (YARE), The Socialist Workers Party (SWP) and many other left wing groups. It was a challenge to the revival of the British National Party (BNP), the rise of Nazi activity in Europe, and an increase in racial attacks in Britain. The media coverage of this event did not reflect the rationality behind gathering and mobilisation of the crowd. As the following newspaper headlines demonstrate, the media coverage mainly concentrated on the violence of the crowd, directly and indirectly backing, and therefore legitimating, the use of force by the police. One newspaper, even went on to argue that, "Like urban terrorists these mobsters have adopted the dress and manner of the IRA" (*The Mail on Sunday,* 17 October 1993, p.3).

MASKED MOB STONE POLICE: 100 hurt as riot erupts on march - *The Mail on Sunday,* 17 October 1993.

THEY WANTED TO CONFRONT POLICE - *The Mail on Sunday,* 17 October 1993.

TOO COWARDLY TO SHOW THEIR FACES - *The Mail on Sunday,* 17 October 1993.

POLICE CLASH WITH RIOTERS OVER NEO-NAZI BOOKSHOP - *The Sunday Times*, 17 October 1993.

RACE MARCH EXPLODES INTO RIOT - *Independent On Sunday*, 17 October 1993.

Organisers and participants regarded the BNP and its members as a threat to freedom and democracy. On the one hand, the media has exaggerated the event itself, whilst on the other hand, it downplayed the extent of any threat stemming from the far right. It was argued that Fascism could only be a fad in England, rather than being a real danger (Ascherson, 1993, p.17). Ascherson concluded that, "In other countries, like Germany, the new racist right is a serious political calling, not a lifestyle, which takes precedence over everything else" (p.17). The general media coverage oversimplified the danger of the BNP while some argued that, "The far left and the right need each other and are often indistinguishable from each other" (*The Sunday Times,* 17 October 1993).

The media coverage of the event, as usual, consisted of one side blaming the other, for the violence which occurred that day. Paul Condon, the Metropolitan Police Commissioner, for instance, accused the organisers and the participants saying that, "Again in London we have seen a cowardly mob of extremists with no intention of demonstrating for a cause, turn up to cause disorder, violence and damage" (*Independent On Sunday,* 17 October 1993). On the other hand, the organisers countered that the police had over-reacted. Julie Wareson, national Anti-Nazi League (ANL) organiser and chief steward of the march said that:

> The police were out of control. What did they expect? People were tremendously angry. The police should have handled it less aggressively. This is no way to negotiate, by hitting the chief steward round the head with a truncheon (*Independent*, 17 October 1993).

The coverage failed to give an accurate picture of events let alone examine the real threat which might come from the far right or left. Media coverage of certain events serves many functions. The first is that the media might distort the truth and put the blame on the crowd and organisers without paying attention to their cause. It also encourages the police use of heavy methods for future events by legitimating the use of force in their reporting. The third is that media coverage often conceals the extent of the threat which might come from an arbitrary use of force by the police or other groups whilst creating a perceived threat which may have in fact no basis at all.

Accordingly, the arrangements are sometimes made on the basis of a perceived rather than an actual threat. An attentive study of the pre-planning of events which are seemingly based on police perception and experiences of past events, are also influenced by other institutions. For example, media coverage of crowd events reinforces police perceptions, which might be biased for various reasons, such as institutionalised conservatism (Waddington et al., 1989, p.162; Reiner, 1992, p.121-124). News reports also tend to focus on spectacular incidents which legitimates the heavy handling of crowd events.

To sum up, media coverage of some crowd gatherings has a profound influence on events. "The context in which the crowd appears may be defined by prior communications, particularly by those emanating from the mass media" (Waddington et al. 1989, p.2). It may "...exaggerate or minimise the possibility of conflict" (ibid. p.163). The media might distort the truth and place the blame on the crowd and organisers without paying attention to their mobilising causes (*The Independent On Sunday*, 17 October 1993; *The Mail On Sunday*, 17 October 1993; *The Sunday Times*, 17 October 1993) It also encourages the police use of heavy methods for future events by legitimating the use of force in their reporting (Bennetto, 1993; Headfield et al. 1993; Whilsher, 1993). Finally, media coverage conceals the extent of the threat which might come from the arbitrary police use of force, or from the activities of certain groups for example on the 'far right', on the other it creates a perceived threat rather than an actual one.

Police Conduct During Crowd Events

Police conduct at crowd events varies according to the type of crowd. The first police response to an ordinary crowd event is to deploy crash barriers and police cordons and divert the traffic flow. This is generally achieved by the deployment of relatively few officers. For instance, in a recent crowd event on 1st August, the Leicester Afro Caribbean Carnival, about 120 police officers were deployed in controlling a crowd of 20, 000 - 30, 000 (observation 4). Since there was no expectation of violence all arrangements were made according to normal and routine policing. However, if the police expect violence, whatever the size of crowd, the arrangements vary.

The belief that there is safety in numbers dominates the police deployment of violent crowds. Police prefer to have more police officers than needed. It is impossible to guess the scale and extent of violence accurately, therefore, even, if the crowd is a relatively small group of people the police will respond to the incident with sufficient manpower. For instance, the removal of less than fifty New Age Travellers from privately owned land in Coalville in 1992 was conducted by the deployment of 120 police officers including a Police Support Unit from a neighbouring county, the Warwickshire Police Constabulary (observation 3). It was not the sheer size of the crowd but the nature of the crowd and the expectations of violence which determined the nature of the police response to these events. These two examples clearly demonstrate the policy of the police at crowd events. The deployment of police officers upon the expectation of violence rather than with respect to the size of the crowd refutes the conventional crowd theories that see the sheer size of a crowd as the main potential for violence.

One of the recent observations made during the research period has also enhanced this view that it is not the size of the crowd but its very nature which determines the police deployment and expectations of violence. The 'March for Jesus' (observation 31), which was one of the biggest rallies attended during the research period, was extraordinarily well organised and passed peacefully. Despite its large scale with well over 50, 000 participants, there were only a handful of police officers visibly deployed.

So it is not the size of the crowd but the expectation of violence that effects the nature of policing public order events. This expectation of violence is assessed partly, but not exclusively, on the evidence of similar past events. For instance, at the Leicester Afro Caribbean Carnival (1992), which has an eight year peaceful history, the police did not feel it necessary even to deploy police officers in protective clothing. On the contrary, at the Notting Hill Carnival the police always have ready a number of riot trained police officers, including some officers from SO 19 (Special Operations), the specially trained firearms unit of the Metropolitan Police. These precautions are taken in the light of previous years' violent experiences.

Show of Force

Apart from deploying sufficient police officers in ordinary uniform, if there is a possibility of violent confrontation, the first step taken by the police is a show of force which is simply the mere presence of sufficient uniformed officers. However, it is difficult to judge what amount of police officers are enough for a 'show of force', or whether this demonstration of police authority is necessary since it is suggested that it may provoke the crowd into further violence. A number of studies have pointed out the provocative effect of over policing and use of police equipment, but no academic research or manual has offered clear guidelines for police officers to be applied in real situations. Authors such as Northam (1989) and Jefferson (1987 and 1990) have pointed out the provocative effect of recently introduced police equipment and tactics but they did not suggest to the police officers a way of protecting themselves without provoking the crowd. This arbitrary judgement still remains with the individual decision of the event commander.

The show of force might have diverse effects on the crowd members and yield unexpected results. In line with this thesis, at this stage of public order policing special consideration should be give to the *constitutional* aspects of crowd participants because sociological factors become less dominant at this stage. Therefore, depending on the cultural peculiarities of a particular crowd some police conduct may be perceived as provocative rather than intimidating.

Intimidation/Provocation

At ordinary crowd events police officers are deployed with standard day-to-day equipment. It is only those situations with the expectation of violence which are problematic for the police. In those situations the police keep their manpower and equipment out of sight in reserve, for deployment when it is felt necessary. For instance, during the 1992 Notting Hill Carnival, manpower and equipment cover nine schools, located in the carnival area, were used by the police for this purpose. Over 5, 000 officers were deployed in total, but only about 500 officers were visible on street duties, the rest remaining in the schools as reserves waiting to be deployed if necessary.

Provocation implies the deliberate behaviour of an individual or a group to make other individuals or groups react in an angry or violent way (*Collins Cobuild,* 1992, p.1157). However, in the context of public order policing, provocation could be 'intentional' or 'unintentional'. Either side can be deliberately and actively provocative or can be perceived as such even though their intention is not provocation. Communication at all stages of a public order event can minimise the risk of provocation which might be caused by misinterpretation of signalling behaviours. In some cases police behaviour or merely the police presence at a certain location, which may be intended for the safety of the crowd, can be misinterpreted and regarded as provocative. Provocation can be further divided into two broad categories; 'active provocation' and 'passive provocation'. Active provocation on the part of the police is very rare and this is also the case for crowds at most peaceful events. However we cannot rule out the possibility of active provocation particularly at politically oriented demonstrations . Provoking an overreaction by the police may mobilise the support of the silent majority of protesters and so strengthen the volume and nature of the protest.

Some aspects of police conduct, which from the police point of view may be regarded as the routine deployment of police officers, can be perceived as highly provocative by the crowd. For instance, the police use of offensive tactics and equipment such as armoured vehicles and certain weaponry such as baton rounds, plastic bullets and indiscriminate use of baton charges. What is more, so-called protective clothing, which has been defined as 'riot gear' by some, can be perceived as offensive, if not provocative.

Passive provocation can take various forms. As the term implies, it shows that it is not a deliberate action but rather it is something which is perceived as provocative by the other side. The other side does not necessarily mean the crowd, as the police as a crowd are subject to the same psychological influences. Certain acts and behaviours of the crowd may be perceived as provocative by the police and may lead to the use of excessive force. In line with the main theme of this research, public order units have always been considered as a type of crowd because they receive group training and are subject to the same psychological determinants as the other types of crowds.

Passive provocation, however innocent it might appear, should be avoided as it can cause the crowd to react in an angry and violent way. The observations made throughout the research period have shown that at most events police behaviour was perceived as provocative. The mere presence of police officers in large numbers at certain locations was regarded as provocative and this can be termed passive provocation. The reason for the police presence may be to protect certain premises from possible attack or to control roads approaching a significant location or a target, rather than direct crowd control.

The following are two of a number of similar incidents observed throughout the research period. The first one occurred during the anti-BNP march 16 October 1993, in Welling, London (observation 25). The march was one of the highly policed crowd events the researcher has observed during the research period However, the presence of police officers in ordinary uniform among the crowd was not resented nor perceived as provocative. On the other hand, the presence of police officers in large numbers at certain locations - the significance of those locations were and still are unknown to the researcher - and the blocking of certain side roads which led to the controversial Nazi base, the book shop, provoked the crowd. As the marchers passed those locations they were chanting anti-police slogans while there was no action taken against ordinary police officers among the crowd. Their presence was perceived as regulatory and managing rather than being seen offensive and provocative.

A similar case was observed in a local student march which took place in Leicester (observation 26). During the march there was no anti-police chanting. However, when the crowd was passing by a side street in the city centre, the presence of police officers blocking a side street provoked the crowd to chant anti-police slogans. In this incident active provocation on the part of the crowd was apparent as a steward was actively urging the students to chant anti-police slogans.

With respect to spontaneous violent crowd events, since the violence has already occurred, it is suggested that the most sophisticated riot equipment and riot trained officers should be deployed without delay; there is no room to deploy traditional benign methods. There are two main police responses to spontaneous public disorder. The first is the deployment of highly sophisticated riot equipment and the second is the deployment of riot trained police officers as soon as the violence breaks out. Passing the boundaries of 'normal' social action at the interaction between the police and the crowd seems to be a decisive factor in the use of aggressive crowd control strategies.

Despite the criticism of harsh tactics and swift police responses, police tactics during the inner-city riots of 1980s have been criticised for their failure to anticipate the escalation of violence and pre-empt it by an early display of force. The police were between two fires; on the one hand they were criticised for deploying a paramilitarily equipped and trained police force which is alien to the traditional British policing system and on the other hand they were blamed for not responding to a crowd event as quickly as necessary. The dilemma, of course, is whether the display of pre-emptive force and the deployment of paramilitarily equipped and trained police units undermines police legitimacy founded upon a non-aggressive image and provokes the crowd into further violence. In short, resort to aggressive tactics and methods have been justified as a response to an intolerable level of violence by the crowd. Tactically speaking, it is still a moot point whether the police should await the outbreak of serious violence before taking vigorous action.

However, in some instances, it is suggested that the failure or delay of the police response to particular events may lead to large scale rioting. Turner and Killian (1962) stated that:

> ...the speed with which the police officer operates in these situations is the measure of the extent to which onlookers can accumulate. By cutting short

> such an accumulation, he can prevent an incident from becoming an affair which it will be impossible for him to handle (1962, p.145).

Similar remarks were made by Kenneth Newman, the then Commissioner of the London Metropolitan Police in an address to the ACPO in 1982:

> It is important that if the initiative has been lost to the rioters in the early stages it should be recovered by the police as quickly as possible. Rioting spreads quickly. Any success gained by the rioters or any apparent reluctance of police to put down rioting will serve to encourage rioters and encourage others to join them (Newman, 1982).

Turner and Killian concluded that a police officer often fails to arrive on the scene of an incident until after a crowd has assembled and achieved a degree of aggressive unity. The 1981 Brixton riot was sparked off by a similar incident which was started by the delay in dealing with a trivial incident. Delay in appropriate police response was also noted by the National Advisory Commission as a contributory factor in the growth of many other riots during the 1960s (The Kerner Commission Report, 1968). The delay of appropriate police response to a particular situation may not only be the result of poor judgement or lack of sensitivity on the part of the individual police officers and may stem from the complexities of organisational structures. Whatever the causes of delay in appropriate police response, this can create a false sense of power, or feeling of omnipotence in the crowd and its participants if the police are indecisive in the first stages of disorder.

In addition to the deployment of sufficient police manpower and equipment, the generation of an anti-riot leadership in the violent crowd by dividing them into two groups is a further approach in dealing with public disorders. This can only be achieved by maintaining communication between the crowd members and the police. This method was suggested by ACPO's manual despite its apparent harsh and heavy handed methods. The ACPO manual urges community intervention (Northam 1989 and ACPO 1985) to act on behalf of the police to defuse violence. La Piere (1938, p.542) suggests that "...rioting may, in any given instance, be prevented by the rise of anti-riot leadership at the critical moment during the growth of a mob". However, this has little practical value since once uncoordinated rioting has become general, it is very difficult if not impossible, to recognise the situation in terms of directive leadership. Each member of the mob is so much engaged in their own affairs that it requires a powerful stimulus to disrupt their behaviour pattern. For this reason, no one seemed to listen to Mr. King's appeal for calm and a stop to rioting and looting, during the Los Angeles riots in 1992. This is confirmed by Moore (1995) as he remarked that he was "...unaware of any occasion where community intervenes have been useful once the riot is underway".

Use of Force

The arbitrary use of force by the police in crowd events has been one of the most controversial aspects of public order policing. Arguments surrounding the issues have focused on whether the police should use force indiscriminately and arbitrarily rather than whether the police have the right to use force in the first place. This has led to a fairly unanimous academic acceptance of the notion that the police have the right to use force under certain circumstances.

However, the police use of force during crowd events is still far from being clear because it is left to individual police officers to decide when and how to use force. Despite the fact that team work policing preconditions individual police officers to act as a team under the control and command of their senior officers, some still argue that use of force is left to the discretion of each single police officer. This view, which is perhaps commonly held, was articulated by an inspector, Keith Wood, from the Metropolitan Police Public Order Training Centre, Hounslow, during one of the ESRC seminar series (Appendix 2). Surprisingly, this view was not challenged by any members of the seminar, and later on Professor John Benyon and Dr Mike King from the Centre for the Study of Public Order made clear their view that they regard each individual police officer during a crowd event as acting under their own discretion. However, the researcher is convinced, in line with some radical thinkers in the field such as Northam and Jefferson, that public order training is a major shift from traditional individually based British policing and that consequently individual police officers working as a team are very much influenced and preconditioned by senior officers and the team of which they are a member. Although Tony Moore (1995) shares similar view with this research he also points out that "...at the end of the day, in law, the individual officer is responsible for the amount of violence he personally used".

The observations made at various public order training sites in London, Manchester and Leicester have led the researcher to believe that in public order policing, which is a dramatic shift from individually based British policing, preconditions the police officer as each officer is expected to act as part of a team rather than an individual responsible for their own actions. Although the researcher witnessed no direct instruction in this respect, it is evident that the nature of team work requires each team member to act in unison. In this context the command given by senior commanders such as 'engage in baton charge' is a command to act as a team. No individual police officer is expected to make his own personal decision about whether to engage or not in the charge. When it comes to the level of force used, it is inevitably up to each individual police officer to adjust the degree of force used in the crowd.

Advocates of paramilitary policing such as P. A. J. Waddington (1987 and 1991) attempt to justify the paramilitarisation of the British police as the only way of dealing with public disorder. For Waddington, the paramilitarisation of public order policing reduces the abuse of force rather than provoking the crowd into further violence. He argues that deploying untrained, ill-equipped, often unsupervised officers with neither a coherent strategy nor tactics has frequently produced both ineffectual policing and encouraged the use of excessive force (McEvoy and Gamson, 1972; Misner, 1972). Waddington (1987) cites Bayley saying that "...the skilful manoeuvring of heavily equipped squads controls violent protests with comparatively little police violence" (p. 41).

It is obvious that the deployment of large numbers of police officers wearing protective clothing and using sophisticated riot equipment and tactics cannot be the only way of dealing with public order situations. Other countries may have quite different methods and it may not be practically possible to adapt to the British police or even the Turkish police systems. For instance, Bayley points out that the Japanese police have developed a distinctive style of responding to riots. "In protest situations the police deliberately disarm themselves. They deploy substantial bodies of elaborately trained, highly disciplined men operating with massed precision" (Bayley, cited in Das, 1988, p.113).

However, it must also be borne in mind that these methods can be applied to particular situations in different ways. Even seemingly similar public order situations cannot be dealt with by using exactly the same methods and tactics and various tactics may be deployed at different stages of a riot situation; it is difficult, if not impossible, to formulate practical tactics which can be applied to all situations in the same way. In the selection below, five main methods of controlling and terminating a potentially riotous crowd are suggested by a manual, *The Police and Minority Groups*, prepared for the Chicago Park District Police by a sociologist in collaboration with supervising police officers:

> 1- Removal or isolation of the individuals involved in the precipitating incident before the crowd has began to achieve substantial unity.

2- Interruption of communication during the milling process by dividing the crowd into small units.

3- Removal of the crowd leaders, if it can be done without use of force.

4- Distracting the attention of the crowd from its focal points by creating diversions at other points.

5- Preventing the spread and reinforcement of the crowd by isolating it (Turner and Killian, 1962, p.144).

If all these methods and tactics can be utilised, which is not always possible, the crowd may disperse peacefully without the use of force. T. Moore (1995), however, sees the attempt to remove the crowd leaders, as the most difficult to achieve and a possible trigger for violence. Otherwise, there is only one way of dealing with the crowd which is to disperse it by using physical force.

In the following quotation Tony Moore, formerly a Chief Superintendent in the Metropolitan Police, London, introduces a sequence of using force once all attempts to mediate with the crowd have failed:

> Firstly, he [the incident commander] can instruct people to leave the area, hoping that community leaders, march organisers or whoever might have some influence on the crowd, will be able to calm the situation; secondly, he can maintain normal policing or a defensive role again hoping that persons holding some sway within the community will calm the situation; or thirdly he can go on the offensive (Moore, 1986, p.93).

A final point to make in relation to the use of force is that it is not seen as solely a method for dispersal but is regarded as having other purposes. For instance, the use of police force and certain acts of violence, such as hitting people on the head with a truncheon, particularly at non-politically oriented events such as football and recreational crowds, are perceived as a kind of 'correctional training' rather than being an abuse of force. This is widely tolerated and accepted among the lower ranks as a part of routine police work rather than being regarded as abuse of authority and power. However, abuses of force of this nature are more apparent in Turkish public order policing than its British counterpart.

Dispersal and Aftermath

One of the most controversial aspects of public order policing is the dispersal of violent or unruly crowds by the use of force. This is described as "...an act of force by the police designed to intimidate members of a crowd so that they flee" (Waddington, 1987, p.42). It is obvious that not all crowds need to be dispersed using force by the police or any other agency; some crowds disperse even without the intervention of a single police officer. The crowd of 62, 500 at a pop concert in Castle Donington on 22 August 1992 (observation 5), for instance, dispersed within ten to twenty minutes without even being warned by the police. With regard to the unruly image of riotous behaviour, some people do in fact disperse or at least move away from the police. Some members of the crowd may be unable to leave the area because others are blocking their way or because no escape routes are available.

Numerous studies on the topic have pointed out that unnecessary and excessive use of force may impose a danger to peaceful participants and provoke them into violent action. Therefore, the use of force during the dispersal as well as arrests should be made sensitively and selectively. First of all, an attempt should be made to persuade crowds to disperse peacefully, without the need for direct or indirect physical contact with the people. As Northam (1989) has stated "...crowd dispersal, like crowd assembly, is infectious and once a crowd begins to disperse it should normally be allowed to melt away" (p.71).

The way in which the dispersal is carried out may significantly vary according to the type and nature of the crowd. For instance, it is very difficult to be selective in the use of force in spontaneous riot situations such as inner city riots in Britain in the 1980s. However, in relatively less unruly crowds such as the 1991 anti Poll-Tax riot in London, a limited and selective use of force could have minimised the scale of violent confrontation. It is important to remember that the nature of a crowd can very easily change, transforming itself depending on the way the police use the force. It has been clearly proven that the decision to march into the crowd without warning dramatically changes the mood of the majority of the crowd.

This was the case when students tried to stop Leon Brittan, the then Home Secretary, during his visit to Manchester University on the evening of 1 March 1985. In the event no request was made by the police to the crowd to clear a passage up to the steps, and at 7.10 pm. 40 police officers in two columns marched along Oxford Road and then turned into the crowd on the steps without warning. This angered many demonstrators who would have been content with a noisy but passive demonstration, and they joined the ranks of the minority who had always intended to resist police attempts to clear a passageway up to the steps (*Police,* Vol. XXI No. 2 October 1988, p.16). This and similar incidents have proved that a number of authors have rightly stressed the importance of heavy-handed policing in provoking less violent factions into further violence alongside other already violently inclined members of the crowd. This was one of the immediate reasons of the inner-city riots in 1980s in Britain (Scarman, 1983; Benyon and Solomos, 1987; Fielding, 1991).

Since the use of excessive force, even the inappropriate display of weapons, may be inflammatory and lead to even worse disorder, "...force should only be used in the last resort and then selectively, not out of cowardice, but because the alternative is an escalating spiral of violence" (Waddington et al. 1989, p.186). Therefore, during the dispersal, as well as in making arrests, necessary police action should be directed against isolated and specified individuals rather than the crowd as a whole.

It is evident that the most militant members of crowds have always been a minority group. However, "...within the crowd, a kernel of 6 or more (1% of the crowd) is generally sufficient to set off some form of abnormal behaviour" (Greater Manchester Police, 1980b, p.6). For instance, after the anti Poll-Tax demonstration in London in 1990, the police reported that, "...the hard core of violent demonstrators among the estimated 40, 000 people attending was believed to be about 3, 000" (Metropolitan Police, 1991, p.9).

Although the most ardent and militant members of the crowd are usually a relatively minor group since they are at the centre of the circle, this presents the police with a problem. The police have to get through the less militant to reach the militant. If this is not handled in a courteous way, which presents enormous difficulties, the less militant members of a crowd can be alienated.

It has become clear that the use of force in public order events both during dispersal or in making arrests must be handled sensitively and carefully. A number of recent public order events at which the researcher has been a participant observer have proved that the police are not as willing to use force as many would believe. To some extent, it might be true that the policemen like most of the rest of us, may prefer to respond in kind to the actions of people they confront. However, it is clear that it is neither practicable nor advisable to use force in dealing with public order situations, although at first it seems the most appropriate method. The police are always reluctant to use force for their own protection in the long run. They are generally slow to deploy counter-violence against violence since they believe that this may increase the violence they confront.

Sometimes authorities may hesitate in using wholesale lethal force out of fear of sanctions from the other governments. The killing of Chinese students by the police in 4 June 1989, in Tian An Men Square, Beijing, for instance, was criticised by the Western world and discredited China in the eyes of the world. In some instances, the use of force may be curtailed by the simple realisation that it may enlarge the scope and intensity of disorder. It is very widely documented that the unrestrained use of force against one group may bring other groups into the conflict.

The gradual shift towards the use of extreme forms of force begins with displays of the use of truncheons and CS gas and leads to the most severe forms of overt coercion which is the deployment of firearms or even military equipment in repressing a particular group, or in some cases a whole nation. However the assumption, which lies behind this gradual move, is that extralegal methods must be used to stop 'extremists' from activities that might threaten public order and the government and the state itself and that, in any case, if the agents of the state adhere to the letter of the law at every turn, the state would be paralysed. For this very reason, every small move towards militarisation has been a centre of controversy. Once the first move is made it is expected that other stages will follow.

The use of lethal force by authorities has often served as a justification for the use of lethal force by the victims. For this reason, not only the British public but also the police themselves have always been against having an armed police force. Finally, it is obvious that the use of lethal weapons toward its citizens will cost the state dear both politically and financially. As the quotation below from H. Arendt sums it up nicely:

> In a contest of violence against violence the superiority of the government has always been absolute; but this superiority lasts only as long as the power structure of the government is intact - that is - as long as commands are obeyed and the army and the police forces are prepared to use their weapons. When this is no longer the case, this situation changes abruptly (Arendt, 1970, p.48).

Therefore, not only in so-called liberal democratic systems but even in totalitarian regimes, the use of lethal force in public order situations is not desirable. This is so because some police and soldiers may realise that their people may be guilty of criminal acts but they are not the enemies to be destroyed, and therefore, feel a sense of sympathy for those they are expected suppress.

Summary

Within this chapter the implications of the CFA model have been applied to public order policing practices. The first section of the chapter deals with the implications of the model on pre-event arrangements and places a special emphasis on the role and the influence of media coverage of events which provides long term communication between the police and certain sections of the society. As a case study, the media coverage of the anti-BNP march of 16 October 1993 has been analysed and it is concluded that the media plays a crucial role in shaping police perceptions of a particular crowd and subsequent police deployment of crowd events.

The second section of this chapter is more concerned with the implications of the CFA model at a face to face level between the police and the crowd and shows that at this stage, both police and crowd action is determined more by psychological imperatives rather than long term sociological considerations.

Conclusion

> It is now commonplace that policing *per se* is a political activity. How could it be otherwise when the police are the custodians of the state's monopoly of legitimate force?...No police task is more political than the policing of political protest, for what is being policed is the political behaviour of fellow citizens (P. A. J. Waddington, 1994c, p.1).

Crowds help individuals to achieve goals which require co-operative and collective action and they provide support for opinions and behaviour patterns. They can also satisfy a need for approval or status. Most changes in society are the result of collective effort; fundamental changes cannot be brought about without the approval and unified efforts of large numbers. Therefore, crowds gather to achieve things which cannot be achieved individually. Wars and many other collective actions can be considered within this category. Throughout history crowds have gathered to accomplish a particular task and therefore crowd action appears to be as meaningful as the individual action, if not more so.

In an overwhelming majority of the observed events crowds have expressed political or social aims. Even apparently diverse crowds such as the mourning crowds of the late Turkish president Turgut Ozal (observations 17 and 18), the Notting Hill Carnivals (observations 6 and 23) and the Bridgwater Guy Fawkes Festival (observation 32) have either immediate or historical political ingredients (chapter two). This leads to the verification of the researcher's theory that sees crowd events not as random occurrences caused by short-term grievances such as the mishandling of a crowd event by the police. Rather it is the argument of this research that crowd events mostly have a story or they are an outcome of accumulated small stories. As the quote cited in Keith (1993, p.72) nicely summarises "There are no stories in the riots, only the ghosts of other stories (Handsworth Songs, 1986)". They also have a message for the future as the crowds mostly express some demands from the existing political arrangements.

Besides the 33 observations carried out by this research (Appendix 1) 21 interviews were made in Turkey with a number of police officers between the ranks of Sergeant and Chief Superintendent (Appendix 2). All the interviewed were working in Public Order Units (Cevik Kuvvet) of

Ankara, Istanbul and Izmir, and some of whom were responsible for the training and operation of these units. In addition, in England three major public order courses, organised by the Central Planning Unit (CPU) and designated for the training of senior officers, were attended by the researcher (Appendix 2). The researcher also took advantage of being a permanent member of Economic and Social Research Council (ESRC) seminar series by attending five seminars which included a number of presentations made by eminent academicians and practitioners in the field. (Appendix 2). Finally, the researcher attended seven more lectures, seminars and meetings (Appendix 2) which he found relevant to the research topic.

CFA and Observations

Conclusions reached by this research are the result of above mentioned activities and besides its practical implications on public order policing practices in both countries, this research has, in relation to the hypothesis of the book, reached the following conclusions.

Throughout the observations made within the research period, social factors have been identified as the most significant cause of crowd events. This observation was true not only in potentially violent political crowd events; leisure and entertainment crowds and even mourning crowds have indirect social and political connotations. However, it has also been identified that the nature of the relationship between the police and crowd during an event is subject more to psychological than sociological considerations.

The model of the research, the CFA, is inspired by secondary data collected and read within the research period. After establishing the model, observations have been made to see whether the crowd events observed fitted and supported the model. The events have been chosen on the basis of their anticipated size, the social and political context and the expectation of violence. Although particular emphasis was placed upon potentially violent and disorderly crowds, observations have been made of a wide range of crowd events including peaceful leisure crowds so that comparisons can be made.

The existing public order policing policies and practices, both in Turkey, England and Wales, perhaps as is the case elsewhere, have proved clearly the validity of our second hypothesis which see the police in almost all events playing the role of a control agency on behalf of its political masters (Brewer et al., 1988; McCabe and Wallington, 1988; Waddington et al. 1989, p.198-200). Despite frequent denials of this role even the advocates of so-called consensus policing such as Waddington (1994c, p.1) admit to the political nature of public order policing.

Throughout the research period a total of 33 observations were made at various public order events. Among the observations made, 23 had direct social and political causes which are classified as 'dissenting' crowds in the second chapter of the book. The remaining 10 events could be classified as 'non-dissenting' crowd events and included leisure crowds and sporting events. However, some of the crowd events which are classified as non-dissenting, such as the Notting Hill Carnivals of 1992 and 1993, mourning crowds of the late Turkish President and the Bridgwater Guy Fawkes Carnival had either immediate or historically social and political connotations despite their being leisure, carnival and mourning crowds (chapter two).

First of all, no crowd was identified as being particularly 'violent' or 'revolutionary'. However, depending on the circumstances, crowds which are classified as 'dissenting' seem to be more likely to act violently in comparison with other types. One of the crucially important conclusions which this research has reached is that crowds in liberal democracies were mostly peaceful and not revolutionary. However, this was not simply because they lack revolutionary elements and spirit; rather the condition of the society in general was not conducive to revolution. Therefore, crowd activities are not to be examined solely by their being violent/peaceful or revolutionary/non-revolutionary. Besides this, the nature of the state and its response to a crowd and general condition of society from which crowds are derived becomes vitally important in terms of its being peaceful or violent. It is this distinction which makes a crowd activity in Algeria 'revolutionary' while a similar event in England poses no political threat to the existing regime.

Secondly, almost all of the demonstrations which originated from a political or social grievance were attended by the members of politically, socially and economically marginalised groups such as the members of Revolutionary Workers Party, Red Aid, Militant Labour, the Irish community, and members of ethnic groups such as the black community, and immigrants and refugees who felt themselves vulnerable. These crowds mostly involved participants who were very articulate in their view rather than being ordinary members of a 'silent majority'. However crowds which affect the stability of their existing political arrangements, such as the Algerian and Russian crowds, are mostly drawn from the 'silent majority'.

Thirdly, the observations have revealed that crowds in liberal democracies may sometimes be violent and seem to be portrayed as revolutionary by the media. However, as long as they are made up only by 'marginalised groups' rather than attracting the members of 'silent majority' amongst its rank they can be destructive and economically costly but not revolutionary and politically threatening.

Finally, in terms of crowds being organised it proved impossible to make observations at spontaneous crowd events for practical reasons, therefore the information concerning spontaneous crowd events rests upon secondary data. However, the nature of the crowd was found to be a contributory factor in the organisation of the crowd rather than simply its sheer size.

In contrast to conventional beliefs about the crowd and its activities this book demonstrates that a crowd is not merely a collection of psychologically motivated individuals and that their acts are no less rational or 'inferior' compared to individual behaviour. However, this research acknowledges that crowds provide an opportunity for participants to do things which they could not or would not undertake as isolated individuals. It also firmly argues that the crowd and police interaction at ground level during a given crowd event is more determined by psychological and biological than social and political determinants (chapter six). Therefore, the CFA model of public order policing suggests a combination of the two disciplines, sociology and psychology, in order to formulate an appropriate police response to crowd events. Therefore, attempts to verify or to test the validity of the first hypothesis has led the researcher to develop a new approach, the Combined Factors Approach, to collective action/behaviour.

The model of this research, the Combined Factors Approach, is applicable at all stages of a crowd movement, starting from the assembling process in the long term, to the interactional level and dispersal. But some factors gain priority over others at certain stages. For example, during the assembling process, it is not feasible to argue that the gathering of the crowd is the result of psychological motivation and it might be more appropriate to refer to the social causes of the gathering. On the other hand, it is not helpful to examine or explain crowd behaviour or individual behaviour at an interactional level using social explanations. While in the assembling process, sociological factors determine the gathering of a crowd, at an interactional level sociological factors are dominated and overwhelmed by psychological factors (chapter six).

In relation to the second hypothesis of the book, the findings of the research have strengthened the broadly Marxist critical view on the role of the police in general and public order policing in particular.

First of all, public order policing practices in both countries have proved that the police, rather than being a neutral institution, are the apparatus which ultimately work in the interest of the state and the ruling class. Despite the various minor differences with regard to policing practices which stem from variations in social, cultural and historical backgrounds, the police both in Turkey, England and Wales, perhaps as elsewhere in the world, seem to be serving the interests of what some radical thinkers call 'the ruling bloc'. Police forces of the both countries play the same role of defending the state and therefore the interests of certain groups. However, the nature and degree of this control varies in accordance with the degree of legitimacy of each state and its nature, namely being openly or indirectly oppressive. In other words, the variations are by degree rather than by nature.

A significant fact this research has discovered is that the claim of the British police to be in the service of the whole community rather than being the apparatus of the state and therefore the power holders is essentially hypocritical. On the basis of its 'expressive' and 'service' role it is argued that the British police uniquely functions with the consent of its people. In fact the expressive and service role of the police has nicely aimed and added into the core mandate of the police to conceal its wider aims as being the apparatus of the state. The contrary may be demonstrated in the case of the Turkish police where the police's role as the apparatus of the state is clearly articulated in the relevant statutes (Police Act 1934, Article 2:A, II, III and IV, cited in Icel and Yenisey, 1990, p.95-96; Police Organisation Act, 1990, Article 9:B, cited Icel and Yenisey, 1990, p.131).

The Police role as protecting the state from possible political opposition was again evident in the fact that political demonstrations were very highly policed even though they were relatively small in size. For instance in one of the recent demonstration which took place in Leicester, the event was policed by over fifty police officers while the size of the crowd was between 150-200 (observation 33). Similar overpolicing was evident in many other politically oriented demonstrations (observations, 14, 19, 23, 25, 27, and 33).

Secondly, any decline in economic and social circumstances will inevitably have a derogatory effect on certain groups who experience the effects of deterioration more directly and acutely and this will be followed by expressions of accumulated dissent as collective action. These groups do not necessarily have to be ethnic minority groups; it is likely that sub-groups in mainstream society will be affected too. Because economic decline victimises indiscriminately, crowd activities involving the expression of political, social and economic grievances will be multi-racial and will cut across economic and class boundaries.

Finally, those countries which are in a transitory period, or resistant to transition are more likely to experience more oppressive policing practices than those who have experienced less coercive forms of transition. This seems to be a truism for all societies. Should a state gradually lose the consent of its public, the nature of policing practices inevitably becomes more oppressive and coercive. Regardless of the name of a particular political system any political system is bound to be perceived by its subjects as oppressive and coercive unless it takes the implications of the CFA into account.

As the state's pressure on its subject increases, the pressure from its public becomes increasingly threatening to the interests of power holding elites. This ends up with a vicious circle which creates more pressure from the bottom and a tougher response from the state's social control agencies, the police. As the pressure from the bottom becomes politically threatening, the role of the police as the provider of the peace for the general public switches to one of protecting the interests of power holders.

In England and Wales the introduction of the recent Police and Criminal Justice Act 1994 may be regarded as a response to the opposition which the British government faces from its public. The research suggests that this opposition was mainly caused by the state's failure in social, economic and political areas. The research concludes that the state's response to opposition which takes the form of collective action is the introduction of increasingly tough laws. That is what the British public in general and the working classes in particular have been subject to since the miners strike of mid eighties and Poll-Tax opposition in the late eighties and early nineties (Card, 1987; Brewer et al., 1988; MacCabe and Wallington, 1988; Uglow, 1988; and Waddington et al., 1989; Sherr, 1989; Townshead, 1993). The Security Service Act 1989 considers some 'political' and 'industrial' activities by putting them in the same category with violent means as a source of potential danger to "overthrow or undermine parliamentary democracy" (Security Service Act 1989, Chapter 5, Article 2).

The police in both countries have and play the same role in relation to public order policing practices, namely to protect the status quo which may equate to protecting the interests of the ruling class. However, the methods used to carry out this task may vary according to the training and experience the police receive and the availability of equipment they need to fulfill this function. The British police, in dealing with public order events, seems to be better equipped and relatively better trained and accordingly, does its job more professionally than its Turkish counterparts. As for Turkish public order policing practices, inadequate training and lack of practical experience coupled with lack of proper equipment lead the police to use more offensive and aggressive methods of crowd control.

Public order policing practices occupy an exceptional place amongst other routine police work as it is high profile, attracting the attention of the print and broadcasting media. However, in Turkey the officers working in these units are the least experienced or have just graduated from police cadet schools. Some of the officers are sent to these units either because they are not successful in other units or as a part of institutional disciplinary punishment. Therefore, the officers who work in these units have the lowest morale and may try to hide the fact that they work in them because they attract little respect from the public.

The senior officers responsible for the training and deployment of Cevik Kuvvet (Rapid Action) units in Turkey complain of the lack of time they have for physical and tactical public order training. However, unlike England, much police time and manpower is wasted by the deployment of these units in a number of private or commercial entertainment and leisure crowds. In England, police deployment at football events has gradually been reduced and in commercial entertainment events, security has been left to private companies. In Turkish Public Order Policing, the time saved from withdrawing the police from private and commercial crowd events might provide enough time and funds for the units to train and equip their officers adequately to deal with potentially more contentious crowd events. This would also minimise negative police and public contact for unnecessary reasons.

The CFA and Policing Systems

Perhaps historical and cultural differences make it neither possible nor even desirable to envisage one police system acceptable to all nations. As Le Bon stated, "Peoples are governed by their character, and all institutions which are not intimately modelled on that character merely represent a borrowed garment, a transitory disguise" (Le Bon, 1969, p.89). This does not lead us to the commonly used dictum which states that 'the people have the police they deserve', but it explains to us why the expectations of the people and the police of a particular event vary from one country to another. Therefore, the examination of the nature of public order policing in two countries will, inevitably, reveal a number of variations. Styles will vary according to political, economic, social and cultural conditions. For instance, a society which is homogeneous, monocultured, and classless will require less adaptability from the police than the one in which there are ethnic, religious, cultural and other differences.

Despite the fact that Turkish culture and ideology has been forcibly moved from its original roots to Western standards, the Turkish-Islamic perception of the state and the police still bears the traces of Islamic influence (chapter four). In contrast, the state's perception of the people and the police and their practices is much more Westernised than that of the people. While the present Turkish state still wants to enjoy a deference which stems from Islamic ideology, its practices towards its people are quite at odds with the expectations of the people.

Obviously, it is not only the policing styles which are influenced and shaped by cultural factors, but also crowd behaviour towards the police is influenced by cultural and political peculiarities of each of the countries. As Mannheim argued, "...as a rule a crowd will behave differently in the Southern Mediterranean and in Northern countries, in a country with a long-established democratic tradition and in one ruled by a rigid totalitarian regime" (Mannheim, 1965b, p.646). Secondly, social values and norms may influence crowd behaviour. For instance, "...a French crowd lays particular weight on equality, an English crowd on liberty" (Le Bon, 1969, p.158), while Turkish crowds give priority to abstract concepts such as chastity, honesty and so on. These differences of emphasis on different concepts explain why there are almost as many different grievances for riots as there are nations. It follows from this that crowds of different countries display very considerable differences of belief and conduct, and are not to be influenced in the same manner. For instance, while a verbal assault on a local girl in the street by an army officer in Turkey provoked a crowd into violent action (Emin, 1992), the same crowd would perceive police beating up a young man in the street as 'correctional training'.

With regard to the police response to public order events, cultural differences between the two countries can easily be observed at each stage of policing. At the general level, unlike the British public who wants to see its police as ordinary citizens in uniform, the Turkish people wants to see its police as a permanently armed military force. The Turkish police have been criticised for being mild and poorly equipped and trained rather than using harsh methods and tactics. In recent terrorist events, the police were criticised by the public for failing to meet violence with violence and vice versa (Meydan, 1994). The generally held idea is that the police should be equipped more heavily than the terrorists in order to suppress the violence. On the contrary, in Britain it is believed by the people as well as the police that an increase in the use of heavy weapons and equipment of any kind will inevitably lead to an increase in violence by terrorists and criminals. Therefore, it is reasonable to argue that an unarmed London policemen would certainly not be able to meet the demands of Istanbul and vice versa.

Moreover, the amount of injured civilians and police and the public perception of this may reflect the differences between the two countries. British public order policing was defined by Robert Mark's proposed strategy of 'winning by appearing to lose', a notion which proved to be rarely practical. The contrast between the two countries is that while the British public are willing to tolerate injured police more readily than dead civilians, the Turkish public does not want to see its police overwhelmed by a crowd in any way. It was evident in recent inner city riots in Britain that the majority of injuries were inflicted upon the police (Brearley and King, 1993, p.10; Benyon, 1993, p.6-7) while in the USA and Turkey, in similar events, the majority of the injured were civilians. This does not necessarily mean that the Turkish public do not criticise its police in cases of abuse of force and authority. Rather, the account given above reflects the overall view and expectations of the Turkish public of its police. When it comes to particular incidents, of course, each act of police violence and abuse of force is criticised, by both the public and the media. In abstract terms, the Turkish public wants to have a police force which will not be overwhelmed either by armed terrorists, nor even by relatively violent crowds, but at the same time they are not as tolerant of police violence and abuse of force, as this would imply.

It must also be noted that violent confrontations in public order events are frequent occurrences both in countries which respond to public order situations with relatively more paramilitarily equipped and trained police units such as Turkey, the USA and many European countries and in countries such as Britain which are policed by the so-called 'non-military consensus policing' (Inan, 1993, p.39; Benyon and Solomos, 1987; Benyon, 1993, p.4-7). With regard to Britain, although the paramilitarisation of the British police has increased dramatically in the last two decades, violent confrontation between the police and crowds dates back to the early days of the police (Cerrah, 1991, passim). The brutal character of riot control tactics used in Britain during the industrial riots of the eighteenth and nineteenth centuries is well documented by a number of studies in the field (Miller, 1985; Benyon and Solomos, 1987; Benyon, 1993, p.4-7). It is evident that in the past the British police have used brutal methods of crowd control. This leads to the conclusion that no country is 'culturally immune' from the use of harsh riot control tactics in preventing or suppressing violent or non-violent crowd events. Not only the relatively paramilitary police forces but also British public order policing, which is established and acts by the so-called consensus of the general public, has not always been so refined.

The conclusion to be drawn from this is that there are cultural differences in the ways that societies view the use of harsh tactics of crowd control. Not only between the distinct cultures; even more or less similar cultures may reveal significant differences in dealing with crowd events. For instance, there are significant differences between British and American policing, particularly in the area of crowd control tactics, in spite of apparent similarities in areas such as ethnic origin, religion, language and so on. It is not surprising that there would be a number of differences between the Turkish police and the British police, both in terms of the public's expectations of police and the police response to public order events.

With regard to the direction of the trend in British and Turkish public order policing they seem to be divergent. As for the British police, this is evident in the extension of police powers and the restriction of the right to assembly and protest introduced by the 1986 Public Order Act (Public Order Act 1986, Chapter 64; Smith, 1987) and expanded by the 1994 Criminal Justice Act. These statutory changes were accompanied by a dramatic increase in police public order training, which involves highly equipped and trained PSUs and joint regional exercises with neighbouring forces on a regular basis (Appendix 1 and 2). Neighbouring forces are required to hold joint training exercises four or five times a year to familiarise themselves not only with their own PSUs but also PSUs from other forces.

Further evidence of this drift towards coercive policing in Britain is the gradual move towards centralisation of existing police forces (Aydin, 1991). One of the earliest moves in this direction was the mutual aid arrangements. Under the Mutual Aid Agreements (Police Act 1964, Chapter 48) the British police established the National Reporting Centre (NRC) which enabled the police to confront the Miners' Strikes of 1984-5 almost as a national force. The National Reporting Centre has developed and changed into the Mutual Aid Coordinating Centre (MACC) which will enable the British police forces to form an *ad hoc* national third force when the situation arises.

This research has discovered, in the context of British public order police training and practices, a move from historically claimed consensus policing to coercive policing. The present *Public Order Guide to Tactical Options and Related Matters,* (1985) prepared by the Association of Chiefs of Police Officers (ACPO) aims to introduce national standards to public order training in order to achieve a degree of co-operation and standard working practices between forces to enable joint operations at large scale public order events.

One of the important points showing the direction of the change in the British public order policing training is the omitting of 'defensive' tactics which was included in the earlier version of the 1985 ACPO manual. The latest version of the ACPO manual reduces the options into two 'offensive', and 'withdrawal' omitting the previously held 'defensive' tactics. In this case the PSUs either have to be 'offensive' which includes more mobile and active tactics or to lose face by 'withdrawal', which is something the police is not very happy to accept.

An important point to make is that public order policing is bound, by its very nature, to be paramilitary as it removes the individuality of police officers by preconditioning them to work in unison and obey the commands given by senior officers. The removal of individuality will inevitably bring the feeling of anonymity. This is one of the reasons why the classification introduced earlier (chapter two) considers the police as a type of crowd, subject to the same psychological considerations. Whether public order training as units is inevitable and unavoidable constitutes another issue but the training in its very nature seems to be a gradual shift from consensus to coercive policing.

What is more, increasing specialisation in various aspects of public order policing witnessed by the researcher over the research period suggest that this trend will continue. For example, 'Rapid Entry' exercises included in the regular public order training (Appendix 2) have become a distinct area of expertise and are now entitled 'Rapid Entry/Intervention Courses' (Appendix 2). Use of military terms, such as 'MoE Men' (Methods of Entry Men) and availability of military like equipment such as 'gas masks', 'stun grenades', and 'ballistic clothes' all herald the possibility of their use in mainland Britain.

To sum up, direction of the change towards centralisation which began for co-operational considerations and ended up with collaboration leading to a greater amalgamation and regionalisation of existing forces and finally, to a complete centralisation.

On the contrary, in Turkish policing in general and public order policing in particular, a piecemeal move towards consensus policing has been noticed. Yet the gap between the Turkish and British public order policing, in terms of being a coercive force or a consensus service, still remains as wide as ever. What is more, the move towards consensus policing, in Turkey, is something forced upon the police rather than being a readily accepted gradual and evolutionary move towards this direction. Whether this trend will continue and will end in the full consensus of a wider public is open to speculation. There are a number of reasons which cast doubt upon these imposed trends in the Turkish police.

First of all, the improvement in Turkish policing has taken place more at the individual level rather than being at organisational level. It partly stems from the liberalisation of the economy and the political spheres during the then prime minister T. Ozal's years in the government following the 1980 military coup. The implementation of a free market economy and moves towards liberalisation have inevitably affected the make-up of the police along with many other social institutions. Many of the senior officers, who are presently serving in Cevik Kuvvet Units, joined the national Turkish Police Academy after graduating from various universities. Cevik Kuvvet Units today involve senior officers having degrees in various social sciences such as law, politics and even theology, and the researcher is one of the first who joined the police force as a university graduate. It seems to be the case that the general academic qualification and educational level of senior officers working in Cevik Kuvvet Units are comparatively higher than their British counterparts. Yet, this general qualification is not backed up by occupational specialisation; training and academic qualifications of individual officers seem to have little positive effect on policing practices as this knowledge and expertise is quickly subsumed by operational police culture.

The second factor affecting the move towards consensus policing is the increasing influence of the broadcasting media. One of the effects of liberalisation has been a dramatic increase in the number of privately owned TV channels in the early 1990s. Through media coverage both the people and the police themselves have become familiar with the police handling of crowd events both in liberal democracies as well as non-democratic regimes. The extensive media coverage of local crowd events has also forced the police to restrain particular acts which causes the people to be more critical of police mishandling of crowd events.

However, it must be acknowledged that the above account is more of a personal impression, acquired from comparisons made in the researcher's own experience rather than being a definite conclusion supported by empirical evidence. The comparison made is based on personal experience and impressions acquired within the period when the researcher was serving as an inspector in Ankara Police College between 1986-1989, and personal contacts and observations within the research period between 1990-1995. This impression is generated and gained from the observations and the visits made to various public order training sites and schools in both countries. This impression was also enhanced by personal contacts with key figures responsible for the training and operations of public order policing in both countries.

As it is only a personal impression, there is, therefore, an obvious need for further research to verify the accuracy of these assertions. Aydin (1991) in his M.A. work reached similar conclusions, and it is very likely that his Ph.D. work will produce some further evidence confirming his early assertions. Nevertheless, this piecemeal move towards consensus policing, which has been covered by very gradual and imposed outside factors, can easily be snuffed out by a slight policy change or even by an operational order from a senior officer, as this reluctant move has not yet been assimilated by the police organisation to become commonly established practice.

The recent disturbances which took place in Istanbul and Ankara in March 1995, when the army were called in to quell the situation, have once again demonstrated the inability of Turkish public order units to deal with crowd events. The events were sparked off by an incident involving the killing of a member of the *Alevi* community and injuring twenty more people after three unidentified gunmen opened fire on a *cafe* which was frequented by members of the *Alevi* and non-Alevi communities. Extensive national and international media coverage of the event has revealed two important points. First of all there was an obvious provocation to involve the *Alevi* community in violence (Colasan, 1995; Mengi, 1995a-b; *Hurriyet,* 17 March 1995). This fact was repeatedly stated, not only by the media, but also by some eminent *Alevi* community leaders. The banners held by some members of the crowd belonged to a number of illegal terrorist groups such as *Turkiye Communist Party* (TKP), *Turkiye Revolutionary Communist Party* (TDKP-GKB), *Revolutionary Youth* (DEV-GENC), *Turkiye Workers and Peasants Freedom Army* (TIKKO), and finally, ERNK-PKK, a branch of the Kurdistan Workers' Party (PKK) (*Hurriyet,* 17 March 1995; *Sabah,* 17 March 1995). None of these groups solely represented nor had a direct relationship with the *Alevi* community and this was clear evidence of provocation from outside the *Alevi* community. The police and the press identified a number of prominent members of the various illegal terrorist organisation among the crowd (Colasan, 1995; *Hurriyet,* 17 March 1995; *Sabah,* 17 March 1995). Following the first disturbances the *Alevi* community, confirming this argument, declined involvement in any further violent activities (*Sabah,* 18 March 1995; *Hurriyet,* 18 March 1995; *Cumhuriyet,* 17 March 1995). However, this does not necessarily deny the existence of plausible grievances to which the *Alevi* community has been subject.

The second lesson to be learned from these disturbances was the fragility of the army to be called in to deal with internal disturbances (Barlas, 1995; Dogru, 1995a-b). The incompetence of the police, which basically stemmed from lack of equipment and training, forced the authorities into a financially and politically costly option; to call the army in (Mengi, 1995b; Barlas, 1995; Tan, 1995; Birand, 1995a-b; Dogru, 1995; Goktas, 1995). However, these events could have been handled with relatively little or even no violence by the deployment of better equipped and adequately trained public order units.

This recent experience forced the researcher to prescribe two entirely different solutions to British and Turkish public order policing problems. Unlike its British counterpart, in Turkish public order policing the need for the acquisition of protective clothing and other equipment and intensive public order training has now become urgent. These facilities allow the police to control violent disturbances with comparatively little police violence. More equipment and better training can be recommended to the Turkish police without discrediting the critics of the recent moves in British public order policing. Their concern about the changes in British public order policing may continue to be valid. However, as the Turkish police is already a paramilitary force, heavily equipped and intensively trained public order units will lead to consensus policing rather than being a move towards coercive policing simply because the alternative is to deploy the army.

The findings of this research for practical public order policing, in both countries are diverse. As for Turkish public order policing the recommendations can be summed up in the provision of better 'equipment' and intensive 'training'. Unlike British public order policing which has already been equipped and trained to a high degree, there is an urgent need for Turkish public order units to be equipped and trained in a similar manner.

CFA and Policing Policies

The police may not be familiar with all the academic literature concerning the crowd, in order to be familiar with a particular crowd. Their preparations are made on past experiences, often making judgements from and basing their future plans on experiences of escalating violence or criminal behaviour. Things which are learned by experience tend to be prejudiced and misleading if they are not refined by carefully considered academic wisdom. It might be an idealist hope to expect every single police officer to bear in mind all these academic arguments, in a given violent crowd situation. However, it is feasible to expect the police as an institution to take into consideration academic studies when they formulate public order policing policy. The application of the Combined Factors Approach to public order policing entails future Chief Constables to stand up and say, to their political masters that, 'Unless you provide the essential provisions for a particular community (long-term arrangements) and increase the level and quality of the life in a particular area, I cannot and will not police (short-term arrangements) this area'.

In recent years the practical experience of police officers and the studies of social scientists have together served as the basis for the formulation of principles of crowd control. Despite the existence of numerous academic studies in this field, very few manuals have been prepared by sociologists in collaboration with serving police officers. Close examination of existing manuals has revealed that academic wisdom was dominated by the practical considerations of senior police officers. Instead of improving police tactics according to these studies, it seems that those studies were conducted and shaped according to the needs of the practical aspects of policing. Consequently, academic studies on crowd behaviour had little positive effect on the police response to crowd event. The police continued to use the traditional crowd control methods and tactics with a few slight modifications. However, it would be unfair to completely deny the dramatic change of perception of crowds in the last two decades or so. Although academic studies had little practical effect on the police response to crowd events, the police perception of the crowd has changed dramatically. The police today do not see all crowds as destructive and revolutionary and their right to express their grievances has been recognised by the police as well as other official bodies.

There are a number of indicators which show the nature and direction of change in police and crowd perceptions of each other. It is important to note that the police and public perceptions of each other reflects the relationship between the state and its people. For this reason, the confrontation of the frustrated crowd with the police is not a random coincidence, rather it is the direct or indirect manifestation of the discontent of the people which erupts as violent confrontation with the police. The nature and degree of violence and the police response to this also reflects the overall level of the society in other social arrangements as well. "As a society becomes more civilised, free, educated, and informed at all levels, its expectations of the police also with other public servants are raised" (Das, 1988, p.109). As people become more aware of the dignity of the individual and of human rights they are likely to criticise and complain about police behaviour which in other ages or in other countries would not have been regarded as wrong. Police public relations in crowd events are more overt than any area of police work, and is a vital factor in the workings of democracies. In democracies, since parliament is directly accountable to the public in frequent general elections, crowd events such as rallies, political demonstrations and mass meetings play an important and legitimate role in the political machinery.

In crowd events the police are expected to stand at the point of balance, on the one hand securing human rights and on the other, exercising their lawful powers given to them by governments in the name of the people, to protect the people, property and institutions. From this point of view, the police response may also reflect the type and level of democracy as well. Not only in totalitarian, or less-democratic countries but even in so-called western democracies, police powers and authorities can be abused. The police can become more the master and less the servant; they can snuff out more freedom than they protect. This fact gives the impression, as argued by radicals, that the police may continue to serve as instruments of class oppression under the guise of legality. In abstract terms, the first factor which determines the nature of police response to crowd events is related to its place between the people and the state. In this respect, there is a fundamental difference between the two compared countries. Unlike the British police which is supposed to be politically independent and accountable only to the public, the Turkish police has been politicised both directly and indirectly. For instance, although the status of the chief constable is not regarded as a political post, after each general election most of the chief constables have usually been replaced at the direction of the new Minister of the Interior.

The influence of this political intervention is, however, less visible at ground level public order policing practices. For example, during a right-wing government the response of the police towards a left-oriented political demonstration is not as politicised as would be expected and vice versa. Apart from a few politically motivated individual interventions police and public relations in crowd events remain unchanged. Thankfully, the politically motivated appointments of chief constables do not dramatically change the overall public order policing policy at ground level.

In Britain, the situation is much the same. During the Labour government in the 1970s, which was supposed to be a so-called pro-working class government, the police response to public order events and even industrial disputes was similar to that of the more recent Conservative government. Some commentators have even argued that the paramilitarisation of the British police began when Labour was in power. This fact leads to the conclusion that unlike the changes in government and even in police authority, the overall policy of the police does not change easily or rapidly. One of the reasons for this slow transformation is the universal nature of police organisations. The nature of police organisations all around the world has always been similar and conservative in general terms. Accordingly, the police response to all situations, particularly to public order events, is determined by the organisational conservatism of the police force. Therefore, the police response to crowd events is bound to be conservative in nature, not because all or a majority of the police officers are politically conservative but because of the conservative nature of the organisation.

This argument does not completely deny the influence of political elites on police conduct, rather it is emphasised here that beside the overt political intervention, the nature of police organisation has an inherited perception towards crowd events. Yet, there are numerous examples of politically motivated police responses to public order events, particularly during industrial disputes of the 1980s. As Reiner states "...the police tend to share the broad political and legal ideals of the 'respectable' working and middle class" (Reiner, 1985, p.97), and these views are similar to that of the media, "...highly sensitive to overt or coded messages about how political elites expect a public order situation to be handled" (Waddington et al. 1989, p.161). They are expected to know how to act or behave on a particular point without being told what to do.

It was believed that, "...the inherent conservatism of the police occupational culture is uncompromising. The law is an absolute and those who infringe it in any way should be summarily dealt with" (Waddington et al. 1989, p.184). At this point it must be noted that the police conservatism which stems from the occupational police culture is not immune to change. Judging by the lessons of the past, it is now apparent that in a number of points police perceptions have been positively changed. For example, in almost all of the briefings in which the researcher participated it was repeatedly stated by operation commanders that the first priority should be given to public order problems and therefore small infringements of the law should be tolerated. It was clearly stated, confirming Waddington et al.'s (1989) finding that "...minor infringements of the law should be overlooked in the interests of the wider objective of maintaining order" (p.164).

The above account has proved that the police response to a particular public order event is not simply a law and order problem concerning routine police work such as maintaining traffic flow and protecting property and the individual. Rather, the police response to those events can be overt or covertly politically motivated which may undermine the legitimacy of police powers.

To conclude, the relationship between the police and crowds has always been problematic and raised many questions about the legitimacy of particular regimes. Particularly, police intervention in crowd events has been one of the most controversial aspects of police work. The police are not very comfortable in a dynamic democratic society and conversely a democracy is not very comfortable with a politically static police force. The unpopular work of controlling crowds has been, since its inception, a burden for the police as a result of division of labour in the society. As the former Chief Constable of Devon and Cornwall, John Alderson once said, "...the ideal civic condition is for a society to be policed by unarmed officers" (Alderson, 1979, p.71). Perhaps it would be more desirable and ideal, if not utopian, for a society not to need a police force in the first place. If this is too much for a society to expect let us hope for a society to have a *police service* which *serves* with the wider, if not full, consensus of its people rather than having a *police force* which *enforces* the law in the interest of power holding elites.

The more a society achieves a just and fair degree of wealth and power distribution amongst the groups and communities which the society is made up, the less riots it will experience. Otherwise, if a regime tries to survive by the consent of a minority of power holders, and their political and economic allies, the social division will become more entrenched and social disintegration will increase. Consequently, in such a society 'the police will encounter the riots which they deserve'. Unless such a society, as a whole, attempts to change itself and its police, to use a familiar dictum, 'its people will have the police which they deserve'.

Bibliography

ACAB (1990) *Poll Tax Riot: 10 hours that shook Trafalgar Square*, London: ACAB Press.

ACPO (1985) *Public Order Guide to Tactical Options and Related Matters*, London: Metropolitan Police.

ACPO (1987) *Public Order Manual of Tactical Band (In-Force) Training*, London: The Central Planning Unit.

Agirakca, A. (1992) *Emeviler Doneminde Kiyamlar,* Istanbul: Safak.

Ahmad, Z. (1991) *Islam, Poverty and Income Distribution,* Leicester: The Islamic Foundation.

Ahsan, M. M. and Kidwai A. R. (eds) (1991) *Sacrilege versus Civility: Muslim Perspectives on The Satanic Verses Affair,* Leicester: The Islamic Foundation.

Akgun, F. (1986) *Toplumsal Olay Cesitleri ve Polisin Rolu,* Ankara: Emniyet Genel Mudurlugu, Egitim Daire Baskanligi Yayinlari Seri No. 2 Yayin No. 1986/24.

Akgun, F. (1988) *Toplum Psikolojisi*, Ankara: Emniyet Genel Mudurlugu, Egitim Daire Baskanligi Yayinlari, Seri No.2 Yayin No. 1988/25.

Akgunduz, A. (1993a) 'Zimmilere secilme hakki verilmedi', *Zaman*, 8 May.

Akgunduz, A. (1993b) 'Fermanla zimmiler esit sayildi', *Zaman*, 9 May.

Akinci, F. (1990) *Polis: Toplumsal bir Kurum Olarak Gelismesi, Polis alt-Kulturu ve Insan Haklari,* Istanbul: Gumus Basimevi.

Alderson, J. (1979) *Policing Freedom: a commentary on the dilemmas of policing in western democracies*, Estover: Macdonald and Evans.

Alderson, J. (1985) 'Human Rights and the Police', *Police Studies*, Vol. 8 No. 2 Summer 1985: 67-73.

Alikasifoglu, K. and Dogu, E. (1987) *Turk Ceza Kanunu, Ceza Muhakemeleri Kanunu ve Polis Mevzuati,* Ankara: Seckin Kitabevi.

Allport, F. (1924) *Social Psychology,* Boston: Houghton Mifflin.

Altayli, F. (1995) 'Ic mihraklar', *Hurriyet*, 17 Mart.

Althusser, L. (1971) 'Ideology and Ideological Apparatuses', in L. Althusser, *Lenin and Philosophy and other essays*, London: NLB: 123-173.

Ankara Constabulary, Rapid Action Unit Sub-Division (1992) *Operational Order,* 16 October 1992, No.1234.

Apaydin, F. and Alister, P (1994) 'Blissful Years of the Jews in the Ottoman State', *The Fountain*, July-Sept. No.7: 8-11.

Appelbaum, R. P. (1970) *Theories of Social Change,* Chicago: Markham Publishing Company.

Appignanesi, L. and Maitland, S. (1989) *The Rushdie File*, London: ICA.

Archer, J (1977) 'The Psychology of Violence', *New Society,* 13 October 1977.

Arendt, H. (1970) *On Violence,* New York: Brace and World.

Armagan, S. (1987) *Islam Hukukunda Temel Hak ve Hurriyetler*, Ankara: Diyanet Isleri Baskanligi Yayinlari No. 274.

Armstrong, H. C. (1937) *Grey Wolf: Mustafa Kemal, An Intimate Study of a Dictator*, Middlesex: Penguin Books Limited.

Ascherson, N. and Regan, D. (1993) 'At home with the neo-Nazis', *The Sunday Review,* The Independent on Sunday, 17 October 1993.

Atar, F. (1983) *Islamda Adliye Teskilati,* Ankara: Diyanet Isleri Baskanligi Yayinlari.

Au, S. Y. Z. Ryan, M. C., Carey, M. S., Whalley, S. P. (1993a) *Managing Crowd Safety in Public Venues: A Study to Generate Guidance for Venue Owners and Enforcing Authority Inspectors*, London: HSE (Health and Safety Executive).

Au, S. Y. Z., Ryan, M. C. and Carey, M. S. (1993b) 'Key Principles in Ensuring Crowd Safety in Public Venues', in Roderich A. Smith, and Jim F. Dickie (eds) *Engineering for Crowd Safety,* London: Elsevier: 133-143.

Avon and Somerset Constabulary (1994) 'Bridgwater Carnival on Thursday 3 November 1994', *Force Operational Order*, No:119/94.

Aydin, A. H. (1991) *Comparative Policing Policy Making Structures in England, Wales and Turkey: a Case for Centralisation and Decentralisation,* an unpublished MA Dissertation, University of Leicester: Centre for the Study of Public Order.

Ball-Rokeach, S. J. (1972) 'The Legitimation of Violence', in: James F. Short and Marvin E. Wolfgang (eds) *Collective Violence,* Chicago: Aldine-Atherton: 101-111.

Bardakci, I. (1995) *Personal communications via facsimile*, dated 03 February 1995, Ilhan Bardakci is an eminent historian and journalist and lives in Bonn, Germany.

Barlas, M. (1995) 'Gecmisi hatirlamayanlar, surekli gecmisi yasarlar...'. *Sabah*, 17 Mart.

BBC Radio 4 (1993) *News at 12* pm, 30 January.

BBC Radio 4 (1994) *News at 5 O'clock* pm, 19 April, an interview with Robert Reiner.

BBC Radio 4 (1994) *News at 7 O'clock* pm, 26 April, an interview with the Home Secretary Michael Howard.

BBC2 (1992) Public Eye, Tackling Crime, March 1992.

Bellah, R. N. (1958) 'Religious Aspects of Modernisation in Turkey and Japan', *American Journal of Sociology*, Vol. 64, 1-5.

Bellah, R. N. (1961) 'Religious Aspects of Modernisation in Turkey and Japan', S. M. Lipset and N. J. Smelser (eds) *Sociology: The Progress of a Decade, A Collection of Articles*, Englewood Cliffs: Prentice-Hall, Inc: 603-608.

Benewick, R. and Holton, R. (1978) 'The peaceful crowd: Crowd solidarity and the Pope's visit to Britain', in: G. Gaskel, and R. Benewick (eds), *The Crowd In Contemporary Britain*, London: Sage: 200-210.

Bennett, C. (1992) *Victorian Images of Islam*, London: Grey Seal.

Bennett, C. (1993) 'Christian-Muslim Relations: The Agenda for Today', a presentation by Revd Dr Clinton Bennett, on 9th December 1993, University of Leicester.

Bennett, C. (1994) *Interview*, Revd Dr Clinton Bennett is a Lecturer in Study of Religions, Westminster College, Oxford, England.

Bennetto, J. and Connett, D. (1993) 'Race march explodes into riot', *Independent on Sunday,* 17 October.

Benyon, J. and Bourn, C. (1986) *The Police: Powers, Procedures and Proprieties,* Oxford: Pergamon Press.

Benyon, J. and Solomos, J. (1987) *The Roots of Urban Unrest,* Oxford: Pergamon.

Benyon, J. and Dauda, B. Garnet, D. (1991) *African Caribbean People In Leicestershire: Progress Report for the City Action Team*, African Caribbean Support Group Research Project, Centre for the Study of Public Order, University of Leicester.

Benyon, J. and Dauda, B. Garnet, D. (1992a) *African Caribbean People In Leicestershire*: African Caribbean Support Group Research Project, Centre for the Study of Public Order, University of Leicester.

Benyon, J. and Dauda, B. Garnet, D. (1992b) *African Caribbean People In Leicestershire: First Interim Report,* African Caribbean Support Group Research Project, Centre for the Study of Public Order, University of Leicester.

Benyon, J. and Dauda, B. (1993) *African Caribbean People In Leicestershire: Second Interim Report,* African Caribbean Support Group Research Project, Centre for the Study of Public Order, University of Leicester.

Benyon, J. (1993) *Disadvantage, Politics and Disorder: Social Disintegration and Conflict in Contemporary Britain*, Leicester: Centre for the Study of Public Order, University of Leicester.

Benyon, J. (1994a) 'Divided We Fall', an unpublished inaugural lecture given by Professor John Benyon, on 24 May 1994, at the University of Leicester.

Benyon, J. (1994b) *Law and Order Review 1993:* An Audit of Crime, Policing and Criminal Justice Issues, Leicester: Centre for the Study of Public Order.

Berk, R. A. (1972a) 'The Controversy Surrounding Analyses of Collective Violence: Some Methodological Notes', in: James F. Short and Marvin E. Wolfgang (eds) *Collective Violence,* Chicago: Aldine-Atherton: 112-118.

Berk, R. A. (1972b) 'The Emergence of Muted Violence in Crowd Behaviour: A Case Study of An Almost Race Riot', in: James F. Short and Marvin E. Wolfgang (eds) *Collective Violence,* Chicago: Aldine-Atherton: 309-327.

Berk, R. A. and Rossi, P. H. (1972) 'Local Political Leadership and Popular Discontent in the Ghetto', in: James F. Short and Marvin E. Wolfgang (eds) *Collective Violence*, Chicago: Aldine-Atherton: 293-308.

Berki, A. H. (1982) *Mecelle*, Istanbul: Hikmet Yayinevi.

Berkowitz, L. (1962) *Aggression: A Social Psychological Analysis,* New York: McGraw-Hill Book Company, Inc.

Berkowitz, L. (1968) 'The Study of Urban Violence: Some Implications of Laboratory Studies of Frustration and Aggression', *The American Behavioral Scientist*, March-April 1968, Volume II, Number 4, Beverly Hills, California: Sage Publications, Inc: 14-17.

Berlonghi, A. E. (1993) 'Understanding and Planning for Different Spectator Crowds', in: Roderich A. Smith, and Jim F. Dickie (eds) *Engineering for Crowd Safety,* London: Elsevier: 13-20.

Bersani, E. A. (1970) *Crime and Delinquency: A Reader,* London: Macmillan.

Beteille, A. (ed) (1969) *Social Inequality,* Middlesex: Penguin Books.

Bienen, H. (1968) *Violence and Social Change,* Chicago: The University of Chicago Press.

Bilton, T. Bonnett, K. Jones, P. Stanworth, M. Sheard, K. and Webster, A. (1987) *Introductory Sociology,* second edition, London: Macmillan.

Birand, M. A. (1995a) 'Hukumet, asil simdi istofa etmeli...,'*Sabah,* 17 Mart.

Birand, M. A. (1995b) 'Polis ile asker ayrimini asil siz yapiyorsunuz...', *Sabah*, 18 Mart,

Blumer, H. (1975) 'Outline of Collective Behaviour', in: Robert E. Evans (ed) *Readings in Collective Behaviour,* Chicago:Rand McNally College Publishing Company: 22-45.

Bowden, T. (1970) 'Guarding the State: The Police Response to Crisis Politics in Europe', *British Journal of Law and Society,* Vol. 5 No.1 1970, 69-88.

Bowden, T. (1978) *Beyond the Limits of the Law*, Harmondsworth: Penguin.

Box, S. (1988) *Recession, Crime and Punishment*, London: Macmillan.

Brain, D. F. (1990) *Mindless Violence?: The Nature and Biology of Aggression,* [a published inaugural lecture, delivered at the College on 5 February 1990], Swansea: University College of Swansea.

Brake, M. and Hale, C. (1992) *Public Order and Private Lives: The Politics of Law And Order,* London: Routledge.

Brearley, N. (1991) 'Riot Control- Understanding Crowd Psychology', *Intersec,* Vol.1, Issue 6, November 1991: 197-199.

Brearley, N. (1992) 'Public Order, Safety and Crowd Control', *Intersec*, Vol. 2 Issue 1, May 1992: 4-6.

Brearley, N. and King, M. (1993) 'Policing Demonstrations: some indicators of change', an unpublished paper presented to the ESRC (Economic and Social Research Council) seminar series, held at the CSPO (Centre for the Study of Public Order), University of Leicester, on 27 September 1993.
Brewer, J. D.(1994) 'Policing Northern Ireland's Divisions', an unpublished paper presented to the ESRC (Economic and Social Research Council) seminar series, held at Ranmoore Hall, Sheffield, on 7-8 January.
Brewer, J. D., Guelke, A., Hume, I., Moxon-Browne, E. and Wilford, R. (1988) *The Police, Public Order and the State,* London: Macmillan Press.
Bridgwater Guy Fawkes Carnival (1994) Souvenir Programme, Bridgwater: Bridgwater Guy Fawkes Carnival Committee.
Bright, M. (1994) 'From Empire to Modern State', *Guardian Education*, April 12.
Brightmore, C. (1992) *Urban Rioting in Latter Day Britain: An analysis of causes, tension monitoring, disorder prediction and prevention,* an unpublished MA dissertation, Centre for the Study of Public Order, University of Leicester.
Brinton, C. (1965) *The Anatomy of Revolution*, New York: Vintage Books.
BSSRS Technology of Political Control Group (1985) *TecnoCop: New Police Technologies,* London: Free Association Books.
Bunglawala, I. (1994) 'The Face of Fascism', *Trends,* Vol. 5, Issue 6, London: Trends Publications Ltd: 4.
Bunyan, T. (1977) *The History and Practice of the Political Police in Britain,* London: Quartet Books.
Buyukdogerli, E. (1992) *Toplumsal Olaylar ve Mudahale Esaslari:* Polis Okullari Ders Kitabi, [Operational Rules of Crowd Events: a textbook for Police Schools], Ankara: Emniyet Genel Mudurlugeu Egitim Daire Baskanligi: Official Publication.
Bwy, D. (1968) 'Dimensions of Social Conflict in America', *The American Behavioral Scientist*, March-April 1968, Vol. II, No. 4, Beverly Hills, California: Sage Publications, Inc: 39-50.
Campbell, C. (1976) 'Perspectives of Violence', in: N.Tutt (ed), *Violence,* London: HMSO.
Campbell, D. (1994) 'War on the streets of London', *The Guardian* Friday 29 April.
Campbell, J. S. (1972) 'The Usefulness of Commission Studies of Collective Violence', in: James F. Short and Marvin E. Wolfgang (eds) *Collective Violence,* Chicago: Aldine-Atherton: 370-378.
Canetti, E. (1962) *Crowds and Power*, London: Victor Gollancz Ltd.
Card, R. (1987) *Public Order: the New Law*, London: Butterworth.
Carr-Hill, R. A. (1986) 'Moral Panics, Policing and the Politics of Public Order', *The Howard Journal*, Vol. 25 No. (4): 286-301.
Cashmore, E. and McLaughlin, E. (eds) (1991) *Out of Order?-Policing Black Community,* London: Routledge.

Cawziyya, Al-Imamu ibn Al-Celilu ibn Kayyim'a-Lcawziyya (1969) *I'lamu'L-Muki'in 'an Rabbi'l'Alemin*, Daru'l-Kutub.

Cem, I. (1995) 'Siddetin "hammaddesi" ve patlayan gecekondular', *Sabah*, 19 Mart.

Central Planning Unit (1992a) *The Public Order: Command Awareness Programme,* Harrogate, Central Planning Unit.

Central Planning Unit (1992b) *The Public Order: Bronze/Silver Programme,* Harrogate, Central Planning Unit.

CSPO (Centre for the Study of Public Order) (1992) *Leicestershire African Caribbean Survey*, Centre for the Study of Public Order, University of Leicester.

Cerrah, I. (1991) *Police Armament In Britain; a consideration of whether the police are becoming increasingly militarised,* an unpublished MA. Dissertation, University of Leicester: Centre for the Study of Public Order.

Cerrah, I. (1994) 'Classfying Crowds: Implications for Police Response to Crowd Events', an unpublished paper presented to the ESRC (Economic and Social Research Council) seminar series, held at the New Scotland Yard, London, on 15 April.

Chesshyre, R. (1990) *The Force,* London: Pan.

Chris, M. (1977) 'The Soccer Hooligans' honour system', *New Society* 6 October.

Clark, S. (ed) (1992) *Malcolm X : February 1965, The Final Speeches*, New York: Pathfinder.

Clarke, R. V. G. (1978) *Tackling Vandalism*, HORS 47, London: HMSO.

Clinard, M. B. (ed) (1964) *Anomie and Deviant Behavior,* New York: The Free Press.

Clutterback, R. (1978) *Britain in Agony: The Growth of Political Violence*, London: Faber and Faber.

Cohen, L. and Manion, L. (1989) *Research Methods in Education*, London: Routledge.

Colasan, E. (1995) 'Son Olaylar ve Aleviler', *Hurriyet*, 17 Mart.

Cole, T. (1989) 'Researching Race and Racism', *Social Studies Review,* Vol. 5, No. 2 November 1989: 62-65.

Coles, P. (1968) *The Ottoman Impact On Europe,* New York: Brace and World.

Collins, Cobuild (1992) *English Language Dictionary*, London: Collins.

Comer, J. (1994) Personal correspondence with Chief Inspector John Comer, Operational Unit of Avon and Somerset Constabulary dated 28 November.

Connery, R. H. (ed) (1968) *Urban Riots: Violence and Social Change*, New York: Vintage Books.

Cooper, P. (1985) 'Competing Explanations of the Merseyside Riots of 1981', *British Journal of Criminology,* 25 (1) :60-69.

Couch, C. J. (1975) 'Collective Behaviour: An examination of some Stereotypes', in: Robert E. Evans (ed) *Readings in Collective Behaviour,* Chicago: Rand McNally College Publishing Company: 71-85.

Cox, B. (1975) *Civil Liberties in Britain*, Middlesex: Penguin Books.

Croall, H. (1992) *White Collar Crime,* Buckingham: Open University Press.

Cumhuriyet (1995) 17 Mart.

Currie, E. and Skolnick, J. H. (1972) 'A Critical Note on Conceptions of Collective Behaviour', in: James F. Short and Marvin E. Wolfgang (eds) *Collective Violence,* Chicago: Aldine-Atherton: 60-71.

Daftary, F. (1992) *The Isma'ilis: Their History and Doctrines,* Cambridge: Cambridge University Press.

Dahhak, M. F. (1993) *Questions: This modern age puts to Islam,* Truestar, London.

Darbyshire, N. (1992) 'Yes, but is it really a riot?', *The Daily Telegraph* 25 July.

Das, D. K. (1988) 'Police and Violent Protests in London: A Comparative Perspective', *Police Studies*, Vol. 11, No. 3 Fall 1988: 105-115.

Davies, J. C. (ed) (1971) *When Men Revolt and Why: a reader in political violence and revolution,* New York: The Free Press.

De Vaus, D. A. (1990) *Surveys In Social Research,* London: Unwin Hyman.

Deane-Drummond, A. (1975) *Riot Control,* London: Royal United Services Institute for Defence Studies.

Denno, D. W. (1990) *Biology and Violence: from birth to adulthood,* Cambridge: Cambridge University Press.

Denscombe, M. (1994) *Sociology Update 1994,* Leicester: Olympus Books.

Devellioglu, F. (1984) *Osmanlica-Turkce Ansiklopedik Lugat,* Ankara: Aydin Kitabevi.

Dickie, J. F. (1993) 'Crowd Disasters', in: Roderich A. Smith, and Jim F. Dickie (eds) *Engineering for Crowd Safety,* London: Elsevier: 89-97.

Dickson, M. G. (1993) 'Strategies and Methods for Appraising Existing Stands', in: Roderich A. Smith, and Jim F. Dickie (eds) *Engineering for Crowd Safety,* London: Elsevier: 1-11.

Dogan, D. M. (1986) *Buyuk Turkce Sozluk,* Istanbul: Beyan Yayincilik.

Dogru, N. (1995a) 'Bayat oyun: Polis kotu, asker iyi', *Sabah*, 17 Mart.

Dogru, N. (1995b) 'Politikacinin pisligini Askere temizletmeyelim...', *Sabah*, 18 Mart.

Dunning, E. (1990) 'Sociological reflection on sport, violence and civilisation', *International Review for the Sociology of Sport,* 25 (1) : 65-81.

Dunning, E. Murphy, P. and William J. (1986) 'Spectators violence at football matches: Towards a Sociological Explanation', *British Journal of Sociology,* 37 (2): 221-244.

Dunning, E. Murphy, P. and William, J. (1990) *The Roots of Football Hooliganism: A Historical and Sociological Study,* London: Routledge and Kegan Paul.

Dunning, E. Murphy, P. Waddington. I. (1992) *Discussion Papers in Sociology: Violence in the British Civilising Process,* Leicester, University of Leicester, Faculty of Social Sciences, Department of Sociology.

Durkheim, E. (1952) *Suicide: A Study in Sociology*, London: Routledge and Kegan Paul Ltd.

Durmaz, M. (1989) Sorusturma Yontemi, Ankara: Afsar Matbaacilik.

Ece, H. (1991) *The Transition Between The Ottoman Empire And New Turkish Police: A Consideration Of The Dynamics For Change,* an unpublished MA. Dissertation, University of Leicester: Centre for the Study of Public Order.

Edgar, D. (1988) 'Festivals of the Oppressed', *Race & Class,* XXIX, 4 (1988): 61-76.

Edwards, A. (1994) 'Thatcherism, Authoritarian Statism and the Dispersal Discipline: Problems in Conceptualising Law and Order in the 1980s', an unpublished paper presented to the Politics of Law and Order Panel, PSA Annual Conference, University of Swansea, 29-31 March.

Elamin, N. (1993) 'Muslims terrorised in France', *The Muslim News,* 26 November.

Elliston, L. (1992) *The Problematic Relationship Between Public Policing, Private Policing and Social Justice,* an unpublished MA. dissertation, University of Leicester: Centre for the Study of Public Order.

Elliston, L. (1994) 'Marshall Training In South Africa: September-December 1993', an unpublished paper presented to the ESRC (Economic and Social Research Council) seminar series, held at the New Scotland Yard, London, on 15 April.

Emin, M. (1992) 'Ickili Subaylara Tepki Suruyor', *Zaman*, 8 July.

Emniyet Genel Mudurlugu (1983a) *Cevik Kuvvet Birimlerinin Onleme ve Mudahale Planlarina Iliskin Yonerge*, [Regulation concerning with the preventive and responsive plans of Rapid Action Units], Ankara: Official Publication.

Emniyet Genel Mudurlugu (1983b) *Polis Cevik Kuvvet Ozel Timleri Yonergesi,* [Specialised Police Rapid Action Units' Regulation] Ankara: Official Publication.

Emniyet Genel Mudurlugu (1983c) *Polis Cevik Kuvvet Yonetmeligi,* [Police Rapid Action Regulation], Ankara; Official Publication.

Erkal, M. E. (1993) *Sosyoloji*, Istanbul: Der Yayinlari.

Erlen, C. (1992) 'All fall out at the fez', *The Guardian,* Monday July 27.

Esposito, J. L. (1992) *The Islamic Threat: Myth or Reality,* Oxford: Oxford University Press.

Evans, R. (1988) *Bridgwater Carnival: Visitors Guide,* Somerset: Bridgwater Guy Fawkes Carnival Committee.

Evans, R. R. (ed) (1975) *Readings in Collective Behaviour*, Chicago: Rand McNally College Publishing Company.

Farra, Al-Kadi ebu Ya'la Al-Farra (1983) *Al-Ahkamu's-Sultaniyye,* Beirut, Lebanon: Risale.

Feierabend, I. K., Feierabend, R. L. and Gurr, T. R. (1972) *Anger, Violence and Politics: Theories and Research,* Englewood Cliffs, New Jersey: Prentice-Hall, Inc.

Festinger, L. Pepitone, A. and Newcomb, T. (1952) 'Some consequences of De-Individuation In a Group', supplement to *The Journal of Abnormal and Social Psychology,* Vol. 47 April 1952 Number 2: 382-389.

Field, S. (1983) 'Social theory and classification of riot and disorder', *Home Office Research Bulletin*, No. 15.

Fielding, N. G. (1991) *The Police and Social Conflict,* London: The Athlone Press.

Fine, B. and Millar, R. (eds) (1985) *Policing the Miner's Strike*, London: Lawrence and Wishart.

Fink, A. E. (1962) *Causes of Crime: Biological Theories in the United States 1800-1915,* New York: A. S. Barnes and Company, Inc.

Finkel, S. E. and Rule, J. B. (1989) 'Relative Deprivation and Related Psychological Theories of Civil Violence: A Critical Review', *Research in Social Movements, Conflicts and Change*, Vol. 9: 47-69.

Folger, R. (ed) (1984) *The Sense of Injustice: Social Psychological Perspectives,* London: Plenum Press.

Fortas, A. (1968) *Concerning Dissent and Civil Disobedience*, New York: Signet Books.

France, A. (1894) *Le Lys Rouge*, Paris.

Francis, P. and Matthews, R.(eds) (1993) *Tackling Racial Attacks*, Leicester: Centre for the Study of Public Order.

Frank, A. W. (1976) 'Making Scenes in Public: symbolic violence and social order', *Theory and Society,* 3: 395-416.

Freud, S. (1940) *Group Psychology and the Analysis of the Ego,* [translated by James Strachey] London: The Hogarth Press.

Freud, S. (1979) *Civilisation and Its Discontents,* London: Hogarth.

Freud, S. (1994) Toplum Psikolojisi, (translated into Turkish by Kemal Saydam from S. Ferud's work, *Group Psychology and the Analysis of the Ego*, Istanbul: Dusunen Adam Yayinlari.

Fruin, J. J. (1993) 'The Causes and Prevention of Crowd Disaster', in Roderich A. Smith, and Jim F. Dickie (eds) *Engineering for Crowd Safety,* London: Elsevier: 99-109.

Gamson, W. A., Fireman, B. and Rytina, S. (1982) *Encounters with Unjust Authority*, Homewood, Illinois, The Dorsey Press.

Gaskell, G. and Benewick, R. (1987) *The Crowd in Contemporary Britain,* London: Sage.

Gaskell, G. and Benewick, R. (1987) 'Social Scientific Perspectives on the Crowd in Britain', *The Quarterly Journal of Social Affairs,* 3 (1): 53-70.

Geary, R. (1985) *Policing Industrial Disputes: 1893 to 1985,* Cambridge: Cambridge University Press.

Geiss, G. (1970) 'White Collar Crime: The Heavy Electrical Equipment Antitrust Cases of 1961', in: E. A. Bersani (ed) *Crime and Delinquency: A reader,* London: Macmillan.

Gellner, E.(1991)'Islam and Marxism: some comparisons', *International Affairs* 67, I: 1-6.

Gibson, C. and O'Neill S. (1993) 'Pitch Invasion could lead to fences again', *The Daily Telegraph,* 8. 3. 1993.

Giddens, A. Held, D. (1988) *Classes, Power, and Conflict: Classical and Contemporary Debates*, London: Macmillan Education.

Ginneken, J. V. (1992) *Crowds, Psychology, and Politics, 1871-1899*, Cambridge: Cambridge University Press.

Ginsberg, M. (1964) *The Psychology of Society*, London: Methuen and Co Ltd.

Glueck, S. and Glueck,. E. (1962) *Family Environment and Delinquency*, London: Routledge and Kegan Paul.

Gocer, C. (1993) 'Rasim Ozdenoren'le Devlet ve Rejim Uzerine', *Ilim ve Sanat,* Sayi; 34, Ocak: 20-22.

Goktas, E. (1995) 'Koyluoglu: Polisin tutumu cagdisi', *Cumhuriyet,* 19 Mart.

Goldschmidt, A. (1988) *A Concise History of the Middle East,* 3rd. ed. Boulder: Westview.

Graef, R. (1989) *Talking Blues: The police in their own words,* London: Fontana.

Graham, H. D. (1972) 'The Paradox of American Violence: A historical Appraisal', in: James F. Short and Marvin E. Wolfgang (eds) *Collective Violence*, Chicago: Aldine-Atherton: 202-209.

Graham, H. D. and Gurr, T. R. (1969) *The History of Violence in America,* Frederic A. Praeger.

Gramsci, A. (1971) *Selections from the Prison Notebooks of Antonio Gramsci,* London: (edited and translated by Q. Hoare and G. N. Smith) Lawrence & Wishart.

Grant, L. Hewitt, P. Jackson, C. and Levenson H. (1978) *Civil Liberty: The NCCL Guide to your Rights,* Middlesex: Penguin Books.

Greater Manchester Police (1980s, undated-a) 'Facing Up to the Challenge', an unpublished paper prepared by the Greater Manchester Police.

Greater Manchester Police (1980s, undated-b) *Crowd Psychology*, an internal document prepared by the Greater Manchester Police.

Grimshaw, A. D. (1968) 'Three Views of Urban Violence: Civil Disturbance, Racial Revolt, Class Assault', *The American Behavioral Scientist*, March-

April 1968, Volume II, Number 4: 2-7, Beverly Hills, California: Sage Publications, Inc.

Grimshaw, A. D. (1972) 'Interpreting Collective Violence: An Argument for the Importance of Social Structure', in: James F. Short and Marvin E. Wolfgang (eds) *Collective Violence,* Chicago: Aldine-Atherton: 36-46.

Gundogdu, A. (1985) *Toplumsal Olaylar ve Cevik Kuvvet,* (Crowd Events and the Rapid Action Unit), an unpublished MA dissertation, Istanbul: University of Istanbul.

Gungor, S. and Kavalali, A. M. (1990) *Uygulamada Toplanti ve Gosteri Yuruyusleri,* Ankara: Yetkin Hukuk Yayinlari.

Gurr, T. (1968) 'Urban Disorder: Perspectives from the Comparative Study of Civil Strife', *The American Behavioral Scientist,* March-April 1968, Volume II, Number 4: 50-55, Beverly Hills, California: Sage Publications, Inc.

Gurr, T. R. (1970) *Why Men Rebel*, Princeton, New Jersey: Princeton University Press.

Gurr, T. R. (1972) 'Sources of Rebellion in Western Societies: Some Quantitative Evidence', in: James F. Short and Marvin E. Wolfgang (eds) *Collective Violence*, Chicago: Aldine-Atherton: 133-146.

Gurr, T. R. (1980) *Handbook of Political Conflict,* New York: The Free Press.

Gurr, T. R. (ed) (1989) *Violence in America, Protest, Rebellion, Reform,* Vol. 2, London: Sage Publications.

Gutzmore, C. (1982) 'The Notting Hill Carnival', *Marxism Today,* August 1982: 29-33.

Hall, S. (1976) 'Violence and the Media', in: N. Tutt (ed) *Violence,* London: HMSO.

Hall, S. (1979) *Drifting into law and order society,* London: Cobden Trust.

Hall, S. (1987a) 'Urban Unrest in Britain', in: J. Benyon, and J. Solomos (eds) *The Roots of Urban Unrest,* Oxford: Pergamon.

Hall, S. Critcher, C, Jefferson, T. Clarke, J. and Roberts, B. (1987b) *Policing The Crisis: Mugging, The State, and Law and Order*, London: Macmillan Education.

Halliday, F. (1993) 'Islam and the West: Myths of Confrontation', CIES Annual Lecture 1993, Coventry University: Centre for International and European Studies.

Hamid, A. (1989) *Islam: The Natural Way*, London: Mels.

Hamidullah, M. (1993)'Islam ve Devlet Uzerine', *Ilim ve Sanat*, Sayi 34, Ocak 1993: 11.

Hannan, R. (1994) 'The Institution of Slavery', *Al-Mizan*, Volume 1 Issue 1: 87-95.

Haralambos, M. and Holborn, M. (1990) *Sociology: Themes and Perspectives,* London: Unwin Hyman.

Hare, A. P. (1972) 'The Nonviolent Alternative: Research Strategy and Preliminary Findings', in: James F. Short and Marvin E. Wolfgang (eds) *Collective Violence,* Chicago: Aldine-Atherton: 356-370.

Harrington, J. (1976) 'Violence in Groups', in: N. Tutt (ed) *Violence,* London: HMSO.

Hatemi, H. (1993) 'Islam Dusuncesinde Devlet Telakkisi', *Ilim ve Sanat,* Sayi, 34, Ocak 1993: 15-19.

Hatipoglu, A. M. (1986) *Operasyon Duzenleme*, (Operational Arrangements), Ankara: Emniyet Genel Mudurlugu, Egitim Daire Baskanligi Yayinlari, Seri No. 2 Yayin No. 1986-2: Ankara: Official Publication.

Headfield, G. Syal, R. and Rayment, T. (1993) 'Police Clash with rioters over Neo-Nazi book shop', *The Sunday Times,* 17 October.

Heidensohn, F. (1992) *Women in Control: The role of women in law enforcement*, Oxford: Clarendon Press.

Heidensohn, F. (1994) 'Making it even: equal opportunities and public order?', a presentation to the ESRC (Economic and Social Research Council) seminar series, held at the New Scotland Yard, London, on 15 April.

Heper, M. (1993) 'Political Culture as a Dimension of Compatibility', in: M. Heper, A. Oncu. H. Kramer (eds) *Turkey and the West: Changing Political and Cultural Identities*, New York: I. B. Tauris and Co. Ltd: 1-17.

Heper, M., Oncu, A. and Kramer H. (1993) *Turkey and the West: Changing Political and Cultural Identities,* New York: I. B. Tauris and Co. Ltd.

Hesse, B. (1993) 'Racism and spacism in Britain', in: P. Francis and R. Matthews (eds), *Tackling Racial Attacks*, Leicester: Centre for the Study of Public Order: 11-17.

Hibbs, D. A. (1973) *Mass Political Violence: A Cross-National Causal Analysis*, New York: John Wiley & Sons.

HMSO (1993) *The 1992 British Crime Survey, Home Office Research Study 132,* by Pat Mayhew, Natalie Aye Maung and Catriona Mirrless-Black, London: HMSO.

Hobbes, T. (1962) *Leviathan*, London: Collins.

Hobbs, D. (1988) *Doing the Business*, Oxford: Oxford University Press.

Hobohm, M. A. (1986) *Islam's Answer to the Racial Problem,* Birmingham: Islamic Propagation Centre International, IPCI.

Hoffman, J. (1988a) 'Are we free to harm ourselves while not harming others?', *Social Studies Review,* Vol.4 No. 1 September.

Hoffman, J. (1988b) 'Is Political Violence Ever Justified?, *Social Studies Review*, Vol. 4, No. 2: 61-62.

Hoffman, J. (1991) *Has Marxism A Future?*, Discussion Papers in Politics, No. P91/1, University of Leicester: Faculty of Social Sciences, Department of Politics.

Hoffman, J. (1992) *Hedley Bull's Conception Of International Society And The Future Of The State*, Discussion Papers in Politics, No. P92/2, University of Leicester: Faculty of Social Sciences, Department of Politics.

Hoffman, J. (1994) *Is Political Violence Ever Justified?, A Critique of Violence in its Statist and Anti-Statist Forms,* Studies in Crime, Order and Policing, Occasional Paper No.4, University of Leicester: Centre for the Study of Public Order.

Hoffman, J. (1995) *Interview and personal communication via letter,* dated 07. March. 1995, Dr John Hoffman is a lecturer at the Department of Politics, University of Leicester, England.

Holdaway, S. (1979) *The British Police,* Croydon: Edward Arnold.

Holdaway, S. (1983) *Inside the British Police,* Oxford: Basil Blackwell Publisher Limited.

Honderich, T. (1976) *Three Essays on Political Violence,* Oxford: Basil Blackwell.

Honderich, T. (1989) *Violence for Equality: Inquiries in Political Philosophy*, London: Routledge.

Hopkins, I. H. G., Pountney, S. J. Hayes, P. and Sheppard, M. A. (1993) 'Crowd Pressure Monitoring', in: Roderich A. Smith, and Jim F. Dickie (eds) *Engineering for Crowd Safety,* London: Elsevier: 389-399.

Howe, D. (1993) 'Freedom to be Yourself', in *Notting Hill Carnival Guide '93,* London: Ashley House Ltd.

HSE (Health & Safety Executive) (1993) *Managing Crowds Safely,* Sheffield: HSE Information Centre.

Huntbach, S. C. (1994) 'The Training of Police Officers to Meet the Needs of Today's Society in Public Order Events', an unpublished paper presented to the ESRC *(Economic and Social Research Council)* seminar series, held at Ranmoore Hall, Sheffield, on 7-8 January.

Hurriyet (1995) 17 Mart 1995.

Huseyin, A. (1993a) *Islami Radikalizmin Otesi: iman ve amelin sosyolojisi*, Istanbul: Yonelis.

Huseyin, A. (1993b) 'The Islamic State Within the Framework of Islam', *Ilim ve Sanat,* Sayi: 34, Ocak 1993:.12-14.

Hussain, A. (1994) 'Islamic Fundamentalism: A Threat to the West?', an unpublished presentation delivered at the University of Leicester, on 17 May.

Ibn Khaldun (1967) *The Muqaddimah: An Introduction to History*, [Translated from the Arabic by Franz Rosental, in three volumes] London: Routledge and Kegan Paul.

Ibn Khaldun (1987) *The Muqaddimah: An Introduction to History*, [Translated from the Arabic by Franz Rosenthal abridged and edited by N.J. Dawood], London: Routledge and Kegan Paul in association with Secker and Warburg.

Icel, K. and Yenisey, F. (1990) *Karsilastirmali ve Uygulamali Ceza Kanunlari,* Istanbul: Beta Basim Yayim Dagtim AS.

Ilim ve Sanat (1993) Sayi: 34, Ocak 1993, Ankara: Vefa Yayincilik.

Inan, K. (1993) *Devlet Idaresi,* Istanbul: Otuken.

Institute of Criminology (1992) *Crowd Management: Civilian and Police Conduct*, Cape Town: University of Cape Town.

Izmir Constabulary (1992)*Rapid Action Sub-Unit* (Izmir Emniyet Mudurlugu, Cevik Kuvvet Sube Mudurlugu (1992) Operational Order, concerning the sporting events of 13 November 1992, Sayi, 1293, Izmir: Official Document.

Janowitz, M. (1968) *Social Control of Escalated Riots,* Chicago: The University of Chicago.

Jefferson, T. (1987) 'Beyond Paramilitarism', *British Journal of Criminology*, Vol. 27, No. 1 Winter: 47-53.

Jefferson, T. (1990) *The Case Against Paramilitary Policing*, Milton Keynes: Open University Press.

Jenkins, G. (1968) 'Urban Violence in Africa', *The American Behavioral Scientist*, March-April 1968, Volume II, Number 4, Beverly Hills, California: Sage Publications, Inc: 37-39.

Johnson, J. M. (1975) *Doing Field Research,* London: Collier Macmillan Publishers.

Johnson, S. (1993) *Realising the Public World Order,* Order and Policing, Occasional Paper No.2, Leicester: Centre for the Study of Public Order.

Johnston, L. (1992) *The Rebirth of Private Policing*, London: Routledge.

Jones, M. (1993) 'Bobby on the beat', *Trends*, Vol. 5 Issue 3 Halifax: Trends Publications Limited.

Jorgensen, D. L. (1989) *Participant Observation*, London: Sage.

Joseph, S. and Hannon, R. (1994) 'East Side Story', *Trends*, Vol. 5, Issue 6, London: Trends Publications Ltd: 5-6.

Jupp, V. (1989) *Methods of Criminological Research*, London: Unwin Hyman.

Kahan, V. (1976) 'Violence- nature or nurture?', in: N. Tutt (ed) *Violence*, London: HMSO.

Kahn, P., Lewis, L. Livock, R. and Wiles, P. (1983) *Picketing: Industrial Disputes, Tactics and the Law,* London: Routledge and Kegan Paul.

Karaman, H. (1993) 'Kur'an-i Kerime ve Ornek Uygulamaya Gore Devlet', *Ilim ve Sanat*, Sayi: 34, Ocak 1993: 6-11.

Karaosmanoglu, A. L. (1993) 'Officers: Westernization and Democracy', in: M. Heper, A. Oncu. H. Kramer (eds) *Turkey and the West: Changing Political and Cultural Identities,* New York: I. B. Tauris and Co. Ltd: 19-34.

Karim, S. (1993) 'The Cancer of Racism', *Trends*, Vol. 5, Issue 3, Halifax: Trends Publications Limited.

Kassam, K. A. (1993a) 'Integration of Islam in Young Ottoman Thought', *Islamica*, Vol. 1 No. 2: 10-14.

Kassam, K. A. (1993b) 'Integration of Islam in Young Ottoman Thought', *Islamica*, Vol. 1 No. 3: 15-21.

Kavakci, Y. Z. (1975) *Hisbe Teskilati*, Ankara: Baylan Matbaasi.

Kazici, Z. (1987) *Osmanlilarda Ihtisab Muessesi*, Istanbul: Kultur Basin Yayin Birligi.

Keith, M. (1993) *Race, Riots and Policing: Lore and Disorder in a Multi-racist Society*, London: UCL (University College London) Press.

Keith, M. (1994) 'Street Sensibility? 'youth', 'gangs', heroes and villains in the of young Bengalis in the East End of London', a presentation to the ESRC (Economic and Social Research Council) seminar series, held at Ranmoore Hall, Sheffield, on 7-8 January.

Kerner Commission Report (1968) *Report of the National Advisory Commission on Civil Disorders*, New York: Bantam Books.

Kettani, M. A. (1969) *The Muslim Minorities*, Leicester: The Islamic Foundation.

Khilafah (1994) *Khilafah Magazine*, Volume 4, Issue 1, April 1994: London.

Kidder, L. H. (1981) *Research Methods In Social Relations*, Tokyo: Holt-Saunders.

King, M. J. (1987) *The Growth of Police Powers in the Federal Republic of Germany: an analysis of the relations of the State, legitimation and coercion*, an unpublished PhD thesis submitted to the University of Wales.

Komur, R. (1992) 'Gecekonducuya Yikim Iskencesi', *Zaman*, 21 November.

Kongar, E. (1979) *Toplumsal Degisme Kuramlari ve Turkiye Gercegi*, Ankara: Bilgi Yayinevi.

Kutub, S. (1981) *Islamin Dunya Gorusu*, Istanbul: Arslan Yayinlari.

Kutub, S. (1982) *Islamda Sosyal Adalet*, Istanbul: Aslan Yayinlari.

Lacey, D. (1993) 'Pitch invasion recalls the darkest age', *The Guardian*, Monday March 8.

Lang, K. and Lang, G. E. (1968) 'Racial Disturbances As Collective Protest', *The American Behavioral Scientist*, March-April 1968, Volume II, Number 4, Beverly Hills, California: Sage Publications, Inc: 11-13.

LaPiere, R. and Farnsworth, P. R. (1949) *Social Psychology*, New York: McGraw-Hill Book Company, Inc.

LaPiere, T. Richard (1938) *Collective Behaviour*, New York: McGraw-Hill Book Company, Inc.

Le Bon, G. (1898) *The Psychology Of Peoples*, London: T. Fisher Unwin.

Le Bon, G. (1969) *The Crowd*, A Classical of Sociology with a new introduction by Robert K. Merton, New York: Viking Compass.

Lea, J. and Young, J. (1984) *What Is to be Done About Law and Order*, Reading: Cox and Wyman Ltd.

Lee, A. McClung (1969) *Principles of Sociology*, New York: Barnes and Noble Books.

Leech, K. (1995) 'Bengali community betrayed', *The Guardian*, January 17.

Leeds, C. (1992) 'Conflict Theories, Government Policies and the Urban Riots of the Early 1980s', in: T. F. Marshall (ed) *Community Disorders and Policing: Conflict Management in Action,* London: Whiting and Birch.

Leicester City Football Club (Undated) *Stewarding Handbook*, [a small confidential handbook prepared by the club's Safety Officer, ex-chief superintendent Ian Coutts, Leicester.

Leicester Mercury (1993) 'Toddler Murder Probe Held Up; Angry crowds hinder police', *Leicester Mercury*, Wednesday, 17 February.

Leicestershire Constabulary (1991) *Leicester City Football Club Major Incident-Contingency Arrangements,* Divisional Order No. 5/91, Leicester: Official Document.

Leicestershire Constabulary (1992a) *Operational Order,* 20/92: Leicester City Football Club -v- Sunderland Football Club, Wednesday 8 April: Official Document.

Leicestershire Constabulary (1992b) *Operational Order,* 47/92; Leicester Caribbean Carnival, Saturday 1 August: Official Document.

Leicestershire Constabulary (1992c) *Operational Order,* No. 42/92; Leicester City Football Club -v- Newcastle United, Saturday 2 May 1992: Official Document.

Leicestershire Constabulary (1992d) *Operational Order,* No. 63/92; Leicester City Football Club -v- Wolverhampton Wanderers, Sunday 13 September: Official Document.

Leicestershire Constabulary (1992e) *Operational Order*, No. HQ/50/92; The 'Monsters of Rock' pop festival, Donington Park, Leicester, Friday 21st August 1992- Sunday 23rd August: Official Document.

Lenin, V. I. (1969) *The State and Revolution*, Moscow: Progress Publishers.

Leon, C. (1994) 'Militaristic Micawbers or the Happiest Institution? The use of special constables in the policing of public disorder', a presentation to the ESRC (Economic and Social Research Council) seminar series, at the centre for the Study of Public Order, 18th November 1994.

Levy, B. (1968) 'Cops in the Ghetto: A problem of the Police System', *The American Behavioral Scientist*, March-April 1968, Vol. II, No. 4, Beverly Hills, California: Sage Publications, Inc: 31-34.

Levy, S. G. (1972) 'The Psychology of Political Activity', in: James F. Short and Marvin E. Wolfgang (eds) *Collective Violence,* Chicago: Aldine-Atherton: 211-223.

Lewis, B. (1961) *The Emergency of Modern Turkey*, London: Oxford University Press.

Lightfoot, L. and Rayment, T. (1992) 'Police study videos to catch riot ringleaders', *The Sunday Times*, 26 July.

Lindzey, G. and Aronson, E. (eds) (1968a) *The Handbook of Social Psychology,* Volume one, Historical Introduction/Systematic Positions, second edition, Reading, Massachusetts; Addison-Wesley Publishing Company.

Lindzey, G. and Aronson, E. (eds) (1968b) *The Handbook of Social Psychology,* Volume two, Research Methods, second edition, Reading, Massachusetts; Addison-Wesley Publishing Company.

Lindzey, G. and Aronson, E. (eds) (1969a) *The Handbook of Social Psychology,* Volume three, The Individual in a Social Context, second edition, Reading, Massachusetts; Addison-Wesley Publishing Company.

Lindzey, G. and Aronson, E. (eds) (1969b) *The Handbook of Social Psychology,* Volume four, Group Psychology and Phenomena of Interactions, second edition, Reading, Massachusetts; Addison-Wesley Publishing Company.

Lindzey, G. and Aronson, E. (eds) (1969c) *The Handbook of Social Psychology,* Volume five, Applied Social Psychology, second edition, Reading, Massachusetts; Addison-Wesley Publishing Company.

Lindzey, G. and Aronson, E. (eds) (1985) *The Handbook of Social Psychology,* Volume II, Applied Social Psychology, third edition, New York: Random House.

Lipset, S. M. and Smelser, N. J. (1961) *Sociology: The Progress of a Decade, A Collection of Articles*, Englewood Cliffs: Prentice-Hall, Inc.

Lofthouse, M. (1993a) 'State and the Police: The need for and use of legitimation', an unpublished paper presented at a seminar at the CSPO, University of Leicester on 17. 11. 1993.

Lofthouse, M. (1993b) 'The Core Mandate of Policing', an unpublished paper presented to the ESRC (Economic and Social Research Council) seminar series held at Sheffield Hallam University, on 15 April 1993.

Lombroso, C. (1968) *Crime: Its Causes and Remedies,* Montclair, New Jersey: Patterson Smith.

Lord Kinross (1965) *Ataturk: The Birth of a Nation,* London: Weidenfeld and Nicolson.

Lorenz, K. (1967) *Evolution and Modification of Behavior,* Chicago: The University of Chicago Press.

Lorenz, K. (1972) *On Aggression,* London: Methuen and Co Ltd.

MacCabe, S. and Wallington, P. (1988) *The Police, Public Order and Civil Liberties,* London: Routledge.

MacCall, G. J. and Simmons, J. L. (1969) *Issues in Participant Observation*, London: Addison-Wesley.

MacFarlane, L. (1974) *Violence and the State,* London: Nelson.

Mackenzie, I. (1988) 'Bobbies Read the Riot Act', *Police Review*, 22 April 1988, Volume 96: 857.

Madge, J. (1975) *The Tools of Social Science,* London: Longman.

Mannheim, H. (1955) *Group Problems in Crime and Punishment,* London: Routledge and Kegan Paul Limited.

Mannheim, H. (1965a) *Comparative Criminology,* A Text Book, Vol. I, London: Routledge and Kegan Paul.

Mannheim, H. (1965b) *Comparative Criminology*, A Text Book, Vol. II, London: Routledge and Kegan Paul.

Mark, R. (1977) *Policing a Perplexed Society,* London: George Allen and Unwin Ltd.

Mark, R. (1978) *In The Office of Constable:* An Autobiography, London: Collins.

Marsh, P. (1978) *The Rule of Disorder,* London: Routledge and Kegan Paul.

Marsh, P. and Campbell, A.(1978b) 'The Sex Boys on Their Own Turf', *New Society* 19 October.

Marsh, P. and Champbell, A. (1978a) 'The youth gangs of New York and Chicago go into business', *New Society*, 12 October.

Marsh, P. and Kibby, K. F. (1992) *Drinking and Disorder*, London: The Portman Group.

Marshall, T. F. (1992a) 'Theories of Violence and the Principles of Conflict Management', in: T. F. Marshall (ed) *Community Disorders and Policing: Conflict Management in Action*, London: Whiting and Birch.

Marshall, T. F. (ed) (1992b) *Community Disorders and Policing: Conflict Management in Action,* London: Whiting and Birch.

Marx, G. (1972) 'Issue-less riots', in: J. F. Short, and M. E. Wolfgang, (eds), *Collective Violence*, Chicago: Aldine-Atherton: 48-59.

Marx, K. (1957) *Capital*, Moscow: Foreign Languages Publishing House.

Marx, K. (1970) *Critique of Hegel's 'Philosophy of Right'*, London: Cambridge University Press.

Marx, K. (1975) 'Critique of Hegel's Doctrine of the State', in K. Marx *Early Writings*, Penguin.

Marx, K. (1988) *Selected Writings,* Oxford: Oxford University Press.

Marx, K. and Engels, F. (1848) *Manifesto of the Communist Party,* Moscow: Foreign Languages Publishing House.

Marx, K. and Engels, F. (1970) *The German Ideology,* London: Lawrence and Wishart.

Mather, I. (1994) 'Mrs Ciller -and Islam- take Turkey by surprise', *The European*, 1-7 April 1994.

Matthews, R. (1994) *Crime Prevention, Disorder and Victimisation*, Order and Policing, Occasional Paper No.3, Leicester: Centre for the Study of Public Order.

Matthews, R. and Young, J. (eds) (1992) *Issues in Realist Criminology,* London: Sage Publications.

Mawardi, Ebu'l-Hasan 'Ali bin Muhammed bin Habib Al-Mawardi (1989) *Al-Ahkamu's-Sultaniyye ve'l-Velayatu'd-Diniyye,* Al-Kuwayt: Daru ibn Kutaybe.

Mawardi, Ebu'L-Hasan El-Mawardi (1976) *El-Ahkamu's-Sultaniyye,* Istanbul: Bedir Yayinevi.

Mawdudi, Abul A'la (1993) *Human Rights in Islam,* Leicester: The Islamic Foundation.

Mawdudi, E. (1980) *Hilafet ve Saltanat*, Istanbul: Elif Ofset Tesisleri.

Mawsili, Abdu'l-lah bin Mahmud bin Mewdudi'L-Mawsili Al-Hanefi (1975) *Al-Ihtiyar Lita'lili'l-Muhtar,* Beirut, Lebenon: Daru'l-Ma'rife.

May, T. (1993) *Social Research: Issues, Methods and Process*, Buckingham: Open University Press.

McClelland, J. S. (1989) *The Crowd and The Mob: from Plato to Canetti*, London: Unwin Hyman.

McCord, W. and Howard, J. (1968) 'Negro Opinions in three Riot Cities', *The American Behavioral Scientist*, March-April 1968, Vol.II, No. 4, Beverly Hills, California: Sage Publications, Inc: 24-27.

McDonagh, E. (1978) *Violence and Political Change*, London: Catholic Institute for International Relations.

McEvoy, J. and Gamson, W. A. (1972) 'Police Violence and Its Public Support', in: James F. Short and Marvin E. Wolfgang (eds) *Collective Violence*, Chicago: Aldine-Atherton: 330-342.

McPhail, C. (1971) 'Civil Disorder Participation: A Critical Examination of Recent Research', *American Sociological Review*, 36: 1058-1073.

McPhail, C. and Miller, D. (1973) 'The Assembling Process: A Theoretical and Empirical Examination', *American Sociological Review,* 1973, Vol. 38 (December): 721-735.

Meier, R. L. (1968) 'Violence: The Last Urban Epidemic', *The American Behavioral Scientist*, March-April 1968, Volume II, Number 4, Beverly Hills, California: Sage Publications, Inc: 35-37.

Mengi, G. (1995a) 'Korkma, tartis...', *Sabah*, 17 Mart.

Mengi, G. (1995b) 'Pahali bir ders...', *Sabah,* 18 Mart.

Metropolitan Police (1987) *Special Police Order* 1/87, Public Order Act 1986, London: Metropolitan Police.

Metropolitan Police (1991) *Trafalgar Square Riot Debriefing,* Saturday 31 March 1990, London: Metropolitan Police.

Metropolitan Police (1992) 'Operational Order', TO20 Operation No. 118/92, Notting Hill Carnival 1992 Sunday 30th and Monday 31st August 1992, London: Official Document.

Metropolitan Police (1993a) *Notting Hill Carnival 1993, Shield Serials and Reserves Briefing Booklet,* London: Official Document.

Metropolitan Police (1993b) *Notting Hill Carnival 1993, Sector 4 Briefing Booklet*, London: Official Document.

Meydan (1994) 'Teroristlerle catismaya giren...Polislere, halktan buyuk destek', in *Meydan* 10 October.

Milgram, S. and Toch, H. (1969) 'Collective Behaviour: Crowds and Social Movements', in: G. Lindzey, and E. Aronson, (eds) *The Handbook of Social Psychology,* Volume Four, Group Psychology and Phenomena of Interactions, second edition, Reading, Massachusetts; Addison-Wesley Publishing Company.

Miliband, D. (1984) *The State and Capitalist Society*, London: Quartet.

Miller, D. (1984) 'The use and abuse of political violence', *Political Studies*, Vol. 32 September: 401-419.

Miller, D. L. (1985) *Introduction to Collective Behaviour,* Bellmont, California: Wadsworth Publishing Company.

Miller. A. and Warren, P. (1993) 'A Cry from the Streets', *The Sunday Times Magazine*, March 7.

Misner, G. E. (1972) 'The Police and Collective Violence in Contemporary America', in: James F. Short and Marvin E. Wolfgang (eds) *Collective Violence,* Chicago: Aldine-Atherton: 343-351.

Momboisse, R. M. (1964) *Crowd Control and Riot Prevention*, State of California: Department of Justice.

Moore, T. (1985) 'Community Disorder Simulation', *Simulation/Games for Learning*, Vol. 15, No. 2: 73-81.

Moore, T. (1986) 'Public Order; the police commander's role', *Policing*, Vol.2. No.2 Summer 1986: 88-100.

Moore, T. (1988) 'Carnival Saves the Day', *Police*, Vol. XXI. No. 1: 36-37.

Moore, T. (1990) 'Keep it Cool!', *Police,* Vol. XXII. No.11: 32-33.

Moore, T. (1991) 'Crowd Management: Learning from the History', an unpublished paper presented at the Crowdman Conference, London: Wembley Exhibition Centre 5.12 1991.

Moore, T. (1994) 'Command and Control in Riots', an unpublished presentation to the ESRC (Economic and Social Research Council) seminar series, held at Ranmoore Hall, Sheffield, on 7-8 January.

Moore, T. (1995) *Personal communication via a letter*, dated 12 January 1995, Tony Moore is an Ex-Chief Superintendent of London Metropolitan Police and lives in Canary Islands, Spain.

Morgan, R. (1987) 'Police accountability: developing the local infrastructure', *British Journal of Criminology* 33 (3): 87-96.

Morrell, W. J. (1992) *The Management of Civil Disorder in the Metropolitan Police,* an unpublished MA dissertation, Leicester: Centre for the Study of Public Order.

Morris, T. (1985) 'The Case for a Riot Squad', *New Society,* 29 November.

Mortimer, E. (1991) 'Christianity and Islam', *International Affairs*, 67, I (1991): 7-13.

Mouland, B. (1992) 'Farmer forces action against hippie invasion', *Daily Mail,* July 27.

Munawi, 'Abdu'r-Rauf (1972) *Feydu'l-Kadir Serhu'l-Cami'u 's-Sagir,* Beirut, Lebonan: Daru'l-Ma'rife. Vol.5: 33.

Mungham, G, (1977) 'The Sociology of Violence', *New Society* 13 October: 60-63.

Murad, I. (1992) 'Devlet, sayet adaletli ise, saygiya layiktir', *Zaman*, 15 October.

Mustafa, N. A. (1985) *El-Mu'arada Fi'l Fikri 's-Siyasiyyi 'l-Islami,* Cairo, [translated into Turkish by Vecdi Akyuz] as *Islam Siyasi Dusunvcesinde Muhalefet* (1990) Istanbul: Iz Yayincilik.

NCCL (1968) 'Report on the Demonstration in Grosvenor Square', [an unpublished report by NCCL dated March 17 1968] London: NCCL.

NCIS (1994) *Press Release: National Criminal Intelligence Service Reshape Itself*, 1/94 14 June 1994.

Nelken, D. (1994) *The Futures of Criminology*, London: Sage Publications.

Newman, K. (1982) 'Civil Disorder - Planning and Strategy', an unpublished paper containing an abbreviated version of a talk given to the Association of Chiefs of Police Officers at the Police Staff College, Bramshill, on 22nd March 1982.

Newman, O. (1973) *Defensible Space: Crime Prevention Through Urban Design,* New York: Collier Books.

Nicholson, C. E. and Roebuck, B. (1993) 'The Investigation of the Hillsborough Disaster by the Health and Safety Executive', in Roderich A. Smith, and Jim F. Dickie (eds) *Engineering for Crowd Safety,* London: Elsevier: 145-155.

Nieburg, H. L. (1968) 'Violence, Law and the Social Process', *The American Behavioral Scientist*, March-April 1968, Vol. II, No. 4, Beverly Hills, California: Sage Publications, Inc: 17-19.

Nieburg, H. L. (1972) 'Agonistics-Rituals of Conflict', in: James F. Short and Marvin E. Wolfgang (eds) *Collective Violence,* Chicago: Aldine-Atherton: 83-99.

Norman, F. (1994) 'Resisting Western Images', *The Fountain*, Oct.-Sep. No.8: 34-36.

Northam, G. (1989) *Shooting In the Dark: Riot Police In Britain,* London: Faber and Faber.

Notting Hill Carnival (1993) *The Notting Hill Carnival Guide '93,* London: Ashley House Ltd.

O'Reilly, M. (1993) 'A Guide to 8 Area T. S. G., Area 8 Westminster', Metropolitan Police: Official Document.

Ocak, A. Y. (1980) *Babailer Isyani,* Istanbul: Dergah Yayinlari.

Oerton, R. (1968) *Who is the Criminal?*, London: Zenith Books.

Oguz, N. and Sisko, E. (Undated) *Fiziki Yetenegi Gelistirme ve Polis Taktikleri,* Ankara: Emniyet Genel Mudurlugu, Egitim Daire Baskaniligi Yayinlari, Ankara: Official Publications.

Ollman, B. (1968) 'Marx's Use of "class",' *American Journal of Sociology,* 73: 573-580.

Ozcan, Y. Z. and Caglar, A. (1994) 'Who are the Future Police Elites?: Socio-Economic Background of the Students at The Police Academy In Turkey', *Policing and Society,* 1994, Vol. (4): 287-301.

Ozguven, I. (1995) 'Konak'ta gazinokondu', *Hurriyet Ege,* 17 Mart.

Palmer, S. and Humphrey, J. A. (1990a) 'White-Collar, Corporate, and Government Crime', in: S. Palmer and J. A Humphrey (eds) *Deviant Behaviour,* New York: Plenum Press.

Palmer, S. and Humphrey, J. A. (1990b) *Deviant Behaviour,* New York: Plenum Press.

Panayi, P. (ed) (1993) *Racial Violence in Britain, 1840-1950,* Leicester: Leicester University Press.

Parekh, B. (1989) 'Rushdie Affair and The British Press', *Social Studies Review,* Vol. 5, No. 2 November 1989: 44-47.

Parekh, B. (1990) 'The Liberal Discourse on Violence', in: D. McLellan and S. Sayers (eds) *Socialism and Morality,* Basingstoke: Macmillan: 116-138.

Park, R. E. (1967) *On Sociological Control and Collective Behavior:* Selected Papers, edited and with an Introduction by Ralph H. Turner, Chicago: The University of Chicago Press, Phoenix Books.

Parry, G. Moyser, G. and Wagstaffe, M. (1978) 'The Crowd and the Community: context, content and aftermath', in: G. Gaskell and R. Benewick (eds) *The Crowd in Contemporary Britain,* London: Sage: 212-250.

Pearce, F. (1976) *Crimes of the Powerful: Marxism, Crime and Deviancy,* London: Pluto Press.

Phillips, J. D. (1986) 'Riot as a Challenge to Policing', an unpublished paper presented by the Greater Manchester Police, on 10th February 1986.

Pidcock, D. M. (1993) 'Death of Democracy: Algeria', *Common Sense,* Issue Number 10 Second Quarter 1993.

Pirie, K. (1992) 'The Shame of Filbert Street: Riot squads move in to halt violence', *Leicester Mercury,* Monday, May 4.

Platt, T. and Takagi, P. (ed) (1981) *Crime and Social Justice,* London: MacMillan.

Police Act (1964) Police Act 1964, Chapter 48.

Police (1988) Vol. XXI No. 2, October.

Police and Criminal Justice Act (1994) Police and Criminal Justice Act 1994.

Police Review (1993) '28 officers hurt in race clashes', *Police Review* 17 September 1993, Vol. 101 No. 5234.

Popplewell, O. (1986) *Committee of Inquiry into Crowd Safety and Control at Sports Grounds: Final Report,* London: HMSO.

Public Order Act (1936) Public Order Act 1936, Chapter 6.

Public Order Act (1986) Public Order Act 1986, Chapter 64.

Pugh, N. C. (1990) *Public Disorder and Policy,* an unpublished MA Dissertation, Hull: The University of Hull.

Quarantelli, E. L. and Russell R. Dynes (1968) 'Looting in Civil Disorder: An Index of Social Change', *The American Behavioral Scientist,* March-April 1968, Volume II, Number 4, Beverly Hills, California: Sage Publications, Inc: 7-10.

Quinney, R. (1980) *Class, State and Crime*, London: Longman.

Rabia, T. (1994) 'The Making of a Racist', *Trends*, Vol. 5, Issue 6, London: Trends Publications Ltd: 7.

Radzinowich, L. and King, J. (1979) *The Growth of Crime: The International Experience*, Middlesex: Penguin Books.

Rahim, A. (1993) 'Islam's Challenge to Capitalist Economic Principles', *Islamica*, Vol. 1, No. 3, August: 15-18.

Rahman, M. (1994) 'The Nature, Sources and Development of Islamic Law', *Al-Mizan*, Volume 1 Issue 1: 46-58.

Ransford, H. E. (1968) 'Isolation, powerlessness and violence: a study of attitudes and participation in the Watts riot', *American Journal of Sociology,* 73: 581-591.

Reicher, S. and Potter, J. (1985) 'Psychological Theory as Intergroup Perspective: A Comparative Analysis of 'Scientific' and 'Lay' Accounts of Crowd Events', *Human Relations*, Vol. 38, No. 2: 197-189.

Reicher, S. D. (1984) 'The St. Paul's riot: an explanation of the limits of crowd action in terms of a social identity model', *European Journal of Social Psychology*, Vol.14:1-21.

Reiner, R. (1992) *The Politics of the Police*, [Second Edition, fully revised and updated], Hemel Hampstead: Harvester Wheatsheaf.

Renatus, H. and Artzt, E. (1973) *Violence : Causes and Solutions,* New York: A Laurel Original.

Revolutionary Fighter (1994) *Revolutionary Internationalist League Bulletin*, January 29.

Robinson, R. D. (1965) *The First Turkish Republic: A Case Study in National Development,* Cambridge, Massachusetts: Harvard University Press.

Rose, G. (1982) *Deciphering Sociological Research,* London: MacMillan.

Roshier, R. (1978) *Crime and Punishment*, London: Longman Social Science Studies.

Ross, I. (1993) 'Pitch invasion sours Tottenham's victory', *Times* 8.3. 1993.

Rossi, P. H. (ed) (1970) *Ghetto Revolts,* USA: Trans-Action Books.

Rottom, J. (1976) 'A History of Violence', in: N. Tutt (ed) *Violence*, London: HMSO.

Rousseau, J. J. (1968) *The Social Contract*, London: Penguin Books.

Rousseau, J. J.(1952)*The Social Contract and Discourses,* London: J. M. Dent & Sons Ltd.

Rowe, M. (1994) *'Race Riots' In Twentieth Century Britain*, Order and Policing, Occasional Paper No.5, Leicester: Centre for the Study of Public Order.

Rubes, J. M. (1993) 'Crowd Flow Patterns', in: Roderich A. Smith, and Jim F. Dickie (eds) *Engineering for Crowd Safety*, London: Elsevier: 173-185.
Rude` G. (1964) *Revolutionary Europe 1783-1815*, London: Collins.
Rude` G. (1981) *The Crowd in History: A Study of Popular Disturbances in France and England 1730-1848*, London: Lawrence and Wishart.
Rule, J. B. (1988) *Theories of Civil Violence*, Los Angeles: University of California Press.
Sabah (1995) 17 Mart, 18 Mart.
Sacranie, I. (1993) 'PM meeting with Rushdie condemned', *The Muslim News*, 28 May.
Safak, A. (1977) *Mezheplerarasi Mukayeseli Islam Hukuku*, [A Comparison of Islamic Penal Code Between All Islamic Sects] Erzurum: Ataturk Universitesi Yayinlari.
Safak, A. (1989) *Hukuk Baslangici; Ders Kitabi*, [Intruduction to Law: A Text Book] Ankara: Polis Akademisi Baskanligi, Emniyet Genel Mudurlugu, Ankara: Official Publication.
Sah Muimuddin Ahmed Nedvi and Said Sahib Ansari (1967) *Asr-i Saadet*, [Translated from Urdu by Ali Genceli, prepared by Esref Edip], Istanbul: Sebilurresad.
Salmi, J. (1993) *Violence and Democratic Society*, London: Zed.
Samenow, S. E. (1984) *Inside the Criminal Mind*, New York: Times Books.
Saunders, M. (1994) 'A Preventative Approach To Maintaining Public Order', an unpublished paper presented to the ESRC *(Economic and Social Research Council)* seminar series, held at Ranmoore Hall, Sheffield, on 7-8 January.
Scarman, L. (1983) *The Scarman Report;* The Brixton Disorders 10-12 April 1981, London: Penguin Books.
Schwartz, L. R. (1972) 'Conflict Without Violence and Violence Without Conflict in a Mexican Village', in: James F. Short and Marvin E. Wolfgang (eds) *Collective Violence*, Chicago: Aldine-Atherton: 149-209.
Scraton, P. (1985) 'From Saltley gates to Orgreave: a history of the policing of recent industrial disputes', in: B. Fine and R. Millar (eds) *Policing the Miner's Strike*, London: Lawrence and Wishart: 145-160.
Scraton, P. (ed) (1987) *Law, Order and The Authoritarian State*, Milton Keynes: Open University Press.
Security Service Act (1989) Chapter Five, Article 2.
Selcuk, A. (1994) 'Science, Philosophy and Religion: Towards a new Synthesis', *Al-Mizan*, Volume 1 Issue 1: 75-86.
Senel, A. T. (Undated) *Toplu Hareketler ve Polis*, (Mass Crowd Movements and the Police), Emniyet Genel Mudurlugu Onemli Isler Mudurlugu Yayinlarindan No. 2, Ankara: Official Publication.
Sener, S. (1990) *Osmanli'da Siyasi Cozulme*, Istanbul: Inkilab Yayinlari.

Shaffer, J. A. (ed) (1971) *Violence: Award-Winning Essays in the Council for Philosophical Studies Competition,* New York: David McKay Company.

Sharp, G. (1972) *The Politics of Nonviolent Action: Power and Struggle,* Boston: Porter Sergent Publishers.

Sherr, A. (1989) *Freedom of Protest, Public Order and the Law,* Oxford: Basil Blackwell.

Short, F. M. and Wolfgang, M. E. (1972) 'Perspectives on Collective Violence', in: James F. Short and Marvin E. Wolfgang (eds) *Collective Violence*, Chicago: Aldine-Atherton: 3-32.

Short, J. F. and Wolfgang, M. E. (1972) *Collective Violence,* Chicago: Aldine-Atherton.

Sighele, S. (1892a) 'La Foule criminelle: Essai de psychologie collective', Translated from the Italian by Paul Vigny, Paris: Felix Alcan, in: J. B. Rule *Theories of Civil Violence*, Los Angeles: University of California Press.

Sighele, S. (1892b) *La Foule Crimenelle Essai de Psychologie Collective,* [Translation from Italian by P. Vigny], Paris: Felix Alcan.

Sime, J. D. (1993) 'Crowd Psychology and Engineering: Designing for People or Ballbearings?', in: Roderich A. Smith, and Jim F. Dickie (eds) *Engineering for Crowd Safety,* London: Elsevier: 119-130.

Sir Norman Chester Centre for Football Research (1989) *Crowd Control and Membership at Football: A survey of Police Officers with Responsibility for policing Football Matches in England and Wales:* Leicester: University of Leicester.

Sismanov, Dimitir (1990) *Turkiye Isci ve Sosyalist Hareketi: kisa tarih (1908-1965),* Istanbul: Belge Yayinlari.

Skolnick, J. H. (1959) *The Politics of Protest,* a report submitted by Jerome H. Skolnick, Director, Task force on Violent Aspects of Protest and Confrontation of the National Commission on the Causes and Prevention of violence, New York: Simon and Schuster.

Sloan, I. (1995) 'Leaving Turkey out in the cold', *The European*, 29 December 1994 -4 January 1995: 8.

Sloan, K. (1984) *Public Order And The Police,* London: Police Review Publishing Co. Ltd.

Smelser, N. J. (1962) *Theory of Collective Behaviour,* London: Routledge and Kegan Paul.

Smelser, N. J. (1968) *Essays In Sociological Explanation*, New Jersey: Prentice Hall.

Smelser, N. J. (1972) 'Two Critics in Search of a Bias: A Response to Currie and Skolnick', in: James F. Short and Marvin E. Wolfgang (eds) *Collective Violence*, Chicago: Aldine-Atherton: 72-81.

Smith, A. T. H. (1987) *Offences Against Public Order: Including The Public Order Act 1986,* London: Sweet and Maxwell, Police review Publishing Company.

Smith, D. J. and Gray, J. (1985) *Police and People In London,* The PSI Report, London: Gower.

Smith, M. D. (1983) *Violence and Sport,* London: Butterworth.

Smith, R. A. and Dickie, J. F. (1993) *Engineering for Crowd Safety,* London: Elsevier.

Social Studies Review (1989) Vol. 5, No. 2 November.

Socialist Worker (1989) 16 October 1993 No. 1364.

Sonmez, Z. (1989) *Baslangicindan 16. Yuzyila Kadar Anadolu Turk-Islam Mimarisinde Sanatcilar,* Ankara: Turk Kultur Dil ve Tarih Yuksek Kurumu.

Spencer, H. (1982) *The Man Versus the State: with six essays on Government, Society and Freedom*, Indianapolis: Liberty Classics.

Spradley, J. P. (1980) *Participant Observation*, London: Holt, Rinehart and Winston.

Stenson, K. and Cowell, D. (eds) (1991) *The Politics of Crime Control,* London: Sage Publications.

Stern, P. C. (1979) *Evaluating Social Science Research,* Oxford: Oxford University Press.

Stevenson, J. (1992) *Popular Disturbances in England 1700-1870*, London: Longman.

Storr, A. (1968) *Human Aggression,* Middlesex: Penguin Books.

Stouffer, S. A., Suchman, E. A., De Winney, L. C. Star, S. A and Williams, R. M. (1949) *The American Soldier: Adjustment During Army Life,* Princeton, New Jersey: Princeton University Press.

Street, H. (1972) *Freedom, the Individual and the Law*, Middlesex: Pelican Books.

Sutherland, E. H. (1970) 'White-Collar Criminality', in: E. A. Bersani (ed) *Crime and Delinquency: A Reader*, London: Macmillan.

Swanson, H. (1976) 'The Biological Value of Agression', in: N. Tutt (ed) *Violence*, London: HMSO.

Sztompka,P. (1990) 'Conceptual Frameworks in Comparative Inquiry: Divergent or Convergent?', in M. Albow and E. King (eds), *Globalisation, Knowledge and Society,* Sage.

Tabrizi, Wali ad-Din Muhammed b. ‘Abdallah al-Khatib (1991) *Mishkat Al-Masabih,* Lahore, SH. Muhammed Ashraf. [English translation with explanatory notes by James Robson, D. Litt. D.D. Emeritus Professor of Arabic], The University of Manchester.

Tame, C. R. (1991) 'Freedom, Responsibility and Justice: The Criminology of the New Right', in: K. Stenson and D. Cowell (eds), *The Politics of Crime Control,* London: Sage Publications: 127-142.

Tamimi, A. (1994) 'From Tolerance To Violence', an unpublished paper delivered by A. Tamimi at Transmed, The International Symposium on Transmediterranean Interdependence and Partnership, that was held in Rome between 17-19 January 1994 and organised by North-South Centre, Council of Europe.

Tan, A. (1995) 'Agar'la soylesi: nevruz'u kutlamaya haziriz', *Sabah*, 17 Mart.

Tan, Y. H. (1992) 'Police public order manual protected', *Independent*, 11th November.

Tarde, G. (1890) *La Philosophie Penale*, Lyon: Edition Storck.

Tash, A. (1995) 'Terrorism or Jihad?', an unbublished paper by Dr A. Tash, The Editor - in Chief of the Weekly International Newspaper *Al-Muslimun,* published in Jeddah.

Taylor, I. (1971) 'Football Mad: A Speculative Sociology of Football Hooliganism', in: E. G. Dunning (ed) *The Sociology of Sports,* London: Cass.

Taylor, I. (1989) *The Hillsborough Stadium Disorder* -15 April 1989, Some Personal Contemplations, *New Left Review*, 177 Sept.- Oct. : 89-110.

Taylor, I., Walton, P. and Young, J. (1975) *The New Criminology: for a social theory of deviancy*, London: Routledge and Kegan Paul.

Taylor, I., Walton, P. and Young, J. (eds) (1973) *Critical Criminology,* London: Routledge and Kegan Paul.

Taylor, P. (1989) *The Hillsborough Stadium Disaster: Inquiry by the Rt. Hon Lord Justice Taylor, Final Report,* London: HMSO.

Taymiya, I. (1987) *Public Duties In Islam: The Institution of the Hisba,* Leicester: The Islamic Foundation.

Tek, H. (1980) *Toplumsal Olaylar ve Kuramsal Orgutler Dersleri,* [a Textbook for Crowd Events and Organised Groups], Ankara: Emniyet Genel Mudurlugu, Polis Egitim Merkezi Mudurlugu Yayinlari, Ankara: Official Publications.

The Bible Societies (1986) *New Testament: Good News Edition,* Swindon: Bible Society Publishing.

The Constitution of the Republic Of Turkiye (1982) Enacted in 7. 11. 1982 No. 2709, Article 34.

The Gideons International (1988) *The Holy Bible: New International Version,* Lutterworth: The Gideons International

The Independent on Sunday, (1993) 17 October.

The Job (1992) 'Public Order: We're Ready for Anything', *The Job*, Metropolitan Police's magazine, Vol. 25, Issue 638, September 18 1992.

The Light-NUR (1980) 'Social Change in Muslim Societies', *The light-NUR*, Vol 7. No. 2, Nov.-Dec. 1980: 3-6.

The Light-NUR (1981) 'Social Change in Muslim Societies', *The light-NUR,* Vol 7. No. 2, Jan.-Feb. 1981: 3-6.

The Independent On Sunday (1993) 17 October.

The Mail on Sunday (1993) 17 October.

The Sunday Times (1993) 17 October.
The Times (1992) 'Police Manual is Protected', *The Times*, 3 November.
The Watchtower (1993) 'Why is Stealing on the Increase?', *The Watchtower*, October 15, 1993, Vol. 114, No. 20.
Thornton, P. (1985) *We Protest: The Public Order Debate,* London: NCCL.
Tilly, C. (1963) 'Queries on Social Change and Political Upheaval in France', Princeton: Centre for International Studies, mimeographed copy, in: J. B. Rule *Theories of Civil Violence*, Los Angeles: University of California Press.
Tilly, C. (1970) 'The Changing Place of Collective Violence', In: Essays in *Theory and History: An approach to the Social Sciences*, (ed) Melvin Richter, Cambridge, Mass: Harvard University Press, in: J. B. Rule *Theories of Civil Violence*, Los Angeles: University of California Press.
Tilly, C. (1974) 'Town and Country in Revolution', in: J. W. Lewis (ed) *Peasant Rebellion and Communist Revolution in Asia*, Stanford: Stanford University Press.
Tirmizi (1981) *Kitabu'l-Fiten*, Istanbul: Cagri Yayinlari.
Toker, Y. and Dilmac, S. (1990s) *Psikolojik Harekat ve Propaganda*, Ankara: Emniyet Genel Mudurlugu, Istihbarat Daire Baskanligi Yayinlari, Yayin No.22, Ankara: Official Publication.
Tomlinson, T. M. (1968) 'The Development of a Riot Ideology Among Urban Negroes', *The American Behavioral Scientist*, March-April 1968, Volume II, Number 4, Beverly Hills, California: Sage Publications, Inc: 27-31.
Tomruk, M. (1989) *Toplanti-Gosteri Yuruyusu Hurriyeti ve Toplumsal Olaylar Karsisinda Polis*, (The Police Towards the Freedom of Assembly and Demonstrations), Ankara.
Toprak, B. (1993) 'Islamist Intellectuals: revolt against Industry and Technology', in: M. Heper, A. Oncu. H. Kramer (eds) *Turkey and the West: Changing Political and Cultural Identities,* New York: I. B. Tauris and Co. Ltd: 237-257.
Townshead, C. (1993) *Making the Peace: Public Order and Public Security in Modern Britain,* Oxford: Oxford University Press.
Trends (1993) Vol. 5, Issue 3, Halifax: Trends Publications Ltd.
Trends (1994) Vol. 5, Issue 6, London: Trends Publications Ltd.
Turan, I. (1993) 'Politicians: Populist Democracy', in: M. Heper, A. Oncu. H. Kramer (eds) *Turkey and the West: Changing Political and Cultural Identities*, New York: I. B. Tauris and Co. Ltd: 116-141.
Turenc, T. (1995) 'Bu is Tansu Hanim'la Gitmiyor', *Hurriyet*, 17 Mart.
Turner, B. S. (1978) *Weber and Islam*, London: Routledge and Kegan Paul.
Turner, R. H. and Killian, L. M. (1962) *Collective Behaviour*, Englewood Cliffs, N.J: Prentice-Hall, Inc.
Tutt, N. (1976) *Intruduction To Violence,* London: HMSO.
Tutuncu, Z. (1971) *Fatih Sultan Mehmet,* Istanbul: Milliyetci Yayinlari.

Udeh, A. (1990) *Mukayeseli Islam Hukuku ve Beseri Hukuk*, [translated from Arabic by Ali Safak], Ankara: Rehber Yayincilik.

Uglow, S. (1988) *Policing Liberal Society*, Oxford: Oxford University Press.

Unal, T. F. (1992) *Christianity versus the Truth,* Izmir: Kaynak House of Publication.

Unal, T. F (1993a) *The Crossroads*, Izmir: Kaynak House of Publication.

Unal, T. F. (1993b) *Yollarin Ayrilis Noktasi*, Izmir: Isik Yayinlari.

Unal, T. F. (1994) *Interview*, 5 October 1994, Taha F. Unal is sogiologist and author of a number of books both in English and Turkish and lives in Izmir, Turkiye.

Varwell, D. W. P. (1978) *Police and Public*, Plymouth: Macdonald and Evans.

Wacks, R. (1987) *Jurisprudence*, London: Blackstone.

Waddington, D. (1987) 'The Summer of '81 revisited: an analysis of Sheffield's Haymarket fracas', in: A. Cashdan and M. Jordin (eds) *Studies in Communication,* Blackwell.

Waddington, D. Jones, K. and Critcher, C. (1987) 'Flashpoints of public disorder', in: G. Gaskell and R. Benewick (eds) *The Crowd in Contemporary Britain,* London: Sage.

Waddington, D. Jones, K. and Critcher, C. (1989) *Flashpoints*, London: Routledge.

Waddington, D. (1992) *Contemporary Issues in Public Order,* London: Routledge.

Waddington, D. (1995) 'A presentation', made on 6 February 1995, at the CSPO: Leicester.

Waddington, P. A. J. (1984) 'Treading the Tightrope', *Police,* September 1984 Vol. XVII No. 1.

Waddington, P. A. J. (1985a) 'Accountability won't Work', *Police,* May 1985 Vol. XVII No. 9.

Waddington, P. A. J. (1985b) 'Now Send for the Judge', *Police*, April 1985 Vol. XVII No. 8.

Waddington, P. A. J. (1987) 'Towards Paramilitarism? Dilemmas in Policing Disorder', *British Journal Of Criminology,* Vol. 27 No. 1 Winter: 37-46.

Waddington, P. A. J. (1988) 'Rabble without a cause', *Police*, January 1988 Vol.XX No.5.

Waddington, P. A. J. (1991) *The Strong Arm of The Law*, Oxford: Clarendon Press.

Waddington, P. A. J. (1992) 'Another Nail in the Coffin of Justice', *Police*, January 1992 Vol. XXIV No. 5.

Waddington, P. A. J. (1993) 'Dying in a Ditch: The Use of Police Powers in Public Order', *International Journal of the Sociology of Law* 1993, 21: 335-353.

Waddington, P. A. J. (1994a) *Personal communication via a letter*, dated 16 March 1994, Reading, England.

Waddington, P. A. J. (1994b) *Liberty and Order: public order policing in a capital city,* London: University College London (UCL) Press.

Waddington, P. A. J. (1994c) 'The politics of Public Order Policing: a 'typographical analysis'! ', an unpublished paper presented to the ESRC (Economic and Social Research Council) seminar series, held at the CSPO (Centre for the Study of Public Order), University of Leicester, on 18 November.

Waters, I. and Brown, J. (1994) 'Quality versus Force: Mutually exclusive or viable dichotomy?', an unpublished paper presented to the ESRC (Economic and Social Research Council) seminar series, held at the New Scotland Yard, London, on 15 April.

Weeks, J. (1990) 'We cannot show their hatred', *Police,* August 1990 Volume 22: 16-17.

Weinberger, B. (1991) *Keeping The Peace? Policing Strikes in Britain, 1906--1926,* Oxford: Berg.

Whilsher, K. (1993) 'Masked Mob Stone Police: 100 hurt as riot erupts on march', *The Mail on Sunday,* 17 October.

Whitaker, B. (1979) *The Police in Society,* London: Eyre Methuen.

Wiles, P. (1985) 'The policing of industrial disputes', in: P. Fosh and C. R. Littler (eds) *Industrial Relations and the Law in the 1980s,* Farnborough: Gower: 151-175.

Williams, J. Dunning E. and Murphy, P. (1986) *Professional Football and Crowd Violence in England,* Sir Norman Chester Centre for Football Research, Department of Sociology, University of Leicester.

Williams, J. Dunning, E and Murphy, P. (1987) *English Football Fans: A return to Europe?,* Sir Norman Chester Centre for Football Research, Department of Sociology, University of Leicester.

Williams, J. Dunning E. and Murphy, P. (1988) *Football and Spectator Behaviour: 'The Friendly Club',* Sir Norman Chester Centre for Football Research, Department of Sociology, University of Leicester.

Williams, J. E. H. (1988) *Criminology and Criminal Justice,* London: Butterworths.

Wilson, J. Q. (1985) *Thinking About Crime,* (revised edition), New York: Vintage Books.

Wilson, J. Q. and Hermestein, R. J. (1986) *Crime and Human Nature,* New York: A Touchstone Book.

Winstone, P. (1993) 'Racial attacks and Europe', in: P. Francis and R. Matthews (eds), *Tackling Racial Attacks,* Leicester: Centre for the Study of Public Order: 18-26.

Wolfgang, M. E. and Weiner, N. A. (1982) *Criminal Violence,* Beverly Hills: Sage Publications.

Wood, D. R. W. (1995) *Interview and personal communications via letters,* dated 20 December 1994 and 10 January 1995, Derek R. W. Wood is the senior editor of the Inter-Varsity Press (IVP): Leicester, England.

Wood, M. (1977) 'The Iconography of Violence', *New Society,* 13 October 1977: 66-68.

Workers News (1994) 'Smash Fascism! Down With Racism!', a newsletter distributed during the TUC Demonstration on 19 March 1994, London: Workers News.

Wright, P. (1985a) 'A Man Alone', *Police,* February 1985 Vol. XVII No. 6.

Wright, P. (1985b) 'We're Getting Back to Normal Service', *Police,* July 1985 Vol.XVII, No.8.

Yack, B. (1992) *The Longing for Total Revolution: Philosophic Sources of Social Discontent from Rousseau to Marx and Nietzssche,* Berkeley: University of California.

Yildiz, V. (1994) *Interview,* 5 October 1994, V. Yildiz is well known Muslim scholar and lives in Izmir, Turkiye.

Yusuf 'Ali, 'Abdullah (1989) *The Holy Qur'an: Text, translation and commentary,* Brentwood, Maryland: Amana Corporation.

Zakaria, R. (1991) *Muhammed and the Quran,* London: Penguin.

Zaman (1992) 'Hayat, bir mucadele degildir', *Zaman,* 18. 11. 1992.

Zaman (1992) 15 October 1992, 19 October 1992, 21 November 1992 and 8 July 1992.

Zaman (1993) 'Vicdan ve nefis mekanizmalari', *Zaman,* 4. 11. 1993.

Zeydan, A. (1985) *Islam Hukukuna Giris,* translated by Ali Safak, Istanbul: Kayihan Yayinlari.

Appendix I

List of observations and attachments

Date	Venue	Event
1. 12 Feb. 1992	Butterfield Park to Hyde Park, London	Observation: National Union of Students (NUS) rally and demonstration.
2. 8 April 1992	Leicester City Football Ground, Leicester	Observation: Leicester City F.C. versus Sunderland A.F.C., football match.
3. 14 July 1992	Three separate sites in Coalville, Leicester	Attachment: Leicestershire Constabulary, clearance of *New Age Travellers* from the three sites.
4. 23 July 1992	Victoria Park, Leicester	Observation: Leicester Afro-Caribbean Carnival of 1992.
5. 22-24 Aug.1992	Donington Park, Leicester	Attachment: Leicestershire Constabulary at the 'Monsters of Rock' pop festival.
6. 30-31 Aug.1992	Notting Hill, London	Attachment: The Metropolitan Police London during the Notting Hill Carnival 1992.

7. 13 Sept. 1992	Leicester City Football Ground, Leicester	Observation: Leicester C.F.C. versus Wolverhampton Wanderers F.C. football match.
8. 2 May 1992	Leicester City Football Ground, Leicester	Observation: Leicester C.F.C. versus Newcastle United.
9. 26 Sept. 1992	Earls Court, London	Observation: Pop Concert, Chris De Burgh.
10. 18 Oct. 1992	19 Mayis Football Ground, Ankara	Observation: Genclerbirligi F.C. versus Ankaragucu F.C. football match.
11. 14 Nov. 1992	Alsancak Football Ground, Izmir	Observations: Karsiyaka F.C. versus Aydinspor F.C. football match.
12. 20 Nov. 1992	Buca, Izmir	Attachment: Izmir Cevik Kuvvet Unit, the Destruction of Squatter's houses.
13. 29 Nov. 1992	Inonu Football Ground, Istanbul	Observation: Besiktas F.C. versus Kocaelispor F.C. football match.
14. 30 Jan. 1993	Hyde Park to Kilburn, London	Observation: Bloody Sunday March and Rally.
15. 6 Feb. 1993	The Embankment to Hyde Park, London	Observation: Women Against Pit Closures march and rally.

16. 20 March 1993	Stamford Bridge Football Ground, London	Attachment: The Scotland Yard at the Chelsea F.C. v. Tottenham Hotspur F.C.
17. 21 April 1993	Kocatepe, Ankara	Observation: Mourning crowd in President Turgut Ozal's funeral.
18. 22 April 1993	Vatan Caddesi, Istanbul	Observation: Mourning crowd in President Turgut Ozal's funeral.
19. 1 May 1993	Pendik, Istanbul	Observation: May The First Rally.
20. 2 May 1993	Gaziosmanpasa, Istanbul	Observation: An open air meeting organised by The Welfare Party (RP) on the election of the new president.
21. 23 May 1993	Hyde Park to the Embankment, London	Observation: 'Lift the Embargo' a national demonstration organised by various Muslim organisations concerning Bosnia.
22. 5 June 1993	Elephant and Castle to Brixton, London	Observation: an arguably national demonstration, organised by the *Red Aid* and various left wing groups concerning Bosnia.
23. 22 Aug. 1993	Regents Park to Belgrave Square, London	Observation: The National Muslim Unity March.

24. 30 Aug. 1993	Notting Hill, London	Attachment: The Metropolitan Police during the 'Notting Hill Carnival' 1993.
25. 16 Oct. 1993	Bexley, London	Observation: 'Unity March': Close down BNP. Organised by Anti-Nazi League and Youth Against Racism in Europe to close down BNP HQ.
26. 20 Jan. 1994	Victoria Park to City Centre, Leicester	Observation: A local student demonstration.
27. 29 Jan. 1994	Hyde Park to Kilburn, London	Observation: 'Bloody Sunday' march and rally.
28. 19 March 1994	Spitalfields Market to London Fields, London	Observation: 'Unite against Racism' March and Rally, organised by TUC.
29. 23 April 1994	Trafalgar Square to Hyde Park, London	Observation; March and Rally, by 'National anti-Vivisection Society.
30. 31 May 1994	City Centre to Victoria Park, Leicester	Observation: Leicester City Football Club's victory parade.
31. 25 June 1994	The Embankment to Hyde Park, London	Observation: 'March for Jesus', to highlight the importance of religion in everyday life ending with a rally in Hyde Park.
32. 3 Nov. 1994	Bridgwater, Bristol	Attachment: Avon and Somerset Constabulary at Bridgwater Guy Fawkes Carnival 1994.

33. 3 Dec. 1994	Spinney Hill Park to City Centre, Leicester	Observation: A local march and rally against the Criminal Justice Act 1994.

Appendix II

List of Courses Visits and Interviews

1 7 April 1992, **visit** to the Leicestershire Constabulary public order training site, Ashfordby, Leicester.
Level two public order training programme, Phase Two.

2 14 June 1992, **visit** to the Metropolitan Police Public Order Training Centre, Hounslow, London.
One day visit and observation in Level One public order training specifically designed for the forthcoming Notting Hill Carnival of 1992.

3 15 September 1992, **visit** to the Leicestershire Constabulary public order training site, Ashfordby, Leicester.
Joint public order training exercise with the Leicestershire Fire Service.

4 25 September 1992, **visit** to the Metropolitan Police Public Order Training Centre, Hounslow, London.
Level Two Public Order Training.

5 25 September 1992, **interview** with Inspector Keith Wood and Inspector Colin Whitford of the Metropolitan Police Public Order Training Centre, Hounslow, London.

6 1 October 1992, **interview** with Ian Coutts, Leicester City Football Club, Leicester.
The interviewed is an ex-Chief Superintendent and presently the Club Safety Officer for Leicester City.

7 16 October 1992, **interview** with Chief Superintendent Yasar Akbas, the Cevik Kuvvet Unit, Ankara. *The interviewed is the head of Ankara Cevik Kuvvet Unit.*

8 18 November 1992, **interview** with Chief Superintendent A. Mecit Canbaz, Cevik Kuvvet Unit, Izmir.
The interviewed is the head of Izmir Cevik Kuvvet Unit.

9 27-29 November 1992, a three day **attachment** to Cevik Kuvvet Unit, Bayrampasa, Istanbul, and **interview** with Chief Inspector Mustafa Kizilgunes.
The interviewed is the head of a highly trained Special Public Order Team.

10 8 February 1993, **interview** with Dr J. S. McClelland, Department of Politics, University of Nottingham.

11 20 February 1993, **interview** with Sergeant Albert Robenson of PT20 the New Scotland Yard, London.

12 7-9 June 1993, Public Order Command Awareness Programme, Kent County Constabulary, Kent and No 5 Region Public Order Training.

13 10-13 June 1993, **visit** to The Police Staff College, Bramshill, Hampshire.
A four day visit to the Bramshill Police Staff College Library.

14 13-17 September 1993, Bronze/Silver Command Course, Greater Manchester Police Sedgley Park Police Training School.

15 31-Jan. 3 Feb. 1994, Major Sporting Events Course, Greater Manchester Police Sedgley Park Police Training School.

16 1 August 1994, **interview** with Chief Superintendent Cemal Levent, in Burdur.
The interviewed is the head of Siirt Cevik Kuvvet Units.

17 1-4 October 1994, a series of **interviews** were carried out with 7 officers of the Ankara Cevik Kuvvet Unit.
All the interviewed were in the ranks of Sergeant and Inspector working in Ankara Cevik Kuvvet Unit, and each one responsible for separate public order serials.

18 5 October 1994, **interview** with Ali Unal, in Bozyaka, Izmir.
The interviewed is a sociologist and author of a number of books both in English and Turkish.

19 6-10 October 1994, a series of **interviews** carried out with 9 officers of Istanbul Cevik Kuvvet Unit.
All the interviewed were in the ranks of Sergeant and Inspector working in Istanbul Cevik Kuvvet Unit, each one responsible for separate public order serials.

20 28 October 1994, **interviews** with Superintendent Haydar Sahin, one Inspector and one police constable of Izmir Cevik Kuvvet Unit.
The interviewed is the head of Training Department at the Izmir Cevik Kuvvetr Unit.

21 13 December 1994, **visit** and observation to Tactical Firearms Unit (TFU) of Leicestershire Constabulary Police Headquarters.

22 20 December 1994, **interview** and **personal communication** with Derek R. W. Wood, Leicester.
The interviewed works for Inter-Varsity Press (IVP) as a senior editor.

23 12 January 1995, **personal communication** with Tony Moore, an ex-Chief Superintendent of London Metropolitan Police.
Tony Moore has seen the Introduction, Chapter 7 and the Conclusion of this thesis and made some comments and suggestions on the text.

24 18 January 1995, **visit** and **observation** in 'Rapid Entry/Intervention Course', ran by officers of Police Mobile Reserve (PMR), of Leicester Constabulary.
One day course involved classroom based theoretical training and practical exercises which were held at Stretton Hall Hospital, Leicester.